AF904638

# Arendt's Disappointments and Our New Beginnings

# Arendt's Disappointments and Our New Beginnings

## Citizenship and Democracy Reimagined

Peter Iver Kaufman

EDINBURGH
University Press

Edinburgh University Press is one of the leading university presses in the UK. We publish academic books and journals in our selected subject areas across the humanities and social sciences, combining cutting-edge scholarship with high editorial and production values to produce academic works of lasting importance. For more information visit our website: edinburghuniversitypress.com

© Peter Iver Kaufman 2026

Cover image: © Matthew and Eve Levine

Edinburgh University Press Ltd
13 Infirmary Street
Edinburgh EH1 1LT

First published in hardback by Edinburgh University Press 2026

Typeset in 10.5/13pt Bembo
by Cheshire Typesetting Ltd, Cuddington, Cheshire, and
printed and bound by CPI Group (UK) Ltd,
Croydon, CR0 4YY

A CIP record for this book is available from the British Library

ISBN 978 1 3995 3408 6 (hardback)
ISBN 978 1 3995 3410 9 (paperback)
ISBN 978 1 3995 3409 3 (webready PDF)
ISBN 978 1 3995 3411 6 (epub)

The right of Peter Iver Kaufman to be identified as the author of this work has been asserted in accordance with the Copyright, Designs and Patents Act 1988, and the Copyright and Related Rights Regulations 2003 (SI No. 2498).

FSC www.fsc.org MIX Paper | Supporting responsible forestry FSC® C013604

This book is printed using paper from well-managed forests, recycling and other controlled sources

# Contents

# Acknowledgements

Just prior to COVID, Jason Wesley Alvis's invitation to deliver a lecture at the University of Vienna started me thinking about this study. A COVID-cancelled paper prepared at the invitation of colleagues in the Department of Political Sciences at the University of Wisconsin, Madison, pushed it further along. Colleagues at Bard College, notably, custodians of the Hannah Arendt Collection, Helene Tieger and Debra Klein made it a pleasure to read over Arendt's shoulder. Although what follows takes exception to much of what my colleagues have written about an assortment of her views on philosophy and politics, the increasing number of Arendt scholars have helped me tremendously to see her disappointments and contributions more clearly. I'm especially grateful for the consistently perceptive work of the veterans, *inter alia*, Dana Villa, Jerome Kohn, Margaret Canovan, Seyla Benhabib and George Kateb. Suggestions from readers solicited by the press have been enormously helpful, prompting me to think, rethink, and rewrite. Cassie Price and Charlotte Tisdale at the University of Richmond assisted me to put what follows in its penultimate form. Finally, I am grateful for the patience, encouragement, and counsel of Beatriz Lopez, Sam Johnson and especially Ersev Ersoy, and I am thrilled *Disappointments* is emerging from the Press, for I meant from the start to dedicate the book to Gary Dickson (1938–2020), eminent Edinburgh University historian and excellent friend.

# Abbreviations

| | |
|---|---|
| BCSL. | Hannah Arendt Personal Library, Bard College, Stevens Library. |
| USLC. | Hannah Arendt Papers, United States Library of Congress. |

**Arendt Abbreviations**

| | |
|---|---|
| *Between Friends.* | *Between Friends: The Correspondence of Hannah Arendt and Mary McCarthy, 1949–1975*, ed. Carol Brightman. New York: Harcourt Brace, 1995. |
| BPF. | *Between Past and Future: Eight Exercises in Political Thought.* New York: Penguin, 2006. |
| *Briefwechsel.* | *Hannah Arendt / Karl Jaspers, Briefwechsel, 1926–1969*, eds. Lotte Köhler and Hans Saner. Munich: Piper, 1993. |
| CR. | *Crises of the Republic.* New York: Harcourt Brace, 1972. |
| *Denktagebuch.* | *Hannah Arendt: Denktagebuch*, 2 vols. eds. Ursala Lutz and Ingeborg Nordmann. Munich: Piper, 2016. |
| EI. | *Eichmann in Jerusalem: A Report on the Banality of Evil.* New York: Penguin, 2006. |
| EU. | *Essays in Understanding, 1930–1954: Formation, Exile, and Totalitarianism*, ed. Jerome Kohn. New York: Schocken Books, 2005. |
| HC. | *The Human Condition.* Chicago: University of Chicago Press, 1998. |
| JW. | *The Jewish Writings*, eds. Jerome Kohn and Ron H. Feldman. New York: Schocken Books, 2008. |
| *Liebesbegriff.* | *Der Liebesbegriff bei Augustin: Versuch einer philosophischen Interpretation.* Berlin: Springer, 1929. |
| LIOC. | *The Last Interview and Other Conversations.* New York: Melville House, 2013. |

| | |
|---|---|
| LKPP. | *Lectures on Kant's Political Philosophy*, ed. Ronald Beiner. Chicago: University of Chicago Press, 1982. |
| LMT. | *The Life of the Mind: One / Thinking*, in *The Life of the Mind*. New York: Harcourt, 1981. |
| LMW. | *The Life of the Mind: Two / Willing*, in *The Life of the Mind*. New York: Harcourt, 1981. |
| MDT. | *Men in Dark Times*. New York: Harcourt, 1970. |
| OR. | *On Revolution*. New York: Penguin, 1977. |
| OT. | *The Origins of Totalitarianism*. New York: Harcourt, 1985. |
| PP. | *The Promise of Politics*, ed. Jerome Kohn. New York: Schocken Books, 2005. |
| RJ. | *Responsibility and Judgment*, ed. Jerome Kohn. New York: Schocken Books, 2003. |
| RV. | *Rahel Varnhagen: Lebensgeshcichte einer deutschen Jüdin aus der Romantik*. Munich: Piper, 2018. |
| Scholem | The Correspondence of Hannah Arendt and Gershom Scholem, ed. Marie Louise Knott, trans. Anthony David, Chicago: University of Chicago Press, 2017. |
| TWB. | *Thinking Without a Bannister: Essays in Understanding, 1933–1975*, ed. Jerome Kohn. New York: Schocken Books, 2015. |

# Preface

'Freedom is the *raison d'être* of politics.' But, for Hannah Arendt, who proclaimed precisely that, the public realm, as conventionally conceived, could no longer be reckoned as a 'political realm.' Freedom had all but been forgotten there. It was 'overshadowed.' Political practice had become synonymous with administration, specifically, the administration of a 'gigantic and still increasing sphere of social and economic life.'[1] Statements of this sort encouraged Samuel Moyn recently to catalogue Arendt with Karl Popper, Isaiah Berlin, and other 'Cold War liberals.'[2] That has the effect of adding another Arendt to the many that have appeared in print since her death in 1975.

But Moyn should be credited as one of the few to recognise the depth of her disappointments. Nonetheless, he mistakes her realism as insensitivity – and as 'racialism.' He notices how often she conceded that personal freedom required some degree of solvency or security, but he appears to miss her many criticisms of citizens' 'passion[s] for sudden riches.' Their preoccupations with material success troubled her. 'Abundance and endless consumption' seemed to have become 'ideals.' Arendt's assessments seemed realistic, though somewhat condescending. Moyn was distressed by her conclusion that meaningful freedoms would 'escape those who were bent upon living for their desires.'[3] To him, she was among those Cold War liberals who contribute to their readers' dim view of civilisation's progress. Moreover, what Moyn took to have been detestable 'racialism' or racism adds to his dim view of her work. We shall address his misperception later in this study, but perhaps it suffices in an introduction simply to state that Arendt's attempts to comprehend early twentieth-century European settlers in Africa cannot reasonably be construed as 'adopting the[ir] mindset.'[4] Still, the dark picture Moyn paints of Cold War liberals does capture Arendt's wariness of statists who seemed prepared to exploit political opportunities malevolently to undermine 'new vision[s] of freedom.'[5] Even so, her fears are rarely recognised as sources of her originality and of her radical reimagination of citizenship and, therefore, of democratic practice. Despite her disappointments with, *inter alia*, philosophy, democratic republics, nationalism and various colleagues, Hannah Arendt earnestly asked whether public realms could be reconceived for the exercise of freedom and the reinvention of democracy.

What follows contends that she was preoccupied by those possibilities from the early 1930s until her death in 1975. The obstacles were formidable. Politics was thought to be about rule. And, as Ari Adut comments, 'politics in representative democracies' had become, even during Arendt's last decades, 'above all, elite competition in front of an intermittently interested citizenry.' The result, he went on, was 'a reduced sense of reality,' because power-brokers and power-holders were 'require[d] to signal ... that [they were] indeed powerful by performances,' by what he dubbed 'grandstanding.'[6] Against the backdrop of what Étienne Tassin characterises as vast simulation, Arendt looked first to find places and opportunities where persons could present themselves authentically, be genuinely free and, he adds, elevate the dignity of the political.[7]

Political freedom in representative democracies otherwise amounted to little more than electing or periodically rejecting rulers. And statists ensured that citizens were content, complacent and, we may add Arendt's often repeated characterisation, 'superfluous.' Statists are usually depicted favourably as advocates of their regimes' legitimacy – advocates for law and order and, therefore, adversaries of anarchists. To Arendt, for whom the statists' 'lying was a way of life,' they were professional politicians or the professionals' pitchmen who slyly managed and, as the occasions and their clients required, manipulated citizens.[8] They wrote and spoke about freedom, but – for statists and their accomplices in the marketplace and media – power, not freedom, was the chief reason for politics to exist. On Arendt's watch, then, statists corrupted politics, as conventionally conceived. Whereas Moyn, among others, whom we shall encounter in subsequent chapters, read Arendt's disappointments as symptoms of 'caustic scepticism,' we shall find them a staging area of sorts from which freedom, citizenship and politics were, for her, and can be, for us, redefined.[9]

To launch, *Arendt's Disappointments* introduces her alternative to statists' salesmanship, specifically, the values, virtues and virtuosity that she associates with citizen-statesmanship. What emerges is a very different, more positive assessment of self-assertion than the one she supposedly shared with Moyn's other Cold War liberals. But Arendt doubted, as Ned O'Gorman does not, that the virtues and virtuosity associated with statecraft and freedom were 'capacit[ies] that could be cultivated widely within our political culture.'[10] Before this study's second section considers how, where and why their survival might be secured in unconventional collectives to reimagine citizenship and, thereupon, to incubate citizen-statesmanship, its initial two chapters take up Arendt's disappointments and scepticism about the prospects for such survival in more conventional forums.

Arendt's sense of political squalor and her interpretation of the decline of democratic practices bear some resemblance to that of Wendy Brown. Shame and blame, Brown says, rain down on 'neoliberalism,' which has 'vanquish[ed] *homo politicus*.' Brown and Arendt cite the failure of democratic apparatuses and protocols to prevent economics from leaching into politics. Brown complains of 'the ascendancy of neoliberal reason' that leads statists to remake their states as firms. 'The central ruse of neoliberal governance … takes place in the name of freedom,' yet 'citizenship loses its distinctly political morphology and with it the mantle of sovereignty.' But Arendt's departure from Brown is significant. Although she, too, deplored the detrimental effect of the marketplace ascendant, Arendt worried equally, if not more, about political obsessions with sovereignty that have been and continue to be principal obstacles to widespread participation in conventional public realms. Brown is convinced that 'popular and individual sovereignty secure' one another. For Arendt, the latter, much as the concept of citizenship, had been defined by statists to the advantage of political elites, yet so slyly presented that ordinary citizens came unwittingly to support their own captivity. She would have personal sovereignty deemphasised in political discourses and would have freedom performed interpersonally in collegial – though agonistic – exchanges made possible in alternative venues that incubate respect for pluralism along with commitments to a common world.[11]

What Judith Butler admires in Arendt's openness to a common world has yet to be closely associated with Arendt's disappointments. But Butler is suggestive, linking 'flourishing' in Arendt's terms, with citizens' affirmations of plurality, 'interdependency' and 'performativity.' Butler, as Arendt, stipulates that persons must relinquish the sense that politics is about power, dominance and sovereignty, and such renunciation requires their acceptance of 'vulnerability.'[12] Annette Vowinckel, thinks the enterprise courts disaster, inasmuch as Arendt's new beginnings might lead to new iterations of totalitarianism. Her doctrine of natality, which we shall soon sift and find politically promising, strikes Vowinckel and others, differently – as 'unconvincing.'[13]

But Arendt embraced precarity. Stability and stasis increasingly troubled her, although, even in her earliest work, her dissertation on Augustine's concepts of love – or craving – as charity and concupiscence, she identified the fear of oblivion as creatively unsettling.[14] In her wonderfully suggestive study of (and her personal journey with) Arendt, Lyndsey Stonebridge insightfully identifies the origins of 'the puzzle' that 'would stay with [Arendt] for life' as she probed the 'relevance of other people in our lives.' But Stonebridge understates the influence of Arendt's teacher and lover, Martin Heidegger, on her first encounter with Augustine, during which she recognised that, for the prelate, the shadow of dying (precarity and mortality) conditioned the trajectories of living.[15] For Augustine and Arendt, stability, unlike precarity, bred complacence. For the latter, however, natality would come to eclipse mortality. She seemed convinced that she could inspire citizens' stamina to begin anew to practise politics without allowing sovereignty or rule to determine directions that discourse and activity would take in alternative public spheres. And, as we shall see, she would not furnish rules. She expected that citizens, reformed as citizen-statesmen – and, therefore, unrecognisable as citizens conformed to statists' expectations – could set the parameters for their collectives and become catalysts for changes beyond them.

Recollecting her disappointments, Arendt refused to discount the difficulties. She acknowledged the sturdiness of nonconformists' impulses. Take her ambivalent account of the career of Bertolt Brecht, which we shall examine at greater length. She celebrated the liveliness of his early verses but also his sarcasm and satire even after he accepted an invitation to direct a theatre company in East Berlin, where the Stasi and other Stalinists created a culture of fear. But she appears to have missed Brecht's short poem that summarises her approach to beginning anew. His *Die Lösung* or 'Solution' responded to leaflets that expressed authorities' distress with, and mistrust of, citizens after striking German workers and supporters defied the official cease-and-desist. The dissidents were neck-deep in trouble when the Soviet army suppressed their protests and officials from the writers' union advised East Germans to recover the regime's trust. Brecht then came up with his 'Solution.' Whereas his union urged citizens to obey and appease, Brecht's poem countered that it might be 'simpler' for the government 'to elect another people' (*wählte ein anderes*).[16]

Brecht's sardonic 'Solution' was to have the regime choose its electorate. Arendt's solution has citizens remaking themselves – and each other – 'rediscover[ing] the treasure of public freedom' in what Jonathan Peter Schwartz commends as 'robustly participatory,' 'non-sovereign political' collectives. Schwartz, though, is far more ambitious and optimistic than Arendt was. She did not imagine, as Schwartz does, that those collectives should eventually congeal into some 'federated,' 'cosmopolitan' public realm. Schwartz's Arendt gave no quarter to citizens looking to reinforce 'communitarianism,' yet she did. Furthermore, unlike Schwartz, Arendt was unpersuaded that a 'rediscover[y]' of 'the treasure of public freedom' required 'a vast expansion of the public realm.'[17] Indeed, an array of other scholars agree that she favoured what Robert Nisbet calls 'localism.' Her instances of such rediscoveries were small: juries, insurgents' cells and town council meetings. But in what follows we must press beyond structure and size to argue that Arendt cared less about both and more about agency, about the importance of resistance and about the ways to inspire change agents to remodel democracy.[18]

## Notes

1. BPF, 154.
2. Samuel Moyn, *Liberalism against Itself: Cold War Intellectuals and the Making of Our Times* (New Haven: Yale University Press, 2023), 83.
3. Compare OR, 129–30 with Moyn, *Liberalism*, 122–3.
4. Moyn, *Liberalism*, 129.
5. Ibid., 115.
6. Ari Adut, *Reign of Appearances: The Misery and Splendor of the Public Sphere* (Cambridge: Cambridge University Press, 2018), 4–6, 72–3.
7. Étienne Tassin, *Le trésor perdu: Hannah Arendt; l'intelligence de l'action politique* (Paris: Klincksieck, 2017), 351–2.
8. Arendt, 'Home to Roost,' RJ, 264–5.
9. Compare Moyn, *Liberalism*, 138.
10. Ned O'Gorman, *Politics for Everybody: Reading Hannah Arendt in Uncertain Times* (Chicago: University of Chicago Press, 2020), 133–5.
11. Compare Wendy Brown, *Undoing the Demos: Neoliberalism's Stealth Revolution* (New York: Zone, 2015), notably, 108–9.
12. Judith Butler, *Notes Toward a Performative Theory of Assembly* (Cambridge, MA: Harvard University Press, 2015), 148–51, 217–18.
13. Consult Annette Vowinckel, *Geshichtsbegriff und historisches Denken bei Hannah Arendt* (Cologne: Böhlau, 2001), 337–8.
14. LB, 18.
15. Compare Lyndsey Stonebridge, *We Are Free to Change the World: Hannah Arendt's Lessons in Love and Disobedience* (London: Hogarth, 2024), 114–15.
16. Bertolt Brecht, *Poetry and Prose*, ed. Reinhold Grimm (New York: Continuum, 2003), 118–19.
17. Jonathan Peter Schwartz, *Arendt's Judgment: Freedom, Responsibility, Citizenship* (Philadelphia: University of Pennsylvania Press, 2016), 202–4.
18. For 'localism,' see Robert Nisbet, 'Hannah Arendt and the American Revolution,' *Social Research* 44, no. 1 (1977), 76–9. We shall have more to say about the differences between Arendt and Nisbet but also about Arendt's efforts to press beyond others who emphasised her fondness for the miniature and her remarks about 'elementary republics.'

# Introduction: Arendt on Being Political

## Citizen-Statesmen

The raft of 'insights as old as articulated political experience,' which she associated with Greeks touting the importance of practical wisdom, helped Hannah Arendt identify the precondition for statesmanship, specifically, an 'ability to see things [from] the perspective[s] of all those present.' This enabled citizen-statesmen to 'orient [themselves] in the public realm' and to participate or perform as 'political being[s].' The implication is that others, straitjacketed with (or in) their own opinions, are kept from becoming statesmen. They are kept from 'sharing the world with others,' from agilely adjusting to changing circumstances, and, therefore, prevented from judging circumspectly.[1] Such straitjacketed citizens orbit around public life. They have no share in shaping it. Statists, desiring citizens' complacency and conformity, control the script. Citizens fill the public realm, expanded by the ubiquitous media and social networks. The more outspoken vie to be heard but generally echo what they've been told. Fictions frequently create factions. Lyndsey Stonebridge identifies the central 'categor[ies]' of Arendt's political thought, but she seems not to have appreciated how they were forged to resist pressures to conform. For Arendt would not have acknowledged, as Stonebridge does, that the 'laws and frameworks to contain [citizens'] action[s]' are 'frail' and unable to 'withstand the onslaught with which each generation inserts itself into the world.'[2] Statists' laws and customs were formidable. As I write, well into the twenty-first century, fictions and factions abound in modern democratic republics, polarising discourse, paralysing comprehensive dissent. The more circumspect, scandalized, would-be citizen-statesmen are pushed to the periphery.[3]

Arendt, as we shall discover, explicitly complained about the difficulties of being statesmanlike in a cluttered, ill-defined, increasingly squalid public realm. She never underestimated problems one confronts while sharing that world. But she insisted that sharing made one's perspectives as well as those of others 'political.' The give-and-take would require forbearance, she explained, hoping her readers were up to the challenge. For placing one's perspectives alongside those of interlocutors and submitting to their influence determined whether the subjective could be 'generalisable' and, Steffen Hermann continues, turned the interpersonal into the political.[4] Arendt's hopes, on that count, have been contagious as well as controversial. Few endorsed them; some amended them; many discounted them as utopian. Her prescriptions for citizen-statesmen continue to generate lively, informed studies of her career, some of which record Arendt's fretting every so often, from the 1930s until her death in 1975, about the failure of damage control along with the recklessness and ruthlessness in the public realm. Performances there tested her faith in the future of the democratic republic to which she emigrated. Would it turn out that the deliberations of a New York City jury, on which she served in the late 1960s – and which she described as invigorating to Karl Jaspers – were as close as she would come to witnessing genuinely democratic deliberations?[5]

But the jurors' job was to sift evidence and reach consensus. Some suspended their reservations to avoid a hung jury. Yet, as we shall find, Arendt censured conformity and mistrusted closure. She found jurors' sincerity endearing and was impressed by their candour, but her enthusiasm for both can hardly be read back into the privileged positions she reserved for colloquy in alternative public realms. She admired the small flock of founders of the American republic. On her reading of their deliberations, jealousies were overcome to make the necessary arrangements for their territory's independence. True, what she conjured up – her version of early American history – shows signs of selective amnesia, yet it brought her no closer to trusting consensus than did her acquaintance with Marxists who looked forward to a post-capitalist consciousness ushering in a classless future. She retained a fondness for the inconclusive, for plurality and for agonistic exchanges but not for conformity. She had a passion for arguments yet less to say about the merits of agreements. She trusted that lively deliberations would invite (or incite) citizens to extend their horizons, 'enlarge [their] mentalities' and, as citizen-statesmen, extend others' sensibilities and horizons.

She said so emphatically, coupling Kant with the Athenians, whose 'incorporat[ion of] struggle into [the] organizational form' of public life appeared not only wise to her but also 'the highest form of human communal activity.'[6] As for Arendt's Kant, he retrieved from 'the Homeric way' the importance of seeing every subject 'in its full reality,' that is, from 'as many perspectives as there are people to discuss' them. Her citizen-statesmen would subscribe to and enliven such seeing and sifting. But their deliberations, as she envisioned them, had to be something other than differently shaded expositions of principles or policies offered *seriatim*. Exchanges that enlarged mentalities featured 'a back, forth and against' (*das Hin und Her und Wider*), which promoted friendships and reciprocities.[7] Almost as an afterthought, she let on that a willingness to forgive eliminated most sources of friction and reinforced a spirit of compromise preventing interlocutors from unwisely flailing away at each other. But whatever decorum was observed, participants were obliged to assess 'the same thing from two opposing sides and then from all sides' and were bound to keep differences in play. Athenians supposedly had done so, and, by doing so, they passed along the 'first successful creation ... of a political realm.'[8]

Differences were critical for confrontations encouraging citizen-statesmen to develop self-awareness and to foster best political practices. But statists generally preferred what Arendt called the 'politics of obedience' that presumed one party was infallible or at least far better positioned and better equipped to address what David Martin Jones denotes as a government's 'complex, contingent [political] realities.' Statists were realists, on Jones's watch, experts who applied the 'rules of prudence' to 'the predicament[s] of rule.'[9] They demanded deference, and such statists' preference for deference had chilling effects on citizens' sensibilities. As a result, citizens' participation in conventionally conceived public realms was minimal. Arendt stocked her study of totalitarianism with telling examples of their superfluity and irresponsibility, but she explicitly and more accessibly dramatized that chill in a subsequent study of the consequences of conformity, in her *post mortem* for the trial and execution of Adolf Eichmann. As she knew from experience during the late 1930s and 1940s, many Germans and others in central and eastern Europe looked on as unwanted, vilified neighbours were evicted, evacuated, interned, and ultimately exterminated. Witnesses as well as the bureaucrats presiding over the removals self-medicated. They swallowed bogus consolations. Removal was called emigration. Citizens grew numb to the horror, followed orders and refused to see 'from all sides' (and even afterward, to appraise critically or penitently) their indifference to, and dependence on, homegrown fascists parading as an aberrant form of Jones's prudent politicians. Ordinary citizens became statists' accomplices after having forfeited the 'back, forth, and up against' that distinguished self-reflection in civilized societies.[10]

They failed to think critically about their behavior and about the malevolence around them; they failed to take account of the various – and of the victims' – perspectives from which the fascists' frightening political practices should have been assessed. The stakes for so many were so high, yet citizens failed to protest. Such failures haunted Arendt; for her, they undermined political practice. Enlightened authorities should know not to pass laws to restrict citizens from thinking, speaking, assessing or disputing, she asserted, looking to the ancients who, in her reconstruction of classical antiquity's political restraint, had judiciously confined laws to what she took to be their proper function: bridling insatiability. That done, discourses then proceeded, ennobling venues as public realms. And the discourses, in turn, stitched informed, informative individuals into constellations of citizen-statesmen. In their collectives, the distribution of influence would be discussed rather than, as Carl Schmitt would have had it, fixed by a single sovereign power that formulated decisions that applied general rules.[11]

Schmitt's reliance on sovereign decisions tended to stabilise, as long as obedience followed, whereas reliance on deliberations was destabilising. Arendt claimed that collectives' precarity and impermanence were not liabilities. They provided opportunities. Intermittent liquidations and subsequent consolidations of citizens' 'common world[s]' made space for new beginnings, new connections and constellations. She clarified: relatively short shelf lives of public realms where citizen-statecraft was defined and developed were not due to hostility. The competitive agonistic spirit was not antagonistic.[12] The unravelling of old remedies, the unfolding of new issues and the changing circumstances spurred what she called 'natality,' the fearless fondness for new beginnings. In the final three chapters and conclusion of this study, we shall calibrate their importance for Arendt's redefinitions of the public realm as well as the contributions they make to our efforts to reimagine citizenship. But it is sufficient now to specify that insolvency could be cathartic and that new collectives incubating the virtues of citizen-statesmanship after some dissolutions of the old need not have required wholesale, disorienting personnel changes. Agonistic discourse, as Arendt imagined it, preserved friendships and fostered performances – speech and action – that dignified performers and advertised the politically as well as personally enriching possibilities of properly reframed public realms. Significantly, John Macready notices how Arendt 'mov[ed] beyond traditional essentialist accounts of human dignity' and why she insisted that dignity be defined performatively, particularly, in political practices favouring the interpersonal over the impersonal and bureaucratic. Macready defines the result as 'conditional dignity,' dignity conditioned by, as well as revealed in, the quality of every citizen-statesman's performances.[13]

Was Arendt's emphasis on the interpersonal and performative unrealistic? For all her talk about friendship, which we shall revisit, she would not have citizen-statesmen 'fuse with' others. She required distance for 'a space of appearances' to open between interlocutors. But compassion, she believed, 'abolishes the distance' and, therefore, the in-between (the '*inter-est*') necessary for dialogues generating 'argumentative interest[s] in the world.' Compassionate persons grow reluctant to provoke, confront and affront. They flatter. Compassion, Arendt imagined, stymied candour. Furthermore, the compassionate, she continued, would be tempted to 'shun the drawn-out wearisome processes of persuasion, negotiation and compromise.'[14] Contestable opinions would go uncontested. Worse, the compassionate, in Arendt's reconstruction of their intimacy, squandered chances to counter the seductively sedative effects of statists' views. And theorists who touted compassion introduced theology into political theory, allowing generalizations to stand as infallible (and, to her mind, depersonalising) and to render would-be citizen-statesmen powerless to breathe life into or inspire 'the real presence of others.'[15]

But, for Arendt, a greater threat than compassion or fusion to meaningful political conversations in public realms was the intrusion of what she distinguished as the wholly other realms of social and economic life. She contended that management of social and economic striving and rivalries should be left to administrators. Related concerns with production and consumption not only intruded into, but had also 'overshadowed[,] the political realm … since the beginning of the modern age.' She proposed that a redistribution of responsibilities for managing social affairs in agencies somehow separate from politics (but she did not stipulate how) was long overdue. Critics see that Arendt, in effect, was impoverishing politics, interpreting even 'international power problems as ultimately springing from economic factors and interests.'[16] Much like compassion, though in vastly different ways, commerce eradicated the *inter-ests* she thought necessary for political activity and discourse. Only political practice, as she redefined it, created those in-betweens where 'the real presence' of participants inclined each to enact what she characterised as 'a who.' But whatever persons produce, expropriate and accumulate, she went on, turn each of them into a 'what.' The citizen-statesmen's 'real story,' she insisted, was political. They were its heroes. Yet she swiftly issued a disclaimer, for Homeric, heroic qualities were not required for what she had in mind as political practice. The only heroic quality required for what she construed as political endeavour was self-transcendence, the ability and the readiness to transcend self-concern and to engage in the *Hin und Her und Wider* making discourse and action political. Any occasion for such transcendence, we shall learn, was a new beginning and was more than what Linda Zerilli depicts as 'an occasion for response.' It was a revelation of possibilities eliciting a species of response that required resistance and courage.[17]

Arendt identified courage as 'indispensable,' particularly as manifest in a 'willingness to act and speak [and] insert one's self into the world.' There were no dress rehearsals. Either one snatched chances to plunge into 'the living flux of acting and speaking' and thus to become 'a who' – a palpable contrast to 'the citizen' defined by statists – or one sought refuge in making, behaving and conforming that seemed to Arendt to be little more than fidgeting, save that shuffling about tempted producers and consumers to trade their *whos* for what they produced or possessed. On this count, she was not all mockery. She thought properly defined political enterprises could be served quite well by some cultural productions, especially the narratives that condensed and commemorated best political practices, discourses and initiatives, which might otherwise be forgotten. Nonetheless, cultural productions were still fabrications – remote from the 'living flux' of the cultural, political exchanges they recorded. Such distance kept their producers or impresarios (pundits or pollsters in forms more conspicuous now than in Arendt's day) from experiencing what she revered as 'the specific revelatory quality of action and speech.'[18]

## The Marketplace Ascendant

Yet there can be no denying that life is ordinarily organised around the requirements and rhythms of the marketplace. Plurality there simply refers to choices of product. Even statists seem tempted to swap efforts to retain political influence for comforts afforded by successes buying and selling. Citizens value those successes more than political participation, though, as Ari Adut suggests, they are not completely powerless politically. They may enforce what Adut calls 'visibility norms' that, ideally, dispose political officials to brake before cruelly exhibiting their authority.[19] Yet citizens commonly become less scrupulous monitors when their economic interests are well-served. During the 1950s, Arendt wrote about postwar Germany's rubble and recovery. She relayed to readers remote from the wreckage that it became 'a radical stimulant for a … quick, more efficient accumulation of wealth' in what had been partitioned and survived as West Germany. But abundance generated a 'waste economy.' The marketplace ascendant, which promoted the widespread devotion to production and consumption, discountenanced impulses to conserve.[20] Of greater consequence politically, abundance discouraged citizens from answering (or even from asking) what Arendt dubbed the 'anti-nihilistic question': why should they exist? Statists' celebrations of conformity, in effect, made intellectual indolence respectable. Citizens simply settled for being political nobodies and let sovereign powers determine when exigencies summoned them, provisionally, to become a public. But even then, citizens let statists determine their consensus. Outstanding issues were resolved for them rather than by them. From the 1930s into the 1970s, Arendt witnessed statists' cunning management (or manipulation) of their public; she looked on as citizens in ostensibly democratic regimes became casualties.[21]

They conformed; their conformity bred complacency; complacency made them easy prey. And totalitarians were cunning predators. But room in Arendt's rogues gallery was also reserved for capitalists and bureaucrats who, she claimed, put citizens under 'insistent' pressure to produce, consume and conform.[22] Her antidote, as Dana Villa says, was 'a genuine politics centered on human plurality, speech and the exchange of opinion in the public sphere.' The observation is uncontroversial, yet Arendt knew political authenticity would be extremely difficult to nurture. For conformist citizens were relatively clueless, ready and eager to follow rather than to lead, largely incurious about their own commodification, wholly unaware that they were casualties. Statists had an interest in preserving citizens' innocence and disempowerment. A 'fabrication model of action,' Arendt noted, convinced citizens that making and marketing preempted political agency.[23]

But Villa does not seem to accept that citizens' recuperation, under such circumstances, would be unrealistic as long as lively, alternative public realms, free from statists' control, are beyond citizens' reach. In 2007, he was distracted by what he termed a 'deeper problem' with Arendt's 'political formulation of plurality.' It was, he argued, too narrow. It failed to account for moral pluralism. Failure on that front duly noted – although not by her – we ought to contextualise her unwillingness to accommodate the opinions of those whom Villa has trumpeting the advantages of an 'increasingly privatised culture.' Arendt presumably would have dismissed them as statists' unwitting collaborators, as credulous creatures oblivious to their political disempowerment or, as Villa also laments, unconcerned that citizenship has lost its 'luster.'[24] But her dismissal made sense, given her interest in rescuing political agency from what his later, more comprehensive study of Arendt's 'central concerns' identifies as 'the automation' or 'mechanisation' of the life process, which seems the culmination of marketplace ascendancy. Her imperative was to resist.[25]

So, for Arendt, the qualities associated with citizen-statesmanship were non-negotiable. Borrowing from Cicero, she detailed the problems leading to the wreckage of the Roman republic – preeminently, Romans' seemingly contagious indifference to civic responsibility – comparing them with 'privatised cultures' in the twentieth century, steadfastly and mistakenly taking the rhythms of the market (production and consumption) as all-consuming. The sudden squalls of concern for public wellbeing in late antiquity (*cura rei publica*) were too few and far between. In Arendt's version of the Romans' history, citizens, abetted by philosophers 'opposing contemplation to all kinds of activity,' became overprotective of their privacy. Statesmanship, as she defined it, suffocated.[26] She brought her sources to heel in a somewhat eccentric way, turning a blind eye to evidence for civic patronage and pageantry, even from Rome's remote provinces.[27] Yet her analysis corresponds with that of many historians who keenly watch the transition from the Greek to the Roman worlds. Antonio Vázquez-Arroyo refers to the momentous differences between the Greek (predominantly Athenian) conceptions of citizenship that stressed 'common involvement' and Roman notions that did not, permitting the nobility and then their emperors' inner circle to govern. The result: citizens looked less to shape their government than to seek protection from it. Vázquez-Arroyo proposes that the transition 'could be considered the first great experience of depoliticisation in the Western tradition,' whereby the 'politics of interest trumped the politics of participation.' Security and luxury afforded by success in the market led to the degeneration of a political life. Among the Romans, political life was reconceived. It was open to a few; it was 'an organisation' and not, as it supposedly had been for the Athenians, 'an association.'[28] Arendt agreed with political theorists who viewed such changes in the perception and evaluation of politics as steps in the wrong direction. But their remedies were not hers. They sought to reify rehabilitated systems or structures to inspire public participation. But, to her, faith in such reforms was misinformed. Political reflection and participation, she averred, should defy systematisation and commodification. Tactics, therefore, must vary, draw on dissatisfaction and be 'as relentless as life itself.'[29]

We shall discover that Arendt geared up to free judgement from the passion for systems and structures that developed from governments' obsessions with market forces and, as we shall discuss later, from political philosophy's admiration for the sciences.[30] Yet those forces, systems and structures came with conspicuous advantages. Notwithstanding their far from spotless record for defending human dignity and for managing competition to minimise belligerence, structured commercial and political agreements often kept human 'unreliability' from capsizing collectives' best efforts to foster meaningful, agonistic political discourses. Arendt yielded that point, yet she complained about the prevailing systems and structures. They failed to disinfect other polarising discourses, to rid them of such contaminants as spite, scorn and slander. What might have been usefully disputatious deliberations were made dreadfully contentious. But because constituted powers' provisions for conformity were in place as breakwaters against what she identified as history's 'incalculability,' statists and citizens alike shored up their political and commercial arrangements with permanent structures. Quiz Arendt about the desirability of such provisions, and she would almost certainly have replied that openness to the future was the prerequisite and 'price for plurality.' The comforts of conformity were undeniable, yet significant enrichment of political speech and action depended on nonconformity – on plurality. She therefore advised readers to resist 'hitch[ing themselves] firmly to one possible perspective.'[31] Opening up to others was likelier to satisfy the cravings for freedom, equality and new beginnings that she summoned citizens to indulge.

Openness, as noted, would be destabilising and disconcerting at first. But, as Steven Klein says, Arendt was eager to disabuse citizens of consoling misconceptions. She conceded that capitalism once seemed promising. 'The economic' became 'a domain of technical mastery.' Citizens were content to have the economic subsume or 'replace' the political. But Klein's Arendt looked to restore 'stable attachments that mediate between the economic and political.' We shall learn, though, that she was clearly and often sceptical that what he calls 'instrumentalising force[s] of the economic subsystem' could ever 'appear as the shared objects of [a] politics' that would, on her terms, pass muster.[32] Citizen-statesmen, however, would have a more mature understanding of the state of play. They trusted that the 'power, which keeps public sphere[s] in existence, [is] the force of mutual promise,' 'the binding power of promises.' Unlike the systems or structures that boasted 'mastery' and permanence, making and keeping promises did not expect to 'cover the whole ground of the future' or, Arendt added, 'to map a path secure in all directions.' Still, promises propped up her reimagined political cultures that let freedom reign.[33]

For Arendt, promises, friendships and, as we shall see, forgiveness sustained optimal conditions for encouraging citizen-statesmanship in alternative collectives. She believed that promises were sturdier than the structures, systems and ideologies on offer in her time. Promise-keeping relied on the promisers' honour, and, she specified, honour far exceeded 'the virtue of decency,' on which Michael Polanyi, for one, depended to transport civilizations 'beyond nihilism.' Arendt courteously proffered her reservations. She approved of Polanyi's determination to get to that 'beyond' and to recover from the culture shocks, for which the twentieth-century tyrannies in central, eastern and southern Europe had been responsible. She agreed with him that European civilization's convalescence required the repudiation of fascists' 'generalising and radicalising thought.' Yet he seemed intemperate to her, touting pragmatism's and empiricism's 'intellectual virtue.' She reckoned that Polanyi's and pragmatism's dependence on decency had foolishly forsaken all theory. She strikingly suggested one could make the case that 'the root of all our evils' can be 'found in the rise of pragmatism and positivism,' both of which consigned theory to a forbidden zone.[34] But political theory need not be divorced from political reality. Indeed, political practices based on promises to discuss plural perspectives were, for her, far better ways to pass beyond nihilism to the commitments that could represent participation in political discourse and deliberation as attractive without promising closure. Arendtian citizen-statesmen's promises to each other ought to lead to engagements that amount to a more robust counter (more robust, that is, than reliance on 'the virtue of decency') to both depravity and to the depraved indifference to politics Arendt found so maddening in the United States from the late 1940s into the 1960s. Immediately after Nazism's eternal *Reich* collapsed and fifteen years before she mapped her course 'beyond nihilism,' she asserted that confronting 'incalculable evil' was the 'precondition for any modern political thinking.' For thirty years thereafter, she held that 'the binding power of promises,' more effectively than the weak tea of post-war pragmatism and positivism could stir citizens to 'fight ... fearlessly, uncompromisingly, everywhere' against the resurgence of totalitarianism and, more generally, against wickedness.[35]

Promises, plurality and freedom were so consistently enthroned at Arendt's court that one may be pardoned for having missed how rudely truth had been unseated. As early as the 1930s, she was wary that truths tended to force closure on conversations and, doing so, to stifle meaningful political discourse. Public realms were to be protected from truths, from those of capitalism and those of Marxism.[36] Politics, as Arendt redefined it, sifted opinions rather than proclaimed truths, whereas statists' politics used truths to corset citizens' curiosity. But when citizens were allowed to participate in deliberation, statists, brandishing their truths, more or less scripted participation so that the truths citizens voiced, by 'happy coincidence,' she stated facetiously, converged with statists' interests or with citizens' economic self-interest. Broad participation, therefore, proved compatible with the marketplace ascendant. As we shall see, Arendt urged that pressure to have truths 'play a political role' be resisted. 'Truthfulness,' she declared, 'never counted among the political virtues, because it has little indeed to contribute to that change of the world and of circumstances,' which she numbered 'among the most legitimate political activities.'[37]

## The Unconventional

As we contemplate Arendt's unblushing attempts to redefine politics and to reimagine both citizenship and democracy, we shall return to discuss her evaluations of the truthtellers' and ideologues' crippling effect on citizens' participation in conventional public realms. But this introduction cannot conclude without sifting her intention to identify freedom as an insurgent, subversive force. Citizens become citizen-statesmen, she claimed, when they are free and eager to participate in agonistic exchanges and when they also use their freedom to call attention to the commodification conspicuous in conventional political cultures that appeared cluttered to Arendt as well as overly, angrily competitive. But David Arndt suspects she would have had 'economic question[s]' docketed for political conversations. Arndt contends that, if such questions are left out, her 'view of politics,' would be as 'narrow' and 'nearly empty' as her most ardent critics hold. But his contention, we shall argue, misjudges Arendt's determination to having politics redefined in alternative venues, worlds apart from the ascendant marketplace.[38] That distance strikes Horst Mewes as significant. He recalls Arendt's vivid displeasure with covetous citizens' obsessions with production and consumption. In terms borrowed from her, Mewes explains that such obsessions leave too little space for politics to make 'an appearance' because there was too little space for citizens to make theirs. Conventional public realms become too crowded for best political practices when talk of producing, consuming, pricing and marketing stand in for and crowd out political discourse.[39] Arendt's briefs for unconventional alternative political spaces (and for the virtues of citizen-statesmanship incubated there) took the form of a challenge that featured the insurgent, dissident force of freedom as a summons to change. 'That we can change the circumstances under which we live at all,' she wrote, is due to our being 'relatively free from them,' free to inspect an array of opinions and to make new beginnings.[40]

The subversive force of freedom enlivened political discourse in alternative public realms that thereby incubated the virtues Arendt associated with citizen-statesmanship. That process, then, qualified, from her perspective, as politics. We shall elaborate her definition later and often in this study, yet a revealing anecdote seems appropriate here. In 1954, Arendt fumed at Geoffrey Francis Fisher, the Archbishop of Canterbury, who proposed that only two sorts of people knew what they were for and against: communists and Christians. Fisher dismissed others as 'amicable non-entities.' Unpartisan and, he insinuated, unintelligent, they were sent off the prelate's pitch. They may have tussled with peers about ephemera, but they were ciphers tenaciously defending neither of Fisher's options.[41] Arendt trotted out the archbishop's characterisation to contest it. His 'amicable' yet unimportant others, in her universe, were not featherweights. Discussing a variety of alternative perspectives, they proved their *gravitas* and enriched political discourse. Fisher's few supposedly knowledgeable partisans thrive on mutual suspicion and polarisation, whereas Arendt's interlocutors interrogate multiple opinions, thereby 'actualis[ing] plurality,' Sophie Loidolt says, and 'keep[ing Arendt's] public realm … in existence.'[42] Loidolt notices that such 'political intersubjectivity' was fundamentally a 'critique of the Cartesian subject,' a critique as well of all 'forms of collectivity that swallow individuality,' but she does not notice that Arendt's 'democratic form of being together' was also a radical critique of democracy, as conventionally conceived and practised.[43] Communication and competition (but not closure) in alternative venues (or poleis) ensured that distances between interlocutors were preserved and that all agreements were provisional. Plurality was the constant, and the *inter-ests* or distances between interlocutors kept them from 'falling over each other.' Yet, Arendt specified, *inter-ests* also joined them as friends with diverse opinions. Distances, therefore, paid dividends: personal, intellectual and political.[44]

Maurizio Passerin d'Entreves acknowledges that Arendt laboured a fair point: 'warmth can never become political.' Yet, featuring friendship, forgiveness and the importance of promise-keeping, she did not insist that political practices invariably precluded the levels of intimacy one typically finds among pariahs in their communities in diaspora.[45] Politics lived there. For Arendt, politics was not found where statists were preoccupied with sovereignty and rule or where production and consumption devoured citizens' interest and time. Perhaps because Ned O'Gorman has not registered Arendt's disappointments as strikingly as they will soon seem to readers of this study, he locates her political forums close to the 'civic architecture and public media' she found both intractable and distasteful. Citizens, therefore, emerge from O'Gorman's alternative poleis with 'skills in political judgement' but apparently disinclined to render devastating judgement against what conventionally passes as politics.[46] They would have more in common with persons Arendt judged critically as parvenus than with pariahs, whom she admired. O'Gorman, much as David Arndt and Sophie Loidolt, has presented refreshingly coherent accounts of Arendtian political preferences, which previous scholars considered scattershot. But the sense that freedom 'could be cultivated widely within our political culture' would have made no sense to her.[47]

Without elaborating, Sylwia Chrostowska brackets Arendt with Giorgio Agamben and several others coaxing theorists to conjure 'nonstatist' collectives known for their 'oppositionality to, and incommensurability with, democratic state sovereignty' – known for 'undercut[ting] high politics.'[48] Introducing diasporic collectives suggests precisely that 'incommensurability' along with what we shall characterise and soon contextualise as pariah sensitivities that Arendt found politically generative. She recalled an unnamed ancient Greek sage who had offered consoling remarks to reassure grim, grieving exiles: 'wherever you may be,' he allegedly said, 'you will constitute a polis.' Forgetting how fractious communities in diaspora often become, Arendt depicted those Greeks in exile as offshoots replicating political practices developed 'at home.'

Émigrés and their pariah poleis (what she would later depict as 'oases'), at their polished best, upheld the value of freedom, equality and plurality. They established and maintained properly, authentically political performances.[49]

What follows in the next two chapters presents evidence of Arendt's recurring disappointment with what evolved in the twentieth century from the political principles, practices and virtuosity she valued. That disappointment led her to write from the pariah's perspective inspiring readers' resolve (and leaving them resources) to reconstitute democracies. This book's last few chapters underscore the importance of that resolve and of those resources for the twenty-first century, during which statists have become adept at what we characterise as 'citizen capture.' For such statists continue to oversee the turn towards authoritarianism in conventional democracies that behave as oligarchies. As two would-be agents of resistance and change, Alix Olson and Alex Zamalin, suggest, new taboos confront citizens looking to protest that 'turn' and behavior, for 'the "democratic" institutions and mechanisms [once] available for organising and expressing discontent' are no longer accessible in the United States and beyond.[50]

Arendt perceived as much, finding that republican regimes fetishised sovereignty. Democracies in the twentieth century were far from the Athens-of-her-remaking. Statists prattled about unity but perpetuated tribal strife, resentments and envy. She imagined that agonistic exchanges were critically important to the exercise of freedom and relevant to the contributions plurality made to democratic practice. But 'contemporary agonists,' according to Giuseppe Baldacci, have come to rely on contentious politics to consolidate collective identities and to detonate charges against – rather than to dialogue with – unassimilated others.[51] Modern agonists become implacable and incorrigible, 'assault[ing]' each other (and democracy) in India, Israel, Europe, Latin America and the United States.[52] Few leaders care to see the world as adversaries or rivals do, that is, to see from others' points of view. They are uninterested in acquiring discernment and 'enlarged mentalit[ies],' which originate with an appreciation for alterity and the commitment to plurality Arendt characterised as 'the political kind of insight par excellence.'[53] In the third decade of the twenty-first century, so much seems at stake for persons who value democracy in the developed and developing worlds. They will find Arendt an ally to the extent that they are prepared to ponder resistance and radical proposals. Doing so, they become the answer to her critics who suspect that any derivative of Arendtian politics is now *inoperante*.[54]

Arendt's answers: work on citizens' motivation. Agency! Reimagine democratic practice, once change-agents have revealed, resisted and undercut statists' seduction. Reimagine citizenship to inspire citizen-statesmanship and change. And create the alternative venues where the virtuosity and virtues of the former can be developed. Statists, to her mind, were antipathetic towards such endeavours. They beguiled, distracted and deceived citizens until enthusiasm for participation in governance ebbed. Arendt echoed Niccolò Machiavelli to that effect and coupled his analyses of lying in politics with her own, and to oppose deceit she summoned Socrates. For all his missteps, he was still emblematic of citizen-statesmanship, for he constantly questioned himself as well as his interlocutors. Her Socrates 'carried within' a witness from which neither he nor an Arendtian could escape. Conscience called citizens back to binding promises that made alternative poleis plausible. But Arendt's Machiavelli bridled optimism. In her 'conversations' with the Athenian and the Florentine, they proved to be as sobering and astute about political promises as they had been about political hypocrisy. Mendacity marked conventional political practice; both the ruled and their rulers 'created phantoms and apparitions ... to fool others' (while fooling themselves) to gain or retain political advantages. As a result, 'treachery and deceit' were pervasive. What, then, could be done? Arendt figured that the answers or remedies mentioned above required a 'watchful and testifying self.' For her, that was what Socrates recommended and what statists attempt to suppress. Critics tempted to concede the 'inoperability' of her politics might try coupling, as she did, Machiavelli's grim analysis with Socrates' prodding to rediscover the insurgent power of freedom and to appreciate its political relevance.[55]

During the late 1920s and early 1930s, Arendt was interested in freedom and resistance to (as well as the failures to resist) assimilation. She was drawn to Augustine, whose 'estrangement' from (her dissertation's term is *Entfremdung*), and aversion to, Romans' seemingly boundless desire for glory led him to advocate alternative ambitions and affections.[56] As she told Jaspers, the purpose of her next effort after finishing her thesis on Augustine, her *Habilitationsschrift*, was to apply what she called 'pariah standards' to study salonnière Rahel Varnhagen's intermittent efforts to assimilate.[57] She disclosed her intention in 1952, a year after the publication of her *Origins of Totalitarianism*, which could be characterised as a pariah's perspective on various statists' ways of making the assimilated 'superfluous.' It seems unfair, then, to consider Arendt's intent as 'apolitical,' as David Arndt does, while admitting that her 'primary concern' was to 'dismantle the inherited concepts in which politics is commonly understood.'[58] But Arndt underestimates, as Arendt did not, statists' opposition to dismantling. He seems to think that one can change 'the communities in which we live' without choosing a community in which to incubate values that would help citizen-statesmen first change citizens. The route to new beginnings passes through such alternative, unconventional collectives.[59]

At those oases, freedom, plurality, promise-keeping and forgiveness create and sustain conditions contrary to those of the ascendant marketplace and to those statists promote. Citizen-statesmen learn to renounce what C. Wright Mills calls 'the immorality of accomplishment,' which gives greed a good name. That renunciation precedes a restoration of citizenship's 'significance' and of citizens' 'action upon [their] common world.'[60] Reconstructing Max Weber's dismay at the 'decadence' of conventional politics, Wendy Brown expresses a desire for a place to extricate citizens from the politics perpetuated by statists' obsessions with sovereignty and domination, someplace where a revamped definition of citizenship could prosper after taking off from an 'unblinking consciousness of the contingent nature of our convictions,' which interlocutors in good company would review.[61] Arendt could not have said it better. But, as we shall discover, she said it often and as well.

## Notes

1. BPF, 217–18; *Denktagebuch*, 571–5.
2. Stonebridge, *Free to Change*, 211.
3. See Anne Applebaum, *Twilight of Democracy: The Seductive Lure of Authoritarianism* (New York: Doubleday, 2020), notably 37–54, 105–18 and 172–89.
4. For which, see Steffen Herrmann, 'Demokratische Urteilskraft nach Arendt,' *Zeitschrift für praktische Philosophie* 6, no. 1 (2019): 266.
5. *Briefwechsel*, 700–1.
6. PP, 165.
7. *Denktagebuch*, 392.
8. PP, 167–9; HC, 31–7. For Arendt's Athens, see Margaret Canovan, *Hannah Arendt: A Reinterpretation of her Political Thought* (Cambridge: Cambridge University Press, 1992), 115–16, 193–4 and Canovan, 'Hannah Arendt as a Conservative Thinker,' in *Hannah Arendt Twenty Years Later*, eds. Larry May and Jerome Kohn (Cambridge: MIT Press, 1996), 13.
9. David Martin Jones, *History's Fools: The Pursuit of Idealism and the Revenge of Politics* (Oxford: Oxford University Press, 2020), 203–4.
10. EJ, 278–9.
11. Marco Walter, 'Das Politische: eine Begriffsbestimmung mit Hannah Arendt und Carl Schmitt,' *Leviathan* 44, no. 3 (2016): 528–9. Also see Florian Dünckmann, 'Nur für Schwindelfreie? Eine Geographie politischer Praktiken nach Hannah Arendt,' *Geographica Helvetica* 75, no. 2 (2020): 88.
12. PP, 181, 186.

13. John Douglas Macready, 'Hannah Arendt and the Political Meaning of Human Dignity,' *Journal of Social Philosophy* 47, no. 4 (2016): 399–400.
14. OR, 76–7.
15. *Denktagebuch*, 525; HC, 243; Liisi Keedus, *The Crisis of German Historicism: The Early Political Thought of Hannah Arendt and Leo Strauss* (Cambridge: Cambridge University Press, 2015), 176.
16. BPF, 154.
17. Compare Linda M. G. Zerilli, *A Democratic Theory of Judgment* (Chicago: The University of Chicago Press, 2016), 202.
18. HC, 186–7.
19. Adut, *Reign of Appearances*, 112–13.
20. HC, 134–5, 252–3.
21. PP, 204.
22. Arendt, 'The Threat of Conformism,' *The Commonweal* 60 (September 24, 1954): 607–10.
23. Dana Villa, 'Arendt, Heidegger, and the Tradition,' *Social Research* 74, no. 4 (2007): 983–4.
24. Ibid., 998–1001.
25. Compare Dana Villa, *Arendt* (London: Routledge, 2021), 174–6.
26. HC, 85, citing Cicero's *De republica* 5.2.
27. See, for example, Anna Leone, *The End of the Pagan City: Religion, Economy, and Urbanism in Late Antique North Africa* (Oxford: Oxford University Press, 2013), 118–19 and Leonardo Lugaresi, *Il teatro di Dio: Il problema degli spettacoli nel cristianesimo antico (II – IV secolo)* (Brescia: Morecelliana, 2008), 735–52.
28. Antonio Y. Vázquez-Arroyo, *Political Responsibility: Responding to Predicaments of Power* (New York: Columbia University Press, 2016), 67–9.
29. HC, 170–1.
30. LM, 62–5.
31. MDT, 7–8.
32. Steve Klein, '"Fit to Enter the World": Hannah Arendt on Politics, Economics, and the Welfare State,' *American Political Science Review* 108, no. 4 (2014): 867.
33. HC, 244–5.
34. Arendt, 'Challenges to Traditional Ethics: A Response to Michael Polanyi,' *TWB*, 189–91.
35. Arendt, 'Organized Guilt and Universal Responsibility,' EU, 132.
36. OR, 209; EU, 375–6; and Ingeborg Nordmann, '"Fremdsein ist Gut": Hannah Arendt über Rahel Varnhagen,' in *Rahel Varnhagen: Die Wiederentdeckung einer Schriftstellerin*, eds. Barbara Hahn and Ursala Isselstein (Göttingen: Vandenhoeck und Ruprecht, 1987), 196.

37. BPF, 246–7.
38. David Arndt, *Arendt on the Political* (Cambridge: Cambridge University Press, 2019), 78. As previously noted, we shall protest the assessment of Arendt's politics as utopian, but we shall also challenge opinions to which Arndt refers (those of Hanna Pitkin, George Kateb and Dana Villa), opinions that her politics without economics is vapid, 'curiously empt[ied] of content,' talk rather than action and simply too exclusive.
39. Horst Mewes, 'L'action politique selon Hannah Arendt,' *Cités* 67, no. 3 (2016), 82–3, 90–1.
40. BPF, 246.
41. Arendt, 'Concern with Politics in Recent European Thought,' part 2, 8 (image 24); USLC.
42. Sophie Loidolt, *Phenomenology of Plurality: Hannah Arendt on Political Intersubjectivity* (London: Rutledge, 2018), 226.
43. Ibid., 155.
44. HC, 52–3.
45. See the brief discussion of civility, solidarity and 'warmth' in Maurizio Passerin d'Entreve, *The Political Philosophy of Hannah Arendt* (London: Routledge, 1994), 88.
46. O'Gorman, *Politics for Everybody*, 50–1, 64.
47. Ibid., 135.
48. See S. D. Chrostowska, *Utopia in the Age of Survival: Between Myth and Politics* (Stanford: Stanford University Press, 2021), 83–4. For Agamben's experimentation, see Peter Iver Kaufman, *On Agamben, Arendt, Christianity and the Dark Arts of Civilization* (London: Bloomsbury, 2020), 142–7.
49. Arendt, 'Culture and Politics,' TWB, 170.
50. Alix Olson and Alex Zamalin, *The Ends of Resistance: Making and Unmaking Democracy* (New York: Columbia University Press, 2024), 88, discussing Sheldon Wolin's depiction of democracy as 'inverted totalitarianism.'
51. Giuseppe Ballacci, 'Deliberative Agonism and Agonistic Deliberation in Hannah Arendt,' *Theoria* 66, no. 161 (2019): 11–12, referring to Chantal Mouffe, William Connolly, Bonnie Honig and Thomas Fossen's discussions of the 'Agonistic Critiques of Liberalism' in *Contemporary Political Theory* 7, no. 4 (2008): 376–94.
52. For the 'assaults,' see Benjamin Wallace-Wells, 'Democracy Calling,' *The New Yorker* (April 10, 2023): 11–12.
53. Arendt, 'Philosophy and Politics,' *Social Research* 71, no. 3 (2004): 436.
54. Guillermo Zapata, 'El espacio público y su fundamento en la libertad: Pensamiento político de Hannah Arendt,' *Papel Politico* 17, no. 1 (2012): 166, 173 (*La arendtiana es todavía una communidad inoperante*).

55. OR, 91–4.
56. LB, 86; Augustine, *De civitate Dei* 18.54.
57. *Briefwechsel*, 236.
58. Arndt, *Arendt on the Political*, 9 and 24.
59. Ibid, 181–2.
60. OT, 301–2. Arendt's *Origins* was first published in 1951; her exposition of *The Human Condition* appeared in 1958 two years after C. Wright Mills remarked on the influence of the elites' 'immorality of accomplishment' on 'the Machiavellianism of the little man.' Consult Wright Mills, *The Power Elite* (New York: Oxford University Press, 1956), notably, 341–50.
61. Wendy Brown, *Nihilistic Times: Thinking with Max Weber* (Cambridge: Harvard University Press, 2023), 47–9.

# 1

# Salesmanship and Statesmanship: Arendt's 'Acute Awareness of Political Finitude'

## Arendt's Founders of the American Republic

Good company creates common worlds, and common worlds require spaces for interlocutors to assemble. Yet social networks now use sophisticated technologies that expand the meanings of such terms as 'space' and 'assemble.' Here, however, we concentrate on traditional collectives. Although Arendt's common worlds could conceivably be maintained by correspondence, much as those of Renaissance *eruditi* were, she believed the urgent twentieth-century need was for presence, which made it possible to develop what she called *interests*, the spaces between interlocutors required to explore their different perspectives and to experience what she identified as participants' 'agent-revealing capacity.'[1] Into those betweens, she fit diverse opinions prompting discourse and generating a new politics whereby each interlocutor was encouraged to become a 'who.' Bystanders-turned-critics with conventional perspectives on politics and public life commonly dismissed her common worlds as not only unorthodox but irrelevant – as apolitical. After all, Arendt conceded that action and speech in her alternative collectives 'almost never achieve[d their] purpose.' Without purposes realized, without some 'conflicting wills and intentions' suppressed, without campaigners colonising constituencies – without a win, winners and losers – how could speech and action be political?[2]

So, suspicions about the politics of unconventional, alternative public realms are understandable, as are suspicions about the plausibility of Arendt's exclusive definition of political practice and doubts about the cogency of her enthusiasm for new beginnings. We must address those doubts and suspicions as well as her own indignation with respect to statists' definitions and practices. But we must first probe her redefinition of politics as speech and action that seem purposeless, when purposes are measured as policy formulation or enforcement. In what follows, we must also review her readiness to equate compassion with the erasure of spaces in between or *inter-ests* required to enliven public realms. But it is appropriate to begin with the reminder that, for her, the recipe for free, fruitful speech and action demanded distance between interlocutors and distance from conventional ideas about citizenship. She presumed that compassion narrowed or eliminated spaces in between, leading to assimilation and complacence and, therefore, making it impossible for persons to be political. She supposed that excessive affect inhibited intellect and figured compassion precluded candid, interpersonal, political performances. Citizen-statesmen were expected to resist the temptation to let feeling trump thinking and to 'abdicate powers and responsibilities' she characterised as political. For Arendt, overcoming such temptation avoided misunderstandings and misalliances permitting administrative issues to obscure the importance of political discourse. She was determined to underscore the political significance of *inter-ests* and the agonistic exchanges plural perspectives occasioned.

Arendt believed agonistic engagements both developed and demonstrated political virtuosity. Procedures – what she called 'precepts' – she assumed, would 'arise directly out of the will to live together with others in the mode of acting and speaking.'[3] She admired the founders of the American republic who understood the importance of involving 'we, the people' in the ongoing discussions and verbal skirmishes about political priorities and about the shapes that their local, state and federal governments ought to take. Abrasive remarks and the scent of dissent seemed not to have put them off. To her, the founders elicited robust, rival opinions. She was intrigued that Thomas Jefferson looked to have been unafraid of recurring revolutions, whereas many of his colleagues feared protest and sedition would become the rule rather than exceptions; to her, those colleagues appeared reluctant to 'provide space[s] where' 'freedom could be exercised' and distrustful of the very revolutionary spirit that brought their government into existence. Were they unaware that any energetic republic's self-fashioning must be forever unfinished? Did they fail to realise that the new constantly emerged from the old? Some insurgents seemed to her to have turned timid, yet she believed that enough had been done on their 'new' continent during the late eighteenth century to break the cycle of oppression-to-reformation-back-to-oppression.[4]

She was wrong. Her inferences seemed sound when she compared remedies for authoritarianism in late eighteenth-century France with the American founders' revolution. As Arendt repossessed them, the French efforts to pivot to a republic were fatally flawed. French founders misconstrued the power of the people. They were 'intoxicated' and overreached.[5] When misfortunes stirred the multitude, the republicans could not cope. Their commiseration failed to bind the people's power to personalities or to ideologies. Their republic disintegrated.[6] In Arendt's century and adopted country, the founders' heirs and their citizens looked to be courting a related political disaster. The latter were enormously impressed by shabby 'unpolitical gifts'– chief among them, what Dana Villa calls 'salesmanship.'[7] Anne Applebaum mulls over similar developments in the twenty-first century, and her brooding resembles Arendt's; for Applebaum wrestles with the inevitable 'excesses' of democracies. She recalls that the founders of the American republic anticipated that statist salesmanship – what Alexander Hamilton depicted as 'the little arts of popularity' – could give demagogues advantages over democrats. To hold the former in check, the founders put in place an electoral college, providing a squadron of elites the right and power to overturn the choices made by the broader electorate. The founders knew (and the elites surely would have ascertained) 'that any political system built on logic and rationality was always at risk from an outburst of the irrational.'[8] Arendt, much as Applebaum, yearned to return to 'the basis of rational debate' on which the founders of the republic placed their faith in democracy. Neither commoners nor elites, however, appeared to prefer that foundation, faith or 'basis' to statists' 'salesmanship,' which gave what passed as politics a carnival ambience. But Arendt preferred judgement to charm and celebrity. Her 'we the people' was comparable to Jefferson's. He and a few colleagues were prepared to invest their republic's future in an electorate able and inclined to discern candidates' intellect and integrity. Arendt's 'we the people' developed that ability and disposition, incubating citizen-statesmanship. Her 'we' 'came into being' with her 'new politics' whenever 'and where people … bind themselves through promises' to consider multiple opinions, to stoke interest in and agonistic discussions of the same and to extend each other's horizons.[9]

Promise-keeping, the reciprocities it created and the extension of one's and of others' horizons during deliberations mattered more to Arendt than the menu of conventional political products statists valued. Predictably, it featured the maintenance of sovereign powers' sovereignty along with citizens' docility, conformity and some semblance of consensus (and sufficient diversions and distractions to keep citizen indignation from developing). To her, reaching a consensus and minimising displeasure were far less important than training citizen-statesmen. She understood that reciprocities created problems. Cohorts could form factions, the proliferation of which was incompatible with good governance. James Madison admitted that 'factious combinations' were 'inconveniences.' But Arendt found him more compelling when he intuited that an abundance of factions prohibited the tyranny of any single one.

So, although freedom often spawned factions, the freedoms to subscribe or to protest were too precious to sacrifice to purge deliberations of narrow special interests. Madison figured that the new republic was sturdy enough to stand as long as government controlled factions' effects and retained power to negotiate their demands and to arbitrate among them. He trusted that a 'zeal for different opinions' would be a firmer foundation on which to build a republic than fanatical devotion to any single perspective. He hoped to keep controversies from turning interlocutors into inveterate enemies.[10] But Arendt suspected that, in Madison's time and in hers, one could only wish for such restraint and that advocates and adversaries would care more for a collective's continuity than for the ostensible rectitude of their respective views. In her galaxy, collectives prospered only as long as citizens protected interlocutors' freedom to disagree. Jefferson, Madison and most other founders were prudent. They formulated constitutional safeguards to keep disagreements and democracy from undermining the republic. But they trafficked in ideas. As Ron Chernow says, 'the immediate utility of ideas was an incalculable tonic for the founding generation.' Arendt, though, was relatively unconcerned with utility as the founders measured it. Moreover, her annoyance at contemporary philosophers' and ideologues' remoteness from what she took to be 'verifiable reality,' as we shall discover, was responsible for her displeasure with abstractions.[11]

Still, she believed that the founders of the republic acted intelligently. They resisted rebranding as 'a mass' the 'manyness' of their people. To their minds – as Arendt reconstituted them – the 'majesty' of 'their multitude' 'resided in its very plurality.' She seems to have brushed past the founders' failure to empower women or to free slaves. Indigenous Americans did not enter into her calculations. Unsurprisingly, therefore, her celebration of the founders' appreciation for the 'endless variety of their multitude' furrows current scholars' brows.[12] To a point, however, the founders did tolerate diversity, presuming 'the sound reason' of all enfranchised constituents. Their initiative was 'conspicuous and impressive enough' for Arendt, although she conceded their achievement 'never carried with it sufficient persuasiveness and plausibility to prevail in the tradition of revolution.' Paladins of the republic conjured and crafted their 'We, the people' without accommodating the population. She acknowledged as much, specifically, that the founders had not given their 'We' adequate space or compelling incentives to exploit their freedom intelligently.[13] Arendt signalled her disappointment that architects of the American political experiment either forgot or never learned that freedoms must be frequently, forcefully tugged from 'the inward domain,' where philosophers tend to deposit them, then practised (or performed) politically. So, despite their inspiring declarations, their congresses and constitution, Arendt's founders of the American republic had not created a 'realm of politics' where freedom could be known 'not as a problem ... but as a fact of everyday life.'[14]

What they accomplished was far from trivial, but they had not pondered relationships between citizens' ethical and political responsibilities to Arendt's satisfaction. And, at other points, she found them less than circumspect. First, they failed to reserve or structure spaces or venues for subsequent public encounters.[15] What she took to have been another significant oversight might be attributed to her intense interest in 'revolutionary spontaneity.'[16] Although the founders were revolutionaries, they seemed wary of the revolutionary spirit. Furthermore, Jefferson and a few other founders imprudently assumed their fellow citizens were politically savvy or figured that they would welcome informal tutorials on government. But nothing of that sort was on offer.

Her disappointment cast shadows over her otherwise encomiastic accounts of the early American experiment with democracy. As Jeremy Arnold notices, her accounts read less like a eulogy than an elegy or jeremiad 'dominated' by 'a mood of despair.' And prominent among what Arnold inventories as the narrative's 'jeremiadic features,' Arendt's sorrow about 'politically fateful forgetting' during the twentieth century directs attention to the founders' (and to their heirs') regrets about what evolved from the eighteenth-century experiment with democracy. Early on and consistently thereafter, haltingly at first, then enthusiastically, statists weighed down their fledgling republic with 'a party system.' Partisans veered from the founders' objectives. Political parties fostered, alternatively, complacency and polarising partisan antagonisms. Arendt was not pleased. The founders and their successors let lapse local colloquies that had promoted citizens' participation in political deliberations. What might have been assets to those yearning to breathe life back into the young republic's revolutionary enterprise made way for the statists' congresses known for skirmishes between churlish, squabbling conferees. But Arnold suspects that Arendt remained relatively optimistic. He has her smuggling reasons for confidence into her study *On Revolution*, 'counter[ing] its continuous ... shifts between tones of irony and despair with the always-present possibility of renewal.' But there is another way to read those 'tones,' one that promotes radical political innovation rather than renewal.[17]

*On Revolution*, Arendt explained, was an effort to explain Americans and their history to Europeans.[18] She also seems to have wanted citizens of her adopted country to become better acquainted with the founders of their republic and to challenge the distillations of its grandeur scripted for civics courses and history textbooks. Citizens' instruction touted successes; Arendt detected a disastrous drift from a 'council state' to statists' government and to diminished citizen engagement. But to incorporate her critical remarks with those of other progressives (and to read them as a summons to representative democracy) would be a mistake. She suspected the chances were 'very slight' that power could ever again be 'constituted' and distributed 'horizontally and not vertically.'[19] Besides, scepticism was already abroad. Scholars generally conceded that there was no such thing as unredacted history. It would therefore have been inappropriate to have one or another version of the founders' stories achieve creedal status. Statists saw to it that doubt and distrust undermined faith in any 'solid and durable common world,' other than the one they were selling. Arendt's take on the founders' faith was passé, as was the founders' hope (and hers) that 'being seen and heard by others' might derive political significance 'from the fact that everybody sees and hears from a different position.' Yet precisely that derivation as well as the faith or hope that statesmanship emerges from such plurality and reciprocity was and, Arendt finished, 'is the meaning of public life.' Appropriate or not, her version of the republic's founding (and, later, its floundering) inspired her recipe for radical political changes that began with the restructuring of citizens' desires and expectations and then addressed issues of empowerment.[20]

Local council meetings seemed to Arendt to have been incubating the virtues and virtuosity necessary for citizen-statesmanship before the founders convened and deliberated, declaring independence from Great Britain. But even before achieving what they declared, pragmatism replaced the revolutionary spirit. Citizens had surrendered their prerogatives to delegates who formed factions. Arendt still proposed that the Americans' insurgency was a perfect specimen, the model of what a revolution should be, as Helmut König suggests (*zum Modell und Muster*), yet scrappy insurgents, faced with the need to cope with mind-numbing detail, had channelled tasks to others, to bureaucrats.[21] Conducting the nation's foreign affairs, managing its finances, keeping the former colonies cooperating: all seemed to argue for delegation and representation. And representatives, deliberating about their country's business, saw little profit going public, save with rumours of scandals that impeached their rivals. Hence, the public realm, a place for citizens to weigh alternatives to their representatives' proposals – to evaluate their legislators' leadership and laws – Arendt said, 'withered away.'[22]

Despite Jeremy Arnold's doubts about Weberian influence, Arendt appears to have borrowed from Max Weber's studies of the administrative state to explain how and why representatives became statists and formed managerial elites for what Weber described as increased 'political maneuverability.'[23] Faith in the impartiality of the law and in the equality of all before the law, however, was lost. But Arendt was perhaps most caustic about that loss before she turned to the founders of the American republic in the early 1960s. Her *Origins of Totalitarianism*, published in 1951, commented at length on the conviction in France of Alfred Dreyfus for treason in 1894. Even after forgers confessed that they created the evidence against him and their miscarriage of justice was widely acknowledged, 'class-conscious generals' successfully 'cover[ed] up for the members of their own clique' and, she explained, made a mockery of the law. Arendt admired Émile Zola and others who campaigned for Dreyfus's exoneration, but not Dreyfus. He was an assimilated Jew – a parvenu – and a spendthrift. But her point was that 'the state machine' had proven itself a poor custodian of justice.[24] The French – much as the founders of the American republic and especially the latter's heirs – left Arendt with what Mira Siegelberg calls an 'acute awareness of political finitude.' And this observation suggests, though Siegelberg does not, that Arendt thought modest repairs to conventional political cultures incapable of stirring something similar to a revolutionary spirit.[25] Arendt held the founders partly responsible; they failed to put what they envisioned on an irreversible course. Their republic soon haemorrhaged statesmen and ended up with statists. She was disappointed yet still believed Jefferson a superb resource for strategising how to wed citizenship to statesmanship and a model of persistently revisionist thinking that she believed critical for binding thought to experience.[26]

Jefferson seemed to have concurred. Arendt remembered and repeated his declaration that 'the joys of discourse' had given him a 'foretaste of … eternal bliss.'[27] Still, as we discovered, she blamed him and other founders of the republic for having failed to create 'a realm of politics' where conversations prompted interlocutors and onlookers to think intelligently about the relationship between political theory and experience. Yet, to their credit, in her ledger, those founders had suppressed whatever they possessed of the desire to dominate. Had they done otherwise, they would have 'liquidat[ed] all spontaneity' in their deliberations. And their legacy would have suffered significantly.[28] Still, Arendt described the founders' occasional squabbling as a letdown (*Abstieg*).[29] But Jefferson's euphoria served her purpose, and, though nearly all his interlocutors were from the same socio-economic patch – of the same gender and race and caste – she granted that they were remarkable for having advocated transparent discussions of their 'discursive differences.'[30]

So, once Arendt scrubbed what Ron Chernow describes as 'the vile partisanship' of the founders' era, which did sabotage some initiatives, she found their deliberations amiably, admirably agonistic.[31] To repeat, she did not think Jefferson and his fellow founders at their conventions had gotten the formula for a democratic republic quite right, yet she packed her idealised image of early American history into her efforts to address the incoherence of what developed during her century from the founders' reputedly amicable arbitrations.

But Ronald Beiner rightly refers to the lack of back-up: Arendt's 'open-ended pluralism' derived from her tendentious, untenable reconstruction of what should be called the founders' partisan pluralism. For theirs was not at all 'open-ended,' but was, 'in fact, a pluralism of opinions and perspectives held by those already robustly committed to a shared and jointly constituted public world.'[32] To Arendt, however, consultations in eighteenth-century Philadelphia seemed exemplary alongside the disagreements in France that quickened the pace from the republican regime to the Reign of Terror.[33]

Yet Arendt was fascinated with that transformation and with its Jacobin impresarios, Luis Antoine de Saint Just and Maximilien Robespierre. Years before she drafted her impressions of their revolution (1963), however, her *Origins of Totalitarianism* proffered penetrating analyses of subsequent, yet not altogether dissimilar, turmoil. Havoc, she asserted, was one of the many undesirable effects whenever supposedly cunning statists, trying both to appease and to control crowds, circulated exaggerated claims about the sovereignty of the masses. For the chaos in mid-twentieth-century Europe, she held commercial interests, then and during the previous century, responsible. They had tantalised statists with the prospects of protecting, by extending, their nations' sovereignty. Capitalists and statists conspired to spawn rapacious nationalisms until 'expansion [became] the permanent and supreme aim of politics.'[34] Financiers, sure that profit was compatible with proper governance at home and especially abroad, turned nationalists into imperialists. They envisioned constant expansion and ceaseless, financially rewarding domestic mobilisation.[35] They awed ambitious politicians. Ordinary citizens, especially the indigenous populations they conquered, were simply 'superfluous.'[36] The financiers and statists during the late nineteenth and early twentieth centuries were much savvier than the eighteenth-century French and, predictably, in Arendt's account, less principled than her founders of the American republic. What followed was the 'particularly brutal exploitation of overseas possessions for the sake of the nation.' Even the less malevolent nationalists-turned-imperialists, who grew critical of their objectionably self-assured and self-indulgent colleagues, robbed their colonies of timber and minerals and robbed indigenous peoples of their freedom and dignity. Arendt seems to have known full well that no narrative could do justice to the nature and vast extent of such larcenous practice, yet, as we shall see, she devoted years of her life to recording European criminality.[37]

And one might say that her capitalists, imperialists, fascists and French revolutionaries made founders of the American republic look good by contrast. Arendt noticed that the 'export of power' did not end well either for the colonised or for colonising powers in the past, yet only gradually would she come to deplore the effects of her adopted country's gunboat diplomacy.

Her disappointment with the messes of the government's making will concern us shortly, but, more generally, statists' salesmanship and their recourse to force when propaganda failed were constantly at hand. Arendt had experienced both. To her regret, they appeared to be 'the essence of [conventional] political action' and 'the center of political thought' in Europe, to an extent she thought inconceivable in the early American republic – and, for a time, unthinkable in the United States. Yet she was initially preoccupied by statists and nationalists in Europe where police and a combination of military and paramilitary forces, had been closely associated with governance. Seemingly ubiquitous posters set mounted militia as emblematic of the nationalists' ambitions.[38] Wendy Brown, channelling Max Weber's analysis of ethnonationalism, suggests that the posters and other paramilitary paraphernalia 'generate[d] masses' that were 'increasingly indifferent to reason and facts and were thirsty for demagoguery.' Brown finds – as Arendt surely found after having studied the French fiasco during the eighteenth century – that demagogues' salesmanship rather than their statesmanship enabled them to exploit what Weber described as 'the emotional nature of the masses.' Having bought into the statists' version of history and destiny, the masses 'cannot be represented, only led.' Brown's alternative appears to be comparable to Arendt's; the two suggest that the 'political hero of modernity' will emerge as an alternative to 'bureaucratic torpor.' Arendt's paragons of political virtue, we shall see, surface in and from unconventional collectives as citizen-statesmen immune to 'temptations of power stripped of connection[s] to integrity, responsibility, vision and purpose.'[39]

## Tyrannies' Efficiencies

History, though, reveals how hard it would be to have statists' relinquish their ambitions. But it is difficult to see why Patricia Owens maintains that Arendt could imagine freedom flourishing 'only in ... an artificially constructed realm of political equality.' Owens's adverb suggests that opposition to statists would be unnatural, whereas Arendt appeared to associate artifice with the manoeuvring and manipulation statists practised.[40] Their agility was on exhibit in their desires for power and empire in the country of her birth once it survived humiliations when peace had been restored at the conclusion of the first war to end all wars. Statists' greed was evident elsewhere in Europe, within those territories diminished by defeat but also within the states sliced from defeated and dismembered empires. At Versailles, the victors ostensibly aimed to liberate but ended by balkanising much of Europe and by permitting tyrannies to prosper; the result of that peace conference looked to Arendt like a series of 'disastrous experiment[s],' inasmuch as 'it became a matter of course' for the war's winners and losers to prey upon ethnic others.[41] She understood as well as any – and better than most – as Bonnie Honig confirms, that confrontations precipitated by redrawing boundaries in 1919 forced statesmanship committed to pluralism 'to go underground.'[42]

Arendt liked her politics and statecraft compellingly aired out. She not only countenanced but also commended what Hans-Jörg Sigwart now calls 'deviating discourses,' enlivening political communication. Statists were suspicious of dissent yet not averse to feeding status resentments with fictions about the superiority of some and the inferiority of others. Sigwart catalogues the rhetoric of nationalism, notably, its baneful consequences, as Arendt's 'primary ethical concern.' Statists' salesmanship inflated claims for the consolations and satisfactions that ethnic or racial solidarity supposedly sustained. Their pitches emphasized solidarity, rested on ideology and included demands for ideological purity. Arendt recoiled and foregrounded the virtues of statesmanship – freedom, engagements with plural perspectives, the pursuit of equality, friendships, forgiveness, openness to new beginnings – together with the exhilaration she associated with agonistic exchanges. Faced with statists' salesmanship and the tyrannies they glamorised, canonised and sold, she relished the role of sceptic, crying foul whenever statists assailed or excluded ethnic or racial others. Arendt was intent on 'transcend[ing] any concrete collective's political horizon' and devoted to composing 'critique' that 'questioned [statists'] self-confidence and creedal passion.'[43] But xenophobia was contagious. Angry mobs served statists' purposes as long as the statists could channel the anger to their regime's advantages.[44] The 1960s were unlike the 1920s and 1930s, yet Arendt thought ethnocentrism 'stalk[ed]' and ensured injustices proliferated in her time. As for nationalists' rhetoric, rituals and tyrannies, to which we shall return, they 'were never more evil and more fiercely defended,' Arendt asserted, than when they were powerless to rein in resentments they promoted. And the statists' marketing nationalism obviously undercut whatever cosmopolitan colleagues were planning to 'establish a just relationship among different peoples beyond … national borders.'[45]

Statists were tremendously resourceful. Arendt's studies of tyranny documented the enormities that followed when statists' and nationalists' 'unwavering faith in an ideological fictitious world' developed as their unwavering faith in force.[46] She witnessed much of what she studied, and she inferred from the reports that reached her after she immigrated to the United States that tyrants were prepared to eliminate frontiers that got in the way of their ambitions for an ethnically or ideologically 'consistent' Europe. It seemed that whenever nativist sentiment in one territory became an obstacle to those ambitions in another, statists adapted. Bolsheviks, for example, proclaimed a 'permanent revolution' that knew no borders.[47]

She chronicled tyrants' efficiencies. They were skilled at putting their prejudices into politics. Arendt's consideration of Nazi nationalists' efficiency included a book-length study of Adolf Eichmann's competence during the war and his composure during his trial. Her study detailed the horrific outcome of the former, but it cost her many friends who mistook her remarks about the defendant and her complaints about the prosecution's 'show trial' for an acquittal. Was she exonerating Eichmann? True, she noted his 'gifts of organisation,' but what has been called her 'preposterous thesis that [he] could not tell right from wrong,' given the totalitarian statists' efficiencies, is quite defensible. She ranked him with other indoctrinated bureaucrats, who looked to fall in line and be normal in abominably abnormal times.[48] And although she had reservations about the conduct of the trial, she was hardly inattentive to the testimony of the victims. Earlier, she had written her monumental *Origins of Totalitarianism* to shed light on victimization and to show how disinformation routinely becomes lethal. *Origins* disabuses persons who imagined that ethnonationalist extremists' exploitation of patriotism could be contained relatively easily. Arendt chronicled how tyrants outmanoeuvred more benevolent members of the League of Nations scurrying to protect minorities – pariahs – in newly created nation-states once the Austrian, German and Ottoman empires were dismembered.[49] She counted herself among the pariahs. Contrary to Judith Shklar, who thinks that 'remaining … a pariah was a real struggle for her,' she rather easily slipped into that role, taking the pariah's perspective and turning it to good use redefining politics and reimagining citizenship.[50]

*Origins* also records the pariahs' persistence, what Arendt elsewhere described as their 'violent courage to live,' an 'insane optimism,' which she located 'next door to despair.' Despite statists' egregious efforts to erase their juridical-political presence, pariahs, unlike parvenus, for whom she sometimes expressed contempt, resisted the 'organized oblivion' prepared for them.[51] The survivors of the Nazis' camps proved her point, yet she claimed that pariah poets also provided ample evidence that the undesirable often could agilely turn back insults either by 'denying the reality of the social order' or by 'confronting it … with [a] higher reality.' Pariah poets' 'divine impudence' put them at odds with hegemonic discourses but transformed the poets' and pariahs' 'political non-existence and unreality … into [an] effective basis of a world of art.'[52]

Arendt was aware of 'the political power of poetry,' though perhaps not as enthusiastic, as Ian Storey reckons, about its disruptive function. Still, she likely celebrated pariah poetry for telling 'the least welcome truths.' But did it, in her opinion, also 'perform … the essential democratic function of bringing silenced people' into public spaces?[53] Or did she assume that tyrants were sufficiently efficient and statists sufficiently resourceful at keeping dissident poetry from turning citizens against their regimes? Marketing conformity, after all, was statists' métier. They took Machiavelli as their master, learning how to be clever but not how to be good. They knew to censor dissent and to make the unpresentable presentable and even respectable.[54] Occasionally, Arendt seemed willing to suffer the perfidious and their publicists to rule as long as spaces were provided for those interested in developing alternative publics with alternative politics or as long as existing alternatives were not shuttered. Yet her concession looks disingenuous. No fool, she realised that constituted powers would bend every effort and capitalise on any chance to avoid interruption and contestation.[55] But 'the faculty of interrupting and beginning something new,' for her, was the essence of politics.[56] She would have been narrowly focused on the character change agents were to develop, yet statists may have read her differently – as Andreas Kalyvas reads her – as the proponent of a freedom that 'brings into being … higher constitutional-legal structures and [new] regime forms.' Kalyvas is another who misconstrues her interest in political structures and minimises her concern with political agency.[57] Yet speculation about how statists may have read Arendt's concessions and expectations is somewhat beside the point. For it seems more important to sense how she read them and held their protocols responsible for suppressing the unconventional. The statement she found and flagged in J. William Fulbright's *Arrogance of Power* compressed an assessment she thought utterly alien to the tyrannical, for it identified 'the true mark of greatness' not as 'stridency but [as] magnanimity.'[58]

By 1950, Zionist nationalists in Israel were the tyrants in Arendt's crosshairs. She endorsed criticisms of their influence in Israeli politics and echoed Judah Magnes's objections to the expulsion of many Palestinians from the territories. Rabbi Magnes, who had died two years earlier, as the state of Israel was born, was an outspoken advocate for a bi-national state. As chancellor of Hebrew University in Jerusalem, he commanded a considerable following, but Zionists dismissed him as addlebrained. Chaim Weizmann thought him clueless – one of the 'nice Jews' willing neither to see nor to meet the need for a state for Jews.[59] But Arendt echoed what she called Magnes's 'moral point of view,' accusing his critics of 'forfeit[ing] the old proud claim of Zionist pioneerdom.' They proved (though additional proof was hardly necessary during the twentieth century) that political practice and the conventionally circumscribed definition of a public realm had 'outgrown sporadic sinfulness and entered a new stage of criminality,' in which pariahs became persecutors.[60] We shall sift Arendt's logic, on that count, in another chapter, and, though we shall also revisit characterisations of her racism then as well, it seems timely to recall her exposition of, and opposition to, Zionists' rationalisations for the dispossession and removal of Palestinian Arabs.[61]

Zionists wielded laws as weapons. Their statists, passed off the pragmatic as moral – and then legal – with ruthless efficiency. Ordinarily, one associates legislation with politics, yet Arendt did not. To her, laws and regulations inhibited political action; in her lexicon, lawmakers were 'craftsmen.' They preferred 'reliability.' 'It is as though they had said that,' should citizens 'only renounce their capacity for action, with its … uncertainty of outcome,' laws would provide the 'remedy for the frailty of human affairs.' Tyrants relied on statutes as barricades against the 'boundlessness' and uncertainty of such affairs. They confused 'making' laws with 'acting' politically, Arendt explained, professing that unpredictability was what distinguished genuine forms of political action from the impassioned, though insincere and counterfeit gestures and enterprises that statists marketed as political. They were tyrants trying to secure ideologically defined ends – as if they were revolutionary – with restrictive, reactionary means. For Arendt, their means and ends marked off their achievements as fabrication. 'Action can result in an end product, she argued, 'only on condition that its … always fragile meaning is destroyed.' To her, it made no sense to privilege laws or any 'end product' over freedom.[62]

For Arendt, freedom always seemed at stake – and at risk. In her *Origins of Totalitarianism*, she maintained that freedom was best expressed as 'the capacity to begin.' Both were jeopardised by totalitarian ideologues, statists – even moralists – who insisted that their demands for obedience were logical, because only they and their partisans were equipped to decipher the 'the law[s] of history.' *Origins* referred to their scam as 'the tyranny of logicality' obliging citizens to submit. And, by submitting, citizens surrendered their 'inner freedom,' as they surrendered the 'freedom of movement when [they] bow down to an outward tyranny.'[63] Statists sold bogus justifications for tyrants' authority. They associated citizenship with complacency, obedience and conformity, pilfering what Arendt termed citizens' 'public freedom.'[64]

Critical to the exercise of that freedom were chances for citizens to measure themselves 'up against others.'[65] The phrase suggests combative suitors sowing dissension and pressing their advantages. Arendt realised that she could be accused of promoting 'a battlefield of conflicting interests' by advocating agonistic political exchanges, but measuring up against – the *wider* in her aforementioned *Hin, Her, und Wider* – seems to have been meant, instead, to encourage self-disclosures and self-discovery that might inspire the extraordinary 'joy' Arendt identified with 'the political life.' Places where citizens sifted others' opinions, holding others accountable for them and measuring their perceptions against them, became public realms. Opportunities for collaboration emerged, chances to weigh anchor with other interlocutors were chances for new beginnings. Arendt alluded to the possibilities that surfaced as individuals 'inserted' themselves into that 'world by word and deed.' Yet statists sanction only such insertions that are consistent with the duties that they correlate with their sort of citizenship, calculated to ensure tyrannies' efficiencies. Their regimes feared dissent and favoured functional, fashionable and mannered 'insertions' that confirmed the political elites' authority. Arendt was having none of that. She would not deprive citizens 'of the joy and the gratification that arise out of being in company … [and] out of acting together and … inserting [themselves] into the world.'[66] Shmuel Lederman's conclusion is that such statements propose 'a new form of government' that was 'essential to the experience of freedom itself.'[67] The reciprocities recommended, however, hardly seem to rise to 'a form of government.' Undoubtedly, Arendt would have citizens resist tyrannies' efficiencies and find spaces or venues to try unconventional ways to enact what she called a 'compact' that could facilitate a free, lively exchange of opinions. The purpose was not to govern or rule but to inspire and prepare citizen-statesmen as change agents, eager and able to promote the virtues of plurality that, ideally, lead to self-discovery, self-disclosure, an 'enlargement of mentality' and the reimagination of citizenship and democracy.[68]

## Opinions and Truth

So, Arendtian public realms were not without requirements. Promise-keeping and forgiveness were foremost among them. In due course, we shall discuss the importance of each, but Arendt's two other specifications bear directly on the subject of this chapter. The first alleged that citizen-statesmen's self-insertions were unrelated to how often they cast ballots. Arendt never proposed that a regime's reliance on multiple referenda brought on the 'direct regeneration of democracy.' Neither would more frequent chances to inspect candidates' or representatives' competence be satisfactory indications of voters' increasing influence. Given the scope of statists' apparatuses of control, nostalgia for the 'direct handling of public business' conjured up a paradise lost.[69] Direct democracy on a large canvas was unrealistic. Second, Arendt thought citizens baffled; despite statist salesmanship, they could not fathom how their governments were of, for or by them. She suspected that the savvier citizens winced at politicians' promises and clichés. Despite evidence that popular support declined for the United States' interventions in Vietnam, the war escalated, proving to her and, she figured, to alert citizens in the late 1960s and into the early

1970s that their influence on government had shrivelled up.[70] The purportedly unassailable contention, which attended the founding of their republic – the notion that citizens' consent was indispensable – was simply set aside by their government in the twentieth century. Arendt was especially unforgiving of the indifferent or acquiescent. Refashioning their care for *res publica*, for their 'common world,' would require a new beginning and fresh commitments to political empowerment that began with scepticism about the supposedly self-evident truths that statists repackaged as slogans. And that new start would also require the redefinition of citizenship, the reinvention of democracy, a reconception of politics and a rather paradoxical recognition of the paramount importance of 'political action understood non-instrumentally.'[71]

It was paradoxical because Arendt's political action in this context was clearly designed to serve two purposes. She looked to alert citizens to the duties of citizen-statesmanship as she defined them and to summon citizens to address the unsettling circumstances that disappointed and distressed her. Her resistance to 'instrumentalism' was framed selectively (and perhaps naïvely) to relieve citizen-statesmen of the need to defend truths cobbled together from philosophers' abstractions and ideologues' *isms* or from generalisations that social scientists were able to turf from their surveys. From her perspective, truth claims were problematic for politics, which, she argued, ought to traffic in opinions. She urged readers to mull over the obvious, that 'truth, as it enters the market place, changes its nature and becomes opinion.' Truthtellers, therefore, should have their truths measured against others' opinions as interlocutors exercise their 'right to rearrange' data (what experience offers) into facts (what they can make of the data narratively). Then, they were to fulfil the citizen-statesmen's duty to share and, when appropriate, to repair those truths-turned-opinions.[72]

At this point, '*non*-instrumentality' ought to outweigh purpose-driven activity. The recurring rearrangements undoubtedly led to uncertainty. Some political theorists were unwilling to accept that outcome. They fell back on utility. They assumed that the validity of any formula pretending to 'unlock' history's secrets depended on its contributions to 'a better tomorrow.' Having exalted means above ends, they let their means become ends.[73] Arendt ridiculed the circularity. She was ready to embrace uncertainty. To some, her recoil from truths as well as her doctrine of natality recall the prejudices driving pragmatism, even utilitarianism. For she considered the repeated rearrangements of data as jumping-off points, meant to hold for only so long. Diana Taylor invites critics reluctant to indulge Arendt's appreciation for the impermanent and to see how successfully her emphasis on precarity freed citizen-statesmen from having to tidy up structures that failed to accommodate their understanding of the public realm. Truths need not oblige them to restructure what, given statists' changing demands and despite their promises of permanence, would always be makeshift. The agonistic discourses Arendt commended and her appreciation for political action 'understood non-instrumentally' could survive in miniature public realms without long (or presumably permanent) shelf lives.[74]

To free interlocutors from the tyranny of truths, *isms* and the demand for durability that usually accompanies sovereign powers' claims to sovereignty, Arendt forfeited predictability; 'from the viewpoint of [conventional] politics,' she explained, 'truth has a despotic character.' But such a statement, which conjures up lurid, tabloid talk of truth's fascism or of fascism's truths, ought not to be taken as an endorsement of relativism. It merely suggested that, for her, the despotic was the enemy of the 'enlarged mentality' she would have citizens cultivate, although without precluding the multiple perspectives she considered 'hallmark[s] of all strictly political thinking.' Plurality made politics possible; 'the more standpoints' one engages, 'the stronger will be [one's] capacity for representative thinking.' But, yet again, political speech and action seem purposeful or instrumental. We cannot resolve the problem created here, save to say that Arendt's objective, shaped by her disappointments, was to demystify and delegitimise despotism and to free political discourse and action from having to hew to prescribed abstractions or protocols.[75]

Thinking that grapples with multiple perspectives and attends to other thinkers' reservoirs of experience creates and continues to enrich public realms. 'If we lose the ground of experience,' Arendt remarked, 'we get into all kinds of theories' braced by trumped up truths. Nearly every theorist professed impartiality but opposed diversity and fought off precarity with metanarratives congealed into systems statists deployed to market sovereign powers. Yet statists' merchandising and metanarratives fell far short of honouring human experience. Instead, Arendt continued, that constellation reflected statists' (and their clients' and devotees') self-absorption.[76] She looked to privilege experience and to distinguish between opinion and truth. Truths ostensibly underlying the generalisations and *isms* obscured the political importance of experience. We shall reflect more comprehensively on Arendt's distinction between truths and opinions when we dock it alongside our discussion of several theorists who influenced her, but a short visit with two scholars who probed that distinction should clarify her purposes.

Looking to 'contravene' Arendt's distinction, Linda Zerilli steers opinions clear of the 'merely subjective.' She would have opinions, on Arendt's terms, become 'the basis for making claims with validity.'[77] Zerilli cites Arendt's statement that Socrates urged Athenians 'to find the truth in their *doxa*,' to find in conversations 'the inherent truth in [their] own opinion[s].'[78] But Zerilli understands that Arendt's mention of inherency did not signal that she would have attributed inerrancy to any single opinion. Indeed, variations – plurality itself – argued against the truth-value of any single proposition. Arendt's Socrates had not looked to make *doxa* truthful. He wanted to ensure that the value and validity of opinions had nothing to do with their conformity to imposed standards and everything to do with one's registering 'the standpoints of other people when forming an opinion' and 'acknowledging them as potentially revealing of something of the world.' Yet, Zerilli clarifies, the 'enlarged perspective' that results 'does not seek to bring about the single right answer.' 'Mak[ing] citizens more truthful,' therefore, would hardly make their conversations less pluralistic. Instead, when conversations enabled citizens to present opinions more perspicaciously and cogently, they contribute to citizen-statesmen's 'political capacity to make judgements.' Zerilli rightly questions the relevance of that outcome for what she calls an unabated 'truth deficit' in current politics. Yet she seems to have missed the effect of Arendt's recurring disappointments on her efforts to reimagine 'a vital democratic polity.'[79]

George Kateb also burrows into Arendt's distinction between truth and opinions, which was central to her analysis of modernity coloured by what she identified as the moderns' resentment of limitations.[80] Yet Kateb complains that Arendt's criticism was too severe. He was put off by her refusal to defer to any reformer adhering to metaphysical doctrines and proffering cosmetic rather than comprehensive changes to democratic practice. To Arendt, such reformers and their reforms were insufficiently experiential.[81] To her, philosophers' degradation of opinion and of 'verifiable experience' licensed statists to dissemble. Unmasked as opinions, truths on which statists depended to sell and to stabilise their regimes were obviously less compelling. Yet the theorists, ideologues and statists strenuously laboured to keep the masks in place. She disliked the outcome, the disguise and the deception that turned their 'truths' into lies (*zur Lüge*).[82]

Many of Arendt's most acerbic remarks about metanarratives, ideologies, *isms* and philosophy's truths (as lies) were composed to substantiate her suspicion that political philosophers knowingly became politicians' pawns and accomplices. Totalitarianism's ideologues particularly interested her. Her analysis of their truths' passages into politics was indelibly stained by her disdain for what she took as philosophers' contributions to what statists' 'supersense' – the appearance of irrefutability – had acquired. Once their 'claim[s] to total validity [were] taken literally,' 'they became the nuclei of logical systems.' There, 'as in systems of paranoiacs, everything follows comprehensibly and even compulsorily.' Totalitarians' philosophers provided useful premises, then, 'over and above the senselessness of totalitarian society.' Statists deployed them to display what Arendt made out as a brassy, clamorous 'contempt for factuality.' With their favourite (yet flawed) premises in place, statists, from the 1920s and into the 1970s, relied on their marketing and on citizens' 'simple-minded trust in the salvation value of stubborn devotion.' Both statists and guileless citizens inspired Arendt's fear that the embers of much political philosophy could, blown into politics as conventionally defined, ignite unwanted fires. Her tactics: counter statists' salesmanship with riveting redefinitions of citizenship and statesmanship and expose the danger when political philosophies morph into political ideologies. The ideologies enabled statists to 'pretend' they had 'found the key to history' and, with it, to have locked citizens into baseless prejudices. But, as noted, Arendt did not spare credulous citizens. Preoccupied with producing and consuming, they accepted statists' truths, mistaking nonsense for some sort of 'supersense,' for some superior political sensibility that gave regimes the power to look into, and to reshape, the future. Citizens' stupefaction gave totalitarians' 'contempt for reality its cogency, logicality and consistency.' Populism, at its worst, was consent to totalitarians' premises and pretensions, which, as we shall see, entice citizens to relinquish their freedom.[83]

What of the progressives among them? Arendt suspected that they, too, were misled. She allowed that some liberals in central Europe denounced fascism between the two world wars; nonetheless, they timidly refrained from backing measures that might have retarded its progress. They 'escape[d] into some fool's paradise,' failing to confront either fascists or the facts during the 1930s and early 1940s. They seemed numb – unresponsive. Most were exceedingly slow to admit antisemitism's influence. When atrocities became better known, progressives elsewhere in Europe and in North America repudiated ethnonationalism, but even would-be liberators left rail lines leading to internment camps unbombed. Genocide went on unabated. Citizens in Germany and in countries that the Germans had conquered lapped up their leaders' lies. Enmity towards outliers or pariahs was infectious and therefore pervasive. Statists' rhetoric and rituals marketed hostility effectively. Arendt insinuated that the regimes in her time continued to pitch prejudices, although more subtly. After the war, as before, the cultured and uncultured alike overlooked the distinction between states that achieve solidarity by including diverse citizens and states that achieve solidarity by branding and excluding misfits. Forgetful? Yes, though Arendt favoured another explanation as well. She attributed the ease with which political oppression followed from an arrogance of power less to the misperception and misrecollections of elites and ordinary citizens than to liberals' failure of will. Persons who described themselves as humane refused to risk nonconformity. She was disappointed by their caution – or could one call it cowardice – remembering that fascists had bottled an intoxicating brew. Philosophy braced totalitarians' conduct with justifications. They played on the importance many citizens placed on belonging, on playing a part in the parade or political juggernaut. And, as noted, fascists deftly appealed to citizens' resentment of their fate and of others' good fortune. Even progressives were turned and, Arendt discovered, the progressives in her time proved as susceptible to statists' sirens' songs as Weimar liberals. Both sets found conformity more congenial than defiance and resistance, and both sets seemed co-conspirators in their own redundancy. Just as totalitarians' subjects, United States citizens were becoming 'superfluous.'[84]

As we learned, she introduced that last term to describe the effect of statist salesmanship and to denote citizens' conformity and complacency during the 1930s and 1940s.[85] But she saw much the same among – and was disappointed by – citizens of her adopted country during the 1950s and 1960s. She started studying Augustine long before then, and, though she referred derisively to his other- or unworldliness on several occasions, one can imagine her looking for courageous colleagues in her century who possessed that prolific prelate's knack for what Eric Gregory calls 'unmasking.' Arendt would hardly have missed (and Gregory does not) Augustine's aptitude for 'exposing illusions' that only thinly veiled off-putting 'techniques of domination.'[86] But statists expertly camouflaged their own and their regimes' contempt for and control over 'superfluous' subjects. Statists knew how to impress citizen-spectators and consumers. During the 1930s, in Germany, they were especially gifted at fabrication, at paving *Autobahnen* and at erecting grand granite edifices festooned with banners. They knew how to project power. The fascists' material presence – or, to be precise, the material presence of their regime – reassured Germans who had been traumatised by humiliations during previous decades, by the loss of territory, by depression and by inflation. 'Fabrication,' Arendt declared, displaced contemplation and action, as truth had displaced opinion. American and European capitalists followed suit, identifying progress with productivity. They marketed prosperity and boasted about sovereignty to square off against the perpetual perishing or precarity that attends every human endeavour. The supposed 'solidity of quiet and order' consoled citizens and kept them from questioning the legitimacy and the undemocratic character of their democracies' democracy.[87]

The output of fabrication, after all, was more 'solid' than the consequences of most political activity. Truth and dogma seemed more 'solid' than opinions and conventionally were tailored impeccably to seem so. But Arendt preferred volatility to solidity. Marks in her copy of Hegel's *Lectures on the History of*

*Philosophy* suggest her approval of his discussions of the finitude of human initiatives (*beshränkt, abhangig, endlich*), although she thought his trust in some infinite spirit excessive.[88] He was enthusiastic about its purported powers to enlighten and compared it with the power of phosphorous to bring light. Had Arendt known that phosphorous was highly combustible? If so, Hegel's metaphor may have worked differently for her. She preferred the incendiary to the solid and stolid. But Hegel earned kudos, on her reading, for having awarded a certain dignity to the empirical, despite his preferences for truth over opinions. Other truthtellers promised certainty without dignifying experience. They promised their truths – or, she clarified, their opinions masquerading as truths – would stand without further elucidation, adding that such truths could 'withstand further elucidation.' Arendt carved Hegel from that herd, inasmuch as his philosophy drew the infinite close enough to the finite to give the vagaries of political experience philosophical purchase.[89]

There was little she could do about the philosophers who refused to follow Hegel's suit. She berated European colleagues, whose contempt for political practice seemed invincible. To her, however, their condescension was understandable, for citizens in Europe rarely experienced the 'measure of dignity and greatness' that the founders of the American republic had bestowed on its citizens.[90] But what Arendt learned about their attempts made subsequent failures along with the stagnation of the new republic's revolutionary spirit all the more disappointing. Nonetheless, backsliding and defaults in Europe were nearly as disconcerting, disorienting and inexcusable. For centuries, statists there acclimated citizens to despotism. But those 'solid,' sanitised truths that despotic sovereign powers owed to their statists and ideologues – despite an appearance of durability and inevitability – on occasion looked unworkable. Dissidents surfaced. Christopher Clark, for example, hears the 'echoes' of 1789 nearly everywhere during 1848, foretelling yet another 'revolutionary era' and making statists and sovereign powers apprehensive. The latter were as frightened of their subjects as their subjects were frightened of them.[91] But 'fear as a principle of action,' Arendt lectured, can 'only be destructive.' She said so in an undated speech, but, plausibly, she composed it while watching the Stalinist regime in Europe (but also the democratic regime in her adopted country during Joseph McCarthy's tumultuous tenure in its senate) looked to purge dissidents. Already in the early 1950s, although increasingly as tyrants' truths dominated what emerged from the ruins left by the century's second great war, a counter-revolutionary spirit must have seemed to her to have taken hold.[92]

## Brecht

We can get a superb look at her discomfort and disappointment by evaluating what appears to have been her profound ambivalence about the decisions one of her favourite artists made in the late 1940s. She was of two minds, reviewing the trajectory of Bertolt Brecht's career. She was thrilled with the exuberance of his early work, but once he fell under the spell of the Stalinists – or seemed to – his ballads, plays and poems were uncharacteristically subdued.[93] He returned to East Berlin in 1949, reluctant to speak truth to power. Appointed to direct the city's new theatre company, he was 'in infinitely closer contact with a totalitarian state' than other playwrights or poets who stayed safely away from Stalin and the Stasi. But Brecht seemed to Arendt to have been unable to 'break through the rumble of Marxist platitudes.'[94] Jerome Kohn paraphrases Arendt's assessment: between 1949 and Brecht's death seven years later, he 'exchanged the visible appearances of the world as the source of his poetry for a totalitarian ideology.'[95] Yet Arendt would have known that Brecht, as others, found communism a fortress of sorts against fascism, the remnants of which had survived the defeats of Mussolini and Hitler, as well as an alternative to crude capitalism that created – then catered to – consumers' insatiable appetites. Might one make a defensible case that Arendt figured that Brecht's 'irresistible inclination to being good and doing good' brought him back to Berlin?[96]

Conceivably, yet Brecht committed what she considered a cardinal sin: he 'fell in line.'[97] She celebrated his earlier aesthetic and political nonconformity. She singled out 'the lyrical cynicism and sarcasm' of his *Three Penny Opera* that awarded 'the real' pride of place over the ideal. But Arendt resisted exaggerating either Brecht's vices or his virtues. She wanted neither to overlook the latter nor to excuse the former.[98] Even before he moved to Berlin, however, she anticipated his attraction to Bolshevik ideologues. She made a list of the 'subjects he 'understands and a list of those … he misses,' appending it to an essay she submitted to *The Kenyon Review*, in which she included him as one of the few *eruditi* whose refusal to patronise hypocrites previously set them apart from their contemporaries. But she deplored what she called his 'loss of sensibility,' assuming often that it was his failures to gauge the baleful political consequences of tyrannies' efficiencies in Erich Honecker's German Democratic Republic and in Stalin's Soviet Union.[99]

Ambivalence, then: Arendt's Brecht was hardly obsequious, although, he generally appeared oblivious to Stalin's purges. He seemed never to have learned the lesson Domenico Losurdo claimed that Arendt had retrieved from, among others, Thomas Paine: that government must hold citizens' vices in check but must not act viciously.[100] Nevertheless, Cecilia Sjöholm and Gudrun von Tevenar probably go too far, inferring from some of Arendt's comments that she would have been happier had he just stopped writing.[101] But he did not and took no pains to conceal his pleasure at having been given a new start. Arendt later – if not then – would have understood his delight at having been given a chance for a new beginning. He took advantage. Brecht was prolific and left clues in his work that led Arendt, despite her scolding, to conclude that his 'loss of sensibility' was infrequent rather than chronic. For example, the year before his death in 1956, he revised his play *Galileo* for patrons of his repertory company. He had the actor impersonating the play's eponymous protagonist recant onstage and, just as the famed scientist's seventeenth-century recantation, the actor's capitulation was controversial. Playgoers could have construed it as a victory for ideology over reality (as the Communists' and Catholics' ideologies' victories) or, as Arendt preferred, the play dramatized tragedy rather than triumph and Galileo's abjuration was Brecht's 'declaration' against Stalinism's demands for citizens' compliance.[102]

Still, she expected more from Brecht, and she managed to grab it. She found evidence that the playwright's compassion for the poor was a constant. He ranked personal piety or sanctity well below the determination to leave the world a better place for the disadvantaged. He was one of the very few, Arendt wrote, 'who understood the insult added to the poor's injured lives' when others let 'their sufferings remain … in the dark.[103] And, to enlighten, Brecht introduced many insolvent yet fearless and endearing characters into his scripts. And to instruct, he also cleverly weaponised irony, although that effort was lost on some. Dining with a few left-leaning friends in New York City, he proclaimed that the innocent victims of Stalin's purges deserved their punishments. His remark shocked his hosts, but Arendt subsequently interpreted: he was not suggesting Stalin's government was right to persecute those wrongly suspected of disaffection. Had he meant that, her disappointment with him would have been unremitting and not measured. What Brecht meant was that the innocent ought to be punished for their innocence; they failed to recognise the extent of Stalin's treachery and, therefore, were culpably 'innocent.' At dinner, he was 'teasingly cautious,' Arendt explained. He had not condemned the Stalinists as explicitly as his scandalised friends – or as she – wished.[104] He veiled yet voiced his dissent. Vindication? Perhaps, on that occasion, but Arendt was saddened by the too few times Brecht found fault. Proclaiming (and conceivably feigning) loyalty to his patrons, he forfeited her unconditional admiration.[105]

She generally expected pariah poets to be politically responsible, to defend reality against ideology, to shred fictions propping up statists' salesmanship.

It was inconceivable that pariahs and poets (but especially pariah poets) would collaborate with the despotic or, by virtue of their indifference – or, worse, acquiescence – would allow demagogues to appear defensible. Pariahs should prefer realities to ideologies. Arendt thought Heinrich Heine's lyrics, which pressed for sensual emancipation, were infinitely more interesting than were his friend Karl Marx's calls for political emancipation. Heine, she averred, deserved 'his place among the most uncompromising of Europe's fighters for freedom,' 'refus[ing] to give up his allegiance to a people of pariahs.'[106] Brecht was more problematic. His early work, his 'wild and beautiful ballads' defied convention. They cared nothing for a 'respectable life.' Yet Brecht came to care too much for it and to accept statists' and political elites' conviction that 'in order to exterminate meanness there should be no mean thing you were not ready to do.' Nazism haunted him. 'The Party' – Trotsky's then Stalin's party – chased away the ghosts.[107] Arendt understood and partly pardoned Brecht's misreading of the past, present and future. He had 'a fierce temptation to be good,' yet, unlike Heine, he adopted Machiavelli's 'seemingly ambiguous attitude toward goodness.'[108]

Contemplating such ambiguity in one of her cultural heroes seemed to make Arendt even more disillusioned, because she expected poetry and literary culture to cover for philosophy's failures. She was disappointed with Brecht, with art and with the political cultures corrupting them. Ezra Pound, to her mind, had what passed as an excuse. She despised Pound's despicable, antisemitic broadcasts from Italy. His transformation from poet to vile statist was deplorable. Brecht's 'sins' were 'smaller' than those of Pound, Arendt granted, yet Brecht had 'sinned more heavily,' being 'only a poet and not an insane one.' Still, we must not be misled by the 'only' in her observation; she anticipated that poets and playwrights, at their best, would register the priority of reality over ideology and thereby would give the lie to statists' marketing.[109]

Arendt reserved for poets and for literary culture in general prominent roles in conveying what Sophie Loidolt calls a 'verbal sense' of the plurality that philosophy often denied. She explains: for Arendt, plurality was not something 'static' or 'substantial.' It was something that happened. Plurality was an activity, comparable to dance or conversation.[110] Arendt, then, enjoined stories and poetry not only to stir memories and aspirations but also to contest statists' salesmanship in ways that prosaic briefs for citizen-statesmanship, similar to the one in this study's introduction, could not. On this count, she agreed with Karl Jaspers, whose efforts to make philosophy more 'concrete and practical' included publishing a periodical for four years after the war drawing Brecht as well as Thomas Mann, T. S. Eliot, and W. H. Auden onto its pages.[111] Arendt took notice and submitted several essays for a book released under the new journal's auspices. For her, poetry was performance, as was plurality – as was politics.[112] She mourned the passing of Brecht's 'disruptive faithfulness to factual reality.' His fears of fascism, as noted, stole that (and him) from Arendt. She knew others also turned to Stalin, assuming, even after Russia's pact with Hitler, that communism would ultimately prove the best antidote for unbridled desires that fuelled capitalism. Patchen Markell suspects such knowledge helped her contextualise Brecht's return to Berlin but gave her cover for continuing to hold him responsible without insisting that posterity pillory him.[113] She held that poets' vocation opened them to risks. They were so much more sensitive to 'the catastrophes of the[ir] time,' because they had been gifted with a 'penetrating, non-theoretical … intelligence.' And such risks, she added, were worth courting, inasmuch as poets vindicated reality's preeminence or authority. Doing so, they deserved 'forbearance' for their flaws.[114]

True, Arendt found it difficult to get past Brecht's concessions to patrons in Berlin in order to retrieve remnants of her admiration for the 'glorious vitality' his early work possessed. But she had greater difficulty rifling through philosophers' work, from Plato's dialogues to Heidegger's lectures, looking for signs of vitality and fidelity to what she canonised as 'verifiable experience.' Her reactions ranged from embarrassment to anger when she encountered political philosophers exhibiting little interest in what Dana Villa terms the 'robust interactive dimension' that Brecht, at his best, displayed.[115] She pointed out that medieval 'minor renascences' of learning and the surges of interest in classical antiquity during the European Renaissances had been confined to the elites. Arendt was disappointed that erudition had not been put to 'highly practical political purposes.' (Machiavelli, she said, was the exception.)[116] But she was more disappointed by the failure to do so in her time. If she had her way, the alternative political collectives and cultures she conjured would foreground the values, and develop the virtuosity, necessary to reimagine citizenship and reinvent democracy. Yet her way played no part in progressives' forecasts for democratic republics' brighter futures. The last lectures she drafted implicitly warned against submerging reality (and human dignity, as Kant defined it) in ideas about progress. None of those ideas, to her regret, provided inspiration to interlocutors to look around through others' eyes to actualise plurality and perform politically.[117]

## Plato, Pragmatists and 'the Great Reversal'

The route from Brecht back to philosophy in Arendt's search for vitality and reality in political practice returns us to her defence of opinions against truth-tellers who took them as distractions. She cited Socrates, underscoring the attributes he was reputed to have valued among statesmen, particularly their passion for sifting and shaping opinions – theirs and those of others. Whereas Plato disliked sifting or shaping that swerved from what he took to be 'transcending standards,' Arendt's Socrates set such standards aside. Plato, playing the part of his amanuensis, must have been fascinated. Arendt imagined him insisting that arguments must forego trying to tease truth from opinions circulating in political practice. Instead, her Plato, as Athenians who condemned Socrates, 'had no use for political argumentation.' 'The solidarity of the polis' did not require sophists who 'look[ed] ridiculous when they appear[ed] in the marketplace.' Instead, absolute standards; 'the spectacle of Socrates submitting his own *doxa* to the ... Athenians and being outvoted by a majority made Plato despise opinions and yearn for absolute standards.' Most political philosophy followed suit.[118]

Her Plato was unmistakably antisocratic and, to her mind, antisocial as well. He showed no interest in the *Hin, Her und Wider* that was so critical for her. Statists were equally unconcerned with the plurality and freedom that made such conversations, in Arendt's terms, political. They could have referred to Plato's rejection of the idea that 'truth claims in politics' were somehow 'entangle[d] in opinion.'[119] Yet Arendt supposed that statists were uninterested in philosophical reflection. They took to truth claims to place their marketing strategies beyond criticism. Still, she blamed Plato for having given the statists' salesmanship the appearance of philosophical respectability. They represented the 'tyranny of truth' as therapeutic. They were unashamed, parading abstractions as truths and could not be bothered to test their generalisations against political experience. Plato made it respectable to race back from messy realities to comforting, self-serving abstractions. The cabal – statists, sovereign powers, elites and ideologues – could not stave off ambiguity and instability. Arendt was grateful for that. Plurality, ambiguity and a modicum of instability or precarity were preconditions for new beginnings. Citizen-statesmen, exchanging opinions, discover that best political practices indulged ambiguities. For Arendt's Plato, such indulgence and searching signalled that truth had been forsaken.[120]

She borrowed from Alfred North Whitehead to suggest that Plato's tack towards transcendence was 'common sense in retreat.' Plato's heirs and admirers claimed to possess knowledge within. Arendt cautioned them that reliance on 'an inner faculty without any world relationship' would discredit their conclusions.[121] They would seem unhinged to colleagues who had no experience pondering political theory abstracted from political practice. Besides, political theorists fond of silences were caught up along with their critics in what Arendt called a 'great reversal.' Mistrust in 'mere contemplation' was leading many philosophers to assert that 'in order to know, one had to do.' The lanes leading to 'modernity' from Plato were nearly empty. Arendt might have been more enthusiastic, had she not considered most pragmatists reversing the course of philosophy impulsive, often unintelligible and always overconfident.[122] Perhaps sensing some reversal of that 'great reversal,' she reminded readers that Plato had taken many a punch from critics but often returned to colleagues' ovations to 'protect and liberate' philosophy from the realm of human affairs.[123]

Arendt referred to herself as a political theorist, distinguishing her challenges from those of the political philosophers who had been and continued to be partial to metaphysics but also from the challenges faced by pragmatists who were hostile to theory. Nonetheless, like the latter, she took public opinion seriously. Fieldwork and polls were not necessary to do so. One could accumulate insight by watching from afar and reflecting on what one observed. Her approach, though, would jeopardise her standing among pragmatists, who, she imagined, would dismiss her 'reflection[s]' on the wickedness of human nature as irrelevant. She wrote about 'the bankruptcy of common sense in the modern world,' yet pragmatists, exhilarated by the sensibilities they found (or thought they found) among the conventionally politically active, were optimistic. Had they known about Arendt's disappointments and wariness, they would have discounted both.[124] Pragmatists and other progressives believed their 'great reversal' irreversible. They were confident it would usher in a new, improved social and political order. But, to Arendt, no reverses were irreversible as long as Plato's desires to be 'useful to politics' by supplying 'absolute philosophical standards' survived among his admirers.[125] At their peril, then, the optimists, who assumed absolutists and authoritarians had been forever left behind, believed democratic republics could be improved incrementally (progressively) without attending to a radical reevaluation of their citizens' competence. To put it bluntly, Platonists and pragmatists were wrong, inasmuch as politically useful new beginnings would redefine politics, reimagine citizenship and reinvent democracy.

For their part, pragmatists ought to have welcomed her doctrine of natality along with her replies to Plato's partisans, who declared timeless truths more trustworthy than opinions. She welcomed the reversal from contemplation to experience. Jaspers did as well. And what Arendt appreciated most about him appears to have been his readiness to relate theory and thinking in general to 'the fundamental facts of political existence.' Jaspers, though, confided that his analysis of those facts betrayed how unpractised he was at working psychology into political philosophy. He counselled that his tentative conclusions about politics should be questioned, not unequivocally endorsed.[126]

Yet Arendt speculated that political theory's contributions to political practice would have been more advantageously influential during the twentieth century, had philosophers been as immune as Jaspers was to Platonists' contempt for 'the perishable affairs of mortals.' Theorists might have been better prepared and more willing to expose fascism's fictions, had they studied the climate of opinions and noticed the coming storms. Even in calmer times, philosophers should acknowledge that the freedom and leisure required for reflection are 'materially impossible without a halfway reasonable arrangement of all [conventionally political] affairs.'[127]

Integral to Arendt's complaints about the irrationality that fouled that climate and caused the storms, her remarks about philosophers' and citizens' captivity demonised statists for having chained both to their purposes. Had most philosophers, during the late 1940s and 1950s, swiftly gauged the magnitude of the 'great reversal' that defined 'modernity,' they might have helped with the reevaluation of political culture and written their *Origins of Totalitarianism*. But they steered clear of political practices, past and present, letting theorists' 'inward discourse[s]' be 'generalised into philosophical doctrine.' As a result, Arendt lamented, the 'experience of the thinking ego got lost' or, she clarified, lost connections with 'difference and otherness,' the 'outstanding characteristics of [interlocutors'] habitat,' into conversations that 'actualize[d] plurality.'[128]

Philosophy was not the only offender. For Arendt, theology and science were equally culpable. They cared more for the reputedly everlasting and irrefutable than for citizens' 'way[s] of life' and 'ever-changing opinions about human affairs.' Philosophy changed as a result of the great reversal – albeit not to Arendt's satisfaction – but science and theology continued without much opposition to bench opinions and allowed statists' 'organized lying' to 'dominate … the public realm.' All three – philosophy that continued to prioritise metaphysics, science and theology – abdicated 'the ground of experience' and let commerce (and statists' salesmanship) determine what passed as politics.[129] Most theologians, many scientists, and too many philosophers had forgotten that 'generations of philosophers of history' had 'demonstrated the impossibility of ascertaining facts without interpretations.' In laboratories, seminars and pulpits, paradigms shaped opinions, which seemed grotesquely distended when upgraded and touted as truths.[130]

Scientists intended to decipher, theologians endeavoured to enchant and philosophers meant to explain creation. Arendt, as noted, traced the conceits of all three to Plato. He was to blame for the shattered reputations of both Socrates and *doxa*. She conjectured that Plato had deliberately popularised his metaphorical conflict between body and soul to signal that the conflict between philosophy and politics was wired into reality.[131] And his acolytes were everywhere, devaluing experience in twentieth-century philosophy, religion and science. Every sect and subdiscipline strenuously endeavoured to keep its deities, doctrines and absolutes independent of, as well as authoritative over, the public realms as conventionally conceived. The sects and subdisciplines treasured tidiness and discredited liveliness, to Arendt's disappointment. Spontaneity survived, she conceded, yet she also warned that its survival (and, with it, the future of freedom) was not certain, inasmuch as spontaneity introduced inconstancy and unpredictability into places where philosophies, sciences and religions thought consistency and constancy ought to reign.

Arendt conceded that Romans were less philosophically gifted than the Greeks, yet she paid tribute to the former's orators and historians for having spoken and written reverentially about the prominent parts freedom played in their republic's and empire's foundation, refoundations, management and expansion. The Romans 'made … history political.' They were lively, though not always tidy.[132] As she scripted their history, they accepted their obligation – as, she said, the political theorists of her time ought to accept theirs – to confront the ambiguities and exigencies of political practice. No Plato shunted philosophy away from the villainy that Varro, Sallust, Cicero and Livy encountered and recounted. Citizen-statesmen had to cope with power and domination. They needed to test theories, to sift opinions, but statists, as noted, trafficked in truths rather than in theories. And their truths ordinarily objectified citizens and disappointed Arendt. What statists called politics suppressed spontaneity. Her journal referred to them as 'puritans,' probably because what they endeavoured to suppress and were desperate to avoid, spontaneity, on her watch, becomes the *sine qua non* of politics, encouraging genuinely new beginnings.[133]

## Notes

1. HC, 182. For Renaissance humanism's 'common world,' see Constance Furey, *Erasmus, Contarini and the Religious Republic of Letters* (Cambridge: Cambridge University Press, 2006).
2. HC, 184.
3. Ibid., 246.
4. OR, 226–7.
5. Ibid., 124.
6. Véronique Albanel, *Amour du monde: Christianisme et politique chez Hannah Arendt* (Paris: Cerf, 2010), 204–5.
7. Dana Villa, *Arendt* (London: Routledge, 2021), 276.

8. Anne Applebaum, *Twilight of Democracy: The Seductive Lure of Authoritarianism* (New York: Doubleday, 2020), 14–15.
9. OR, 173–4.
10. James Madison, *Federalist* 10, https://avalon.law.yale.edu/18th_century/fed10.asp, accessed April 22, 2020.
11. Ron Chernow, *Alexander Hamilton* (New York: Penguin, 2004), 251.
12. OR, 83: 'The word "people" retained for [the founders] the meaning of manyness, of the endless variety of a multitude whose majesty resided in its very plurality.' We shall address scholars who infer racial prejudice from such exclusions – those furrowed brows – shortly.
13. Ibid., 85.
14. BPF, 144.
15. For which, see the analysis in Vázquez-Arroyo, *Political Responsibility*, 148–9.
16. George Kateb, *Hannah Arendt: Politics, Conscience, Evil* (Totowa: Rowman and Allanheld, 1989), 98.
17. Compare Jeremy Arnold, 'Arendt's Jeremiad: Reading *On Revolution* in a Time of Decline,' *The Review of Politics* 76, no. 3 (2014), 361, 369–70.
18. *Briefwechsel*, 504 (*Grundtatbestände klarzustellen*).
19. CR, 233.
20. HC, 57.
21. Helmut König, 'Die Gründung der Freiheit: Hannah Arendt und die Theorie der Revolution,' *Osteuropa* 67, no. 6–8 (2017), 186.
22. OR, 263–4.
23. See the margin of Arendt's copy of Weber, *Gessamelte politische Schriften* (Munich: Drei Masten Verlag, 1921), 167; BCSL, but see Arnold's alternative, 'Arendt's Jeremiad,' 373–6.
24. OT, 91–4.
25. Mira Siegelberg, 'Things Fall Apart: J. G. A. Pocock, Hannah Arendt, and the Politics of Time,' *Modern Intellectual History* 10, no. 1 (2013), 117.
26. For Arendt's take on revisionist thinking or 'rethinking,' see Luisa G. Musso, 'Formazione della persona ed educazione alla cittadinanza spunti a partire da H. Arendt,' *Rivista di filosofia Neo-Scolastica* 108, no. 3 (2016), 529–30.
27. OR, 122–3.
28. OT, 456.
29. *Briefwechsel*, 393.
30. For that definition or measurement, see Dana Villa, 'From the Critique of Identity to Plurality in Politics: Reconsidering Adorno and Arendt,' in

*Arendt and Adorno Political and Philosophical Investigations*, eds. Lars Rensmann and Samir Gandesha (Stanford: Stanford University Press, 2012), 96. Patricia Owens, 'Racism in the Theory Canon: Hannah Arendt and 'The One Great Crime in which America Was Never Involved,' *Millennium: Journal of International Studies* 45, no. 3 (2017), 411–14 suggests Arendt's definitions of 'a fully human world' often – as did Jefferson's – excluded indigenous and tribal cultures. Owens and others, of late, attribute this to Arendt's 'anti-black racism,' an attribution we shall shortly challenge.

31. Chernow, *Hamilton*, 430.
32. See Beiner's review of Linda M. G. Zerilli's *A Democratic Theory of Government*, in *Perspectives on Politics* 16, no. 3 (2018), 821.
33. For example, OR, 98–9.
34. OT, 125.
35. Peter Wagner, 'Die westliche Demokratie und die Möglichkeit des Totalitarianismus: Űber die Motive der Gründung und der Zerstörung in *The Origins of Totalitarianism*,' in Totalitäre Herrschaft und republikanische Demokratie, ed. Antonia Grunenberg (Frankfurt am Main: Peter Lang, 2003), 137.
36. See Arendt's typescript lecture, 'Outlines and Research Memoranda,' folder 2, image 8 ('*ueberfluessigen Mensche[n]*'); USLC. She elaborated in her *Origins of Totalitarianism*, as we shall see, but consult, in this connection, OT, 444 and 457.
37. OT, 129–30.
38. Ibid., 136–8.
39. Brown, *Nihilistic Times*, 33–4.
40. Compare Patricia Owens, 'Not Life but the World is at Stake: Hannah Arendt on Citizenship in the Age of the Social,' *Citizenship Studies* 16, no. 2 (2012), 306.
41. OT, 271–2.
42. Bonnie Honig, *Political Theory and the Displacement of Politics* (Ithaca: Cornell University Press, 1993), 122.
43. Hans-Jörg Sigwart, *The Wandering Thought of Hannah Arendt* (New York: Palgrave Macmillan, 2015), 126.
44. OT, 458.
45. Arendt, 'Zionism Reconsidered,' in JW, 352.
46. OT, 417–18.
47. Ibid., 389, referring to the Bolsheviks.
48. Compare the contrary assessment in the letter from Michael A. Musmanno to William Shawn, July 22, 1963, in Adolph Eichmann file, Correspondence, 1938–1968, 2–4; USLC.

49. OT, 276–7.
50. Judith N. Shklar, 'Hannah Arendt as Pariah,' *Partisan Review* 50, no. 1 (1983), 71 suggests that Arendt, a non-observant Jew often surrounded by Christians, was tempted to assimilate, to be baptized. But Shklar's connections between Arendt's associations and such temptations are tenuous, at best.
51. OT, 452. For 'insane optimism' and despair, see Arendt, 'We Refugees,' JW, 268 and 273.
52. Arendt, 'The Jew as Pariah: A Hidden Tradition,' JW, 279–81. Arendt referred there to Heinrich Heine. Shortly, and at greater length, we shall discuss her assessments of another pariah poet, Bertolt Brecht, composed early in her career.
53. Ian Storey, 'The Restless Unsaid: Arendt on Political Poetics,' *Critical Inquiry* 41, no. 4 (2015), 870–1.
54. BPF, 136–7.
55. HC, 204.
56. Ibid., 246.
57. Andreas Kalyvas, *Democracy and the Politics of the Extraordinary: Max Weber, Carl Schmitt, and Hannah Arendt* (Cambridge: Cambridge University Press, 2008), 202.
58. See the margin in Arendt's copy of J. William Fulbright's *The Arrogance of Power* (New York: Random House, 1963), 199; BCSL.
59. Hedva Ben-Israel, 'Bi-Nationalism versus Nationalism: The Case of Judah Magnes,' *Israel Studies* 23, no. 1 (2018), 90.
60. Arendt, 'Peace or Armistice in the Near East?' *The Review of Politics* 12, no. 1 (1950), 77–8.
61. For Arendt's work with Zionists in Germany in 1933 and for her endorsement of Magnes's views, see Elisabeth Young-Bruehl, *Hannah Arendt: For Love of the World*, 2nd edn. (New Haven: Yale University Press, 2004), 102–10 and 224–33, respectively.
62. PP, 181; HC, 195–6.
63. OT, 473.
64. OR, 268.
65. HC, 194.
66. BPF, 259.
67. Shmuel Lederman, 'Agonism and Deliberation in Arendt,' *Constellations* 21, no. 3 (2014), 334.
68. LKPP, 74–5.
69. OR, 255.
70. CR, 223–4.

71. The phrase is Ronald Beiner's; see Beiner, 'Rereading 'Truth and Politics'' *Philosophy and Social Criticism* 34, no. 1–2 (2008), 124.
72. BPF, 232–4.
73. Ibid., 80.
74. Dianna Taylor, 'Butler and Arendt on Appearance, Performativity, and Collective Political Action,' *Arendt Studies* 1 (2017), 173–4.
75. BPF, 236–7.
76. For remarks on experience and abstractions, consult, *inter alia*, BPF, 53–4 and Arendt, 'Hannah Arendt on Hannah Arendt,' TWB, 449.
77. Linda M. G. Zerilli, *A Democratic Theory of Judgment* (Chicago: The University of Chicago Press, 2016), 121–2.
78. Arendt, 'Philosophy and Politics,' *Social Research* 71, no. 3 (2004), 434.
79. Zerilli, *Democratic Theory*, 141–2.
80. Kateb, *Hannah Arendt*, 163–4.
81. Ibid., 194.
82. *Denktagebuch*, 621.
83. OT, 457–8.
84. Arendt, 'Destruction of Six Million,' JW, 491–3; Daniela Bassi, 'Verso una politica del limite? Note sur potere e l'azione nel lessico politico di Hannah Arendt,' *Jura Gentium* 15, no. 1 (2018), 89.
85. OT, 311, 444, 457, 475.
86. Eric Gregory, 'Augustine and Arendt on Love: New Dimensions in the Religion and Liberalism Debates,' *The Annual Society of Christian Ethics* 21 (2001), 158.
87. HC, 305–6.
88. See the passages underscored in Arendt's copy of Georg Wilhelm Friedrich Hegel, *Vorlesungen über die Geschichte der Philosophie*, vol. 2 (Leipzig: Felix Meiner, 1040), 181–2; BCSL.
89. BPF, 238.
90. BPF, 140.
91. Christopher Clark, *Revolutionary Spring: Europe Aflame and the Fight for a New World, 1848–1849* (New York: Crown, 2023), 743–4.
92. Arendt, 'On the Nature of Totalitarianism: An Essay on Understanding,' Speeches and Writings File, 1923–1975, 26–26a; USLC.
93. MDT, 217.
94. Ibid., 247.
95. Jerome Kohn, 'Loyalty as Betrayal: Hannah Arendt's Judgment of the Poet Bertolt Brecht,' *Social Research* 86, no. 3 (2019), 666–7.
96. Arendt, 'Remembering Wystan H. Auden,' TWB, 529.

97. MDT, p. 243; Patchen Markell, 'Politics and the Case of Poetry: Arendt and Brecht,' *Modern Intellectual History* 15, no. 2 (2018), 525–6.
98. MDT, 230–1.
99. Arendt, 'Beyond Personal Frustration: The Poetry of Bertolt Brecht,' *Kenyon Review* 10, no. 2 (1948), 311–2.
100. Domenico Losurdo, 'Hannah Arendt e l'analisi delle rivoluzioni,' in *La pluralità irrappresentabili: Il pensiero politico di Hannah Arendt*, ed. Roberto Esposito (Uribino: Edizioni QuattroVenti, 1987), 144–5.
101. Cecilia Sjöholm, 'Voicing Thought: Arendt, Poetry, and Philosophy,' in *Philosophy and Poetry: Continental Perspectives*, ed. Ranjan Gosh (New York: Columbia University Press, 2019), 75; von Tevenar, 'Invisibility,' 39.
102. MDT, 245.
103. Ibid., 238.
104. Arendt, 'Reflektionen über den Dichter Bertold Brecht und sein Verhältnis zur Politik,' 7; Speeches and Writings File, 1923–1975, 022275; USLC.
105. MDT, 227.
106. Arendt, 'The Jew as Pariah: A Hidden Tradition,' JW, 282.
107. MDT, 240.
108. Ibid., 236.
109. Ibid., 211–2.
110. Sophie Loidolt, *Phenomenology of Plurality: Hannah Arendt on Political Intersubjectivity* (London: Routledge, 2018), 77.
111. Young-Bruehl, *Hannah Arendt*, 215, quoting Jaspers.
112. HC, 169–71.
113. Markell, 'Politics,' 503, 521, 532–3.
114. MDT, 225–7.
115. Villa, 'Arendt, Heidegger,' 995–6 suggests Arendt distanced herself from Heidegger's notion that authenticity required being with (or within) the world – *Mitsein* – because that concept 'was surprisingly devoid of a robust interactive dimension.'
116. LMW, 211.
117. LKPP, 77: 'It is against human dignity to believe in progress.'
118. Arendt, 'Philosophy and Politics,' 428–9. Also see the underscored passages in Arendt's copy of *The Statesman*, in *The Collected Dialogues of Plato*, eds. Edith Hamilton and Huntington Cairns (New York: Pantheon, 1961), 1084–5; BCSL.
119. Zerilli, *Democratic Theory*, 120.
120. Arendt, 'Philosophy and Politics,' 431.

121. HC, 283.
122. Ibid., 291.
123. EU, 428.
124. Ibid., 314.
125. Arendt, 'Philosophy and Politics,' 452–3.
126. *Briefwechsel*, 450.
127. Arendt, 'Karl Marx and the Tradition of Western Political Thought,' *Social Research* 69, no. 2 (2002), 313.
128. LMT, 185–7.
129. BPF, 228–9.
130. Ibid., p. 234.
131. Arendt, 'Philosophy and Politics,' 445.
132. BPF, 164–5.
133. *Denktagebuch*, 495.

# 2

# Nationalism and 'Non-thinking': Arend on Parvenus, Pariahs and Philosophers

## Spartacists and Spectators

Apologists for nationalism's contributions to sovereignty and solidarity tend to underestimate the tenacity with which the need to belong grips citizens who deny a sense of belonging to religious, racial and ethnic others. Eventually controversies develop, and some nationalists welcome them. Yael Tamir seems to invite problems with her question, 'how much diversity can be taken in while retaining social cohesion?' She wants to sow 'seeds of a new discourse' but without 'position[ing] people against one another.' Nonetheless, when she inquires about capping diversity, she appears to be suggesting administrative or legislative overreach.[1]

The nationalists whom Arendt studied and with whom twenty-first-century citizens worldwide are all too familiar, looked to create social and ideological solidarity by sowing seeds of discord rather than Tamir's seeds of discourse. And the frequency with which statists resolutely did and do so is distressing. Arendt was upset. The prerogatives of blood and soil (ethnicity, territory, race) latched onto citizens' imaginations and limited their perspectives. Emphasis on origins made it harder to articulate the importance of new beginnings.[2] To the nationalists, plurality mattered far less than conformity, if at all. The elite and ordinary alike seemed indifferent to exclusions associated with ethnonationalism. Many citizens were unfazed when statists serving nationalists declared their neighbours undeserving or undesirable. Arendt remembered how bias and bigotry displaced decency and civic concern during the 1920s and 1930s. But nationalisms threatened civilisations long before Adolf Hitler and Nazi statists persuaded citizens of Aryan ancestry that the reserve of 'the right people' was exclusively Aryan.[3]

In January 1919, members of a nationalist paramilitary murdered Arendt's paragon of political virtue, Rosa Luxemburg, Polish émigré, Marxist scholar and co-founder of the *Spartakusbund*, which was trying to unite the German left. The murderers were apprehended but charged with disposing of Luxemburg's corpse – not with creating it – and were let off lightly. The Weimar Republic kept coddling nationalist paramilitaries during the 1920s, the most militant of which tipped the scales in favour of fascism in the early 1930s, as the republic gave way to the Third Reich. Arendt was mortified by the efficiency with which Nazi statists marshalled support for Hitler's second *putsch* and for what followed. She also marvelled at the popularity of populism. Save for Luxemburg, who cofounded and coordinated the Spartacists, she had nothing good to say about the Marxists who were the Nazis' chief rivals.[4] Arendt preferred Immanuel Kant's analysis of the trajectories of history to that of Karl Marx and Friedrich Engels. The latter two, she complained, foreclosed options. She lampooned the notion that at history's end a classless society supplied with an inexhaustible 'abundance' would allow everyone to indulge 'in some sort of hobby.' History's importance, for Kant and for Arendt, lay in prying open 'new horizons for the future.'[5] Conditions for a modern economy were yet to be calculated. She acknowledged that the poverty and misery of workers and the inhumanity of employers and exploiters ought to be the first post-war problems to be addressed. 'Collective ownership,' though, struck her as 'a contradiction in terms.' 'Our problem' was 'not how to expropriate the expropriators,' Arendt explained, but how to 'arrange matters' to the advantage of ordinary citizens whom capitalists and fascists disempowered.[6]

She believed that Luxemburg's 'brilliant' study of the political structures that had encouraged industrialization and imperialism eventually would prove useful resolving 'our problem.' But, above all, Arendt's tribute to Spartacists' activist and martyred social theorist celebrated her determination to take her savvy into the streets.[7] Whereas many of her Marxist colleagues perched above class struggles, assuming workers' bravado would finish off the capitalists and capitalism without leadership on the left, Luxemburg, 'loyal to reality,' knew better. While Marxists refined their theories about social 'evolution,' she organized. While her comrades were waiting for history to be lugged into crisis, she – weary of waiting – maintained what Arendt described as 'a program of constant friction with society.' For Arendt, Luxemburg unquestionably deserved pride of place on the left. She embodied a revolutionary spirit, which was hostage to no theory and to no logic of history.[8]

To commemorate the *Spartakusbund*'s abortive November uprising, Arendt planned to dedicate her long essay on the Hungarian revolution of 1956 to Luxemburg who, like the Hungarian insurgents, fearlessly challenged statist authorities. But the Hungarians seemed encumbered with ideological baggage, with what Christopher Holman calls 'stale dogmas.'[9] At first, the Hungarians showed striking solidarity and spontaneity. They set up their council system to encourage widespread participation. Arendt's glimpse was sufficient, to her mind, to dignify it as 'the foundation of a new body politic.'[10] The rebels of 1956 were not what Marx anticipated. Most had not emerged from the exploited underclass but from 'over-privileged' families. Yet they were driven, as were the Spartacists, by a 'will for freedom.'[11] Yet within weeks, disagreements divided them and the Hungarian and Soviet statists took advantage of the divisions. Hence, much as Luxemburg and the Spartacists, Hungarian insurgents failed to institutionalise their revolutionary spirit. The two uprisings collapsed. To Arendt, the 'will for freedom' looked destined for defeat in the twentieth century. Disappointed, she nonetheless resolved to remind readers of the Spartacists' stand for, as well as Luxemburg's dedication to, 'justice and freedom and revolution' and to include her own summons to innovate.[12]

She admired Luxemburg for having made principled stands without drawing her principles from absolutes and abstractions, counting that as virtuous, as we should now expect. As she prepared for her own bout with 'insane nationalism,' she recalled Luxemburg's activism, realism and martyrdom as, ten years later, she prepared for her own bout with 'insane nationalism.' But Arendt was no activist. She was no organizer. Instead, she wrote about insurgencies and about the 'experience of total politicisation in totalitarianism' to formulate her alternative definition of politics.[13] 'Deeds and words' qualified as political when they created 'interests' in a 'worldly in-between,' the *inter-ests* we have already encountered. She trusted that such spaces encouraged interlocutors to act and speak directly to each other.[14] The Spartacists, under constant pressure, would unlikely have had time or the inclination to theorise their partisans' interactions, but if the Luxemburg Arendt lionized had survived into the 1930s and beyond, she could only have echoed her eulogist's indictments of contemporaries' tepid reactions to fascist protocols and apparatuses. For Spartacists appear to have looked beyond nationalists' materialism and their statists' efforts to fashion conformity. They certainly seemed so to Arendt who saw nationalisms' obsessions with 'making' and 'building' had come 'to occupy a rank formerly held by political action.'[15]

Statists basically built a mass culture, equating citizenship with conformity. Plurality obviously complicated such work. Nationalism made it easier. At any twist or turn in the development of what Arendt stigmatised as 'mass culture' nonconformity and plurality presented problems for statists. Hence, they valued and urged ideological consistency. Abstractions served them well. Arendt thought otherwise, as we know, and Katherine Arens seems right to pair

Luxemburg's belief that 'public life … need[ed] to be reconceived as engagements in the immediate not in terms of abstract patterns' with Arendt's effort to find alternatives to 'decaying' yet influential 'body politic[s].'[16] Occasions to express her admiration for Luxemburg offered her chances to express her contempt for the persistence of nationalisms and to reconfirm the 'loyalty to reality' she shared with the émigré martyr. The anecdotes and analyses Arendt bundled into her *Origins of Totalitarianism* illustrated regimes' rearmament of ethnonationalism. There and thereafter, she put her contemporaries on notice that nationalisms in the 1950s and 1960s were nearly as sinister as those in the 1930s. Rather than await protests, the Nazis preemptively rounded up, intimidated and eliminated 'carriers of tendencies' that threatened the party. They turned the public realm into a stage for spectators' expressions of fealty. Fast forward to find the 'hustle and bustle' of the public realm in the United States, which, Ari Adut says, 'above all is a sensory experience' ready to be taken in, though not acted upon. It is not a place for 'civic dialogue,' Adut goes on, citing some advantages of spectatorship, defining what he terms its 'emancipatory' dimension. But Arendt would have questioned, if not quarrelled with, Adut's characterisation. To her mind, the impresarios and not the spectators would have justifiably claimed the advantage, insofar as Nazi statists' stagecraft and subsequent nationalists' spectacles' 'indelible inauthenticity' have successfully objectified spectators and subverted dissent to their respective regimes' benefit.[17]

## 'Years of Aberration': War and Race

Adut was less worried than Arendt about the control statists hoped to exercise over the public realm. For him, spectatorship had certain rewards. Spectators could duck under 'civic dialogue' and the responsibilities that came with participation. Arendt relished discussions, which, in the right settings, 'enlarged' interlocutors' 'mentalit[ies].' And, to frame favourably enlargement and enlightenment as well as to warn of the deterioration of the public realms during the second half of the twentieth century, she compared features of totalitarian regimes that discouraged freedom and plurality during the 1930s with subsequent political developments in western Europe and in the United States. Fascists in Germany were intent on erasing the history of Jewish assimilation. They entombed the decades when 'the real vanguard' of German society was 'eager to associate with' Jewish financiers.[18] What fascists wanted forgotten was forgotten. Meanwhile, airbrushed accounts glamorised the nationalists' seizure of power. But Arendt perceived that statists and their patrons among the political elites in the United States were succumbing to similar temptations to rescript history. The last lecture she delivered before her death, paid then President Gerald Ford a backhanded compliment. Bungling by then had led to the Americans' defeat in Vietnam and the disgrace of Ford's predecessor, Richard Nixon. She regarded Ford as rather proficient 'getting rid of unpleasant realities' by pardoning Nixon and promoting the illusion that his humiliated country was about to 'open a new chapter of history.' The president's publicists nimbly 'swept under the rug of imagery' the corrupt practices and lost causes of the previous administration. Often-repeated falsifications were effective brooms.[19] But the redactions and puffery impaired citizens' ability to judge.[20] Arendt touted new beginnings but mistrusted any fresh start – any 'opening' for natality – that depended on what she characterised as 'the defactualisation' of the past.[21]

Totalitarian officials and the statists they retained 'defactualis[ed]' to depict the present (as well as their presence in history) as inevitable and to have their subjects see their own subjection as the culmination of an irreversible, fruitful course of events. Statists were surefooted, confident that their scripts would be taken not simply as plausible versions of history but as incontestable ones. Arendt granted that they could be imaginatively devious. For their part, though, the statists would have been loath to encourage or endorse the 'imaginative seeing' she would have had her citizen-statesmen value and practise to project familiar concepts into new contexts to entice and enable interlocutors to consider alternative perspectives. But statists, Arendt suggested, had put their rhetorical skills to different uses. They were marketing to 'manipulate fact and opinion.' She referred to the 'defactualisation' and rescripting of history circulating in Europe and the United States from the 1950s. She knew that lies and distortions had leavened political cultures for millennia. 'Truthfulness,' she agreed, had never been numbered 'among the political virtues.' Yet something in her time had changed; previously, 'organised lying' had been concerned only with particulars. It 'was never meant to deceive literally everybody.' But, she supposed, recent deceptions were fiendishly circulated to give the deceivers total (or totalitarian) control. 'Mass manipulation' interested the power-brokers who assumed that they were apart from that 'mass' to be managed. Yet she could tell that some recent deceptions were deceiving the deceivers as well as their constituents.[22]

Case in point: information released about the war in Southeast Asia. H. R. McMaster's narrative eviscerates the American government for having 'deceiv[ed] Congress about the nature and cost of its intervention in Vietnam.' President Lyndon Johnson told his Secretary of Defence, Robert McNamara, to filter the news and keep reports of the conflict 'very, very low key.' Citizens were shocked, therefore, when the extent of the American military involvement and its exorbitant cost in casualties became known. McMaster, a former army lieutenant general, suggests that military commanders were contrite reflecting on their capitulation to the statists' demand for deception.[23] Arendt's close friend and frequent correspondent Mary McCarthy, had been reporting about, and often from, Vietnam for years. She suspected deceit, but citizens learned only years later that her suspicions were warranted. In spring, 1971, what came to be known as 'the Pentagon Papers,' stolen from government files, were published. Readers then had a cafeteria of documents and sufficient proof of a concerted campaign of disinformation, no matter what they selected from the counter. Political officials and military commanders fed journalists – and, through them, a public that had become weary of war – from a seemingly inexhaustible menu of falsifications. Years later, when all was revealed, McMaster was scathing. McCarthy was incredulous. How could (and why did) the principal architect of the war strategy, McNamara, set aside the 'criteria of judgement' that he 'applied with such severity' while leading the Ford Motor Company? How could he and his deputies have torched the truth about their unwieldy war's escalation, and why would a democratic government subvert democracy so cavalierly? McMaster's answer amounts to an indictment of what statists considered an airtight alibi: keeping costs of the war 'classified,' they said, shielded from criticism the administration's progressive domestic agenda.[24] McCarthy scoffed at the excuse and accused civilian authorities of what could be classified as an awkward attempt at therapeutic misdirection. They ceased fretting about the accuracy of the information they retailed. They tried to delete the mind-numbing evidence of violence in Vietnam to avoid traumatising citizens who 'could not bear the expense of the truth.' Johnson and McNamara forgot how to 'spot discrepancies' between the real and the reassuring.[25]

McCarthy called them 'discrepancies,' Arendt 'divergences.' Both referred to statists, adept at marketing, who passed off fantasy as fact. They relied on citizens assuming that their country's 'modern mechanised power' would easily overpower an ostensibly backward country.[26] Arendt was equally angry with deceived constituents and deceptive statists, though, after the publication of the Pentagon Papers, she gave the citizens' credulity something of a pass and concentrated her scalding commentary on government mendacity – on statists' divergences. In an essay on 'Lying in Politics,' she tried a clever twist on one of the regime's deluxe untruths, the so-called 'domino theory.' Statists claimed that democracies fall to communism, one after another, as dominoes do when the first one tilts into a second. Hence, some superior power must intervene to prevent the first or the next from falling. Dropping dominoes morphed from a theory to an inevitability. But, in Arendt's revision of the metaphor, dominoes became data – or, to be precise propaganda – as American civilian and military officials put forward lie after lie. She referred to the statists' subterfuge as 'the proliferation and perfection of make-believe.'[27]

Statists rummaged through what informants told them about third-world conflicts to collect evidence that communists crossed borders and conspired with indigenous insurgents to upend purportedly democratic governments. The result: supplemental divergences substantiating the domino theory. Whereas Beijing and Moscow were routinely at daggers drawn, officials in the United States and their friends in the universities claimed that communism was seamless, that a Sino-Soviet bloc was determined to undermine democracies wherever its agents could discover then dupe local malcontents. Seven years after Joseph McCarthy was censured by his senate colleagues for spellbinding slander that convinced many of his countrymen of communists' creeping control over the media, the military and the government, Robert McNamara and his minions tried their hand at dominoes. To Arendt, their most egregious offense against the truth dishonoured the dead. Authorities doctored statistics about casualties to suggest that victory was imminent.[28]

The Pentagon Papers exposed much of the fraud. Civilian control of the military, which founders of the American republic took as a promising step away from Europe's neo-feudal arrangements, led to a politicisation of the country's defenses. The founders had not anticipated consequences of that sort and did not put in place provisions against lying in politics, which, within a century, if not before, became epidemic. A dwindling stock of honest, thoughtful statesmen was left to inspire citizens to think critically and to mistrust statists' explanations and justifications. Such critical thinking (or mistrust), Arendt went on, must 'always' be 'hostile.'[29] To tamp down the hostility, statists counted on intimidation when needed but were generally confident in citizens' credulity, which Arendt described as 'non-thinking.' She conceded that, from the 1950s into the 1970s, statists in the United States were less coercive than fascists had been in previous decades, but, she submitted, statists in every age promoted 'non-thinking' to stave off sedition. Socrates had been its avowed enemy. Arendt adduced that he was persecuted because he looked to slow down Athenians by vexing them and by compelling them to think through rather than to accept others' doctrines. Dana Villa refers to his method as 'dissolvent.' It dissolved others' answers and left citizens with questions.[30] Arendt would have agreed and approved. She reckoned that discourses routinely developed from such dissolutions. Ideally, they would challenge citizen-statesmen effectively to challenge non-thinking peers. But, just as Athenian patriarchs who feared Socrates, statists discouraged dissolvent, disorienting thinking and the exchange of opinions it prompted.[31]

As we discovered, Arendt was profoundly disappointed by what she learned about the early American republic. She was at pains to explain the founders' decision to relieve citizens of responsibilities to think critically. She contended that democracy deteriorated when it became representative democracy. The founders still impressed her by what they dissolved and began. But Jefferson and others, despairing of organising and institutionalising citizens' continuous participation, chose instead to advocate a representative regime and to ask only that electors periodically delegate authority. As for the delegates or representatives, remote from the next election, they had little incentive to be attentive to the electorate and could remain unresponsive without much risk.[32] They could ignore the disaffected, as long as the malcontents were few. Representation was an affliction, which, Arendt noted, lasted into the twentieth century when statists dismissed as ungrateful parasites those protesting policy or war. They were characterised as beneficiaries of an affluent society looking to sabotage benefactors' endeavours. She thought that protesters would have fared much better, had Thomas Jefferson's scheme for a series of 'wards' been implemented. Such 'elementary republics' could have fortified democracy in the United States, she imagined, although not by 'strengthen[ing] the power of the many.' Instead, wards would have drawn on 'the power of everyone,' who would 'count and be counted upon.'[33] She figured that competence would outweigh charisma, and, inasmuch as citizens' passions for the 'commonality' took hold without diminishing their appreciation for plurality, many would become citizen-statesmen, ready to confer, voicing opinions competitively yet collegially.[34]

Such readiness appears utopian. Arendt realised it could not survive in conventional public spheres or in those only modestly reupholstered. It could hardly inspire new beginnings while citizens were untroubled by their governments' or statists' accommodation for, or indifference to, their own 'non-thinking.' Accommodations took a few forms. Perhaps the most conspicuous and preposterous, given the rivalries, even among the 'non-thinking' in every constituency, was and still is the assurance that no elected representative would stray from the electorate's wishes. But assurances of that sort held, Arendt suggested, because the elected instructed statists to sell national identity, to create common prejudices and, in effect, to commandeer 'political life' in the interests of incumbents by dazzling and distracting the electorate. Whatever channels were still open between the represented and their representatives became clogged with other-than-political dramas or spectacles. If amusements failed to depoliticise and disempower citizens, statists proffered scandals.[35] For prurience is usually irrepressible. The statists' salesmanship impresses. Statists were and still are practised opportunists. They repurpose indiscretions and embarrassments to arrest citizens' attention. What they unveil or invent can hold and control citizens' imaginations, and such citizen capture, Ari Adut admits, is 'symptomatic of a degraded public sphere.'[36] Yet Arendt did not overlook the progressive character of the American republic. Workers were gradually emancipated from many of the oppressive conditions under which they long laboured. Sanitation improved. There was more time to think about politics – although less incentive to do so. But there had been no 'progress in the direction of freedom.'[37]

American citizens in the nineteenth and twentieth century were less astute. Participation in the discourses and actions, which she imagined as critical to the creation and perpetuation of public realms, mattered less to them than producing, pricing, possessing and consuming. Ordinary and elite citizens alike were preoccupied with leisure. But they settled for less. Better second in Gaul than first in Rome. Better complacent than creative. Arendt prophesied that the time would soon come when the 'devouring character' of daily existence dominated, when only 'the effort of consumption will be left.'[38] The virtues of citizen-statesmanship that were undervalued after the founders' conventions adjourned, were completely eclipsed by ordinary citizens' (and the elites') desires to acquire with as little effort as possible. Few were interested in holding representatives accountable. Arendt summarised with a nearly audible growl: the electorate's informed consent was 'entirely fictitious.' The prospect of accountability 'lost all plausibility.' Bureaucratization of republican regimes, in effect, licensed partisan delegates to 'represent nobody except party machines.'[39]

Resistance to those party machines was nearly nonexistent. Partisans had little difficulty demonstrating how effective the 'single-minded attention directed to the acceleration of the[ir] movement[s]' could be.[40] In a lecture delivered a year before the publication of her *Origins of Totalitarianism* in 1951, Arendt referred to such movements' success at 'normalising' tyranny. She lectured 'on ideology and propaganda,' intending to illustrate the 'solidarity of [partisans'] gangsterism.'[41] What might have called a halt? Historical study? Residual respect for plurality? Arendt wondered whether either might work in her adopted country. Historical study seemed politically irrelevant in the United States, where political parties were known to collaborate to approve legislation that – far from encouraging plurality – exacerbated the effects of both racial tensions and socio-economic stratification. Furthermore, the suggestion that private interests be sacrificed was exceedingly unpopular. But such sacrifices were precisely what Arendt required. 'The necessary sacrifice of individual interests' to 'the commonweal' must be forthcoming, she advised, if her redefined politics were to prosper and if citizens were to experience a liberation and 'happiness' persons only find there.[42] As for statists, conventional 'politics at once became for them a necessary evil' when they concentrated on systems and structures that, she scowled, ensured citizens developed strictly material and 'pre-political' conceptions of their 'needs and necessities.'[43]

While Arendt was finishing her doctoral dissertation in Germany, in the United States, Walter Lippmann was celebrating citizens' disinterest in politics. He argued their participation could only prevent experts from getting things done. Ordinary citizens were not only self-indulgent, callous, cocooned and, therefore, ill-informed, but they had no business intruding on others better prepared to govern. Citizens thought in stereotypes, he wrote; without them, they were helpless trying to decipher a bewildering world.[44] Arendt harboured similar reservations, though she held statists responsible for their citizens' ignorance, self-absorption and general ineptitude. But one could not pry statists from conventional politics. They were part of its fabric, yet Arendt trusted that plurality, freedom and natality in alternative venues would awaken citizens' enthusiasm for politics as she redefined it, for her 'new politics.' For his part, Lippmann frowned on citizen participation. He declared citizens hopelessly hostage to political factions. 'Most mercilessly maligned' Machiavelli knew as much, he said, reading the Florentine's *Principe* as a telling exposé and implied that citizens tempted to book a berth in their parliaments or congresses should obtain Machiavelli's short treatise, mistrust every political faction's fictions, abjure political participation and permit a reliable and – as required – a ruthless expert to govern.[45]

On one count, Arendt might have agreed with Lippmann. He feared the constant jousting of belligerent, rival, resentful interest groups, which, he imagined, would follow, if widespread participation in the public realm were encouraged. Arendt favoured opening deliberations, yet worried about 'the overlapping of rights and interests' that could disrupt them. Commenting controversially on school desegregation, she shocked progressives by opposing conventional political measures to force schools to integrate. Integrationists' goodwill was offset by their usurpation of what she took to be personal, parental prerogatives or rights. Governments, she conceded, played important roles protecting citizens' rights to an education; authorities should ensure that all the governed were informed. To some extent, then, the content of education was a political rather than just a personal matter. Nonetheless, the context of education ('the context of association and social life'), she suggested, was better left for parents to determine. She endorsed compulsory education but not compulsory integration. She thought that government interference with the freedom of choice – with the freedom to choose with whom to associate – was contrary to the intentions of her favourite founders.[46] And, as Ainsley LeSure argues,

Arendt guessed that 'the inadequacy of … political institutions tasked with realising [racial] equality' would become all too obvious when racial biases were not directly addressed. 'The tragic continuities of old and new forms of racial domination' would persist 'after moments of supposed racial progress' were celebrated.[47]

LeSure's argument is cogent and will be adapted shortly to present some of our assessments of Arendt's remarks on race, but here it seems important to emphasise her regard for the rights to assemble and to associate. She deemed the founders of the American republic far more prudent than their French counterparts, who allowed Isaac René Guy le Chapelier to pass a bill through their General Assembly in 1791 abolishing craft guilds and other intermediate assemblies. The French insurgents, foolishly, to Arendt's mind, prohibited any assembly from coming between the particular interest of an individual and the general interest defined by statists.[48] She berated the French for 'desert[ing]' the local societies they set up, intending to empower citizens, and for leaving Maximilien Robespierre free to improvise an insubstantial notion of political necessity that let the regime extinguish the freedom to associate.[49]

Arendt's mistrust of political solutions to interpersonal or social problems, her aforementioned defence of the right to associate and her distinctions between the social and the political reflect her wholly unflattering appraisal of twentieth-century statists' salesmanship. This observation is not intended to be exculpatory. Focusing on freedom, she failed to see racial discrimination as a political problem. As Richard Bernstein succinctly points out, she could be 'obtuse,' 'imposing her own categories on the world.' She repeatedly stressed the urgency of taking reality into one's political theories, yet, as Bernstein says, she could exhibit an insensitivity to 'the complexities of reality.'[50] Jerome Kohn shrewdly pegs her failure. Selecting eight of her essays for his collection, *Responsibility and Judgment*, Kohn placed her review of Rolf Hochhuth's provocative play, *The Deputy*, immediately after her controversial 'Reflections on Little Rock,' as if to call attention to her inability to spot the connections between white supremacists' furious resistance to integration during the late 1950s and 1960s and the loathsome consequences of Aryan supremacy, especially the fascists' politics of exclusion and extermination. Hochhuth's drama excoriated Pope Pius XII for the Catholic church's silence during, and for Rome's tacit approval of, the persecution of the Jews – for what Arendt's review called a 'disastrous loss of all feeling for reality.' Inarguably, had she been more familiar with the history of racial prejudice and with racial profiling in the United States, her evaluations of the American integrationists' 'usurpation' of the freedom to associate would have been tempered.[51]

But she deplored the politicisation of ethnicity and race. Norma Claire Moruzzi claims that Arendt could not imagine 'a political movement organised around anti-racism.'[52] We shall propose that Arendt expected her 'new politics' to tackle the sources of racism more effectively than legislation. To think that she presumed politics, as she redefined it, would overlook issues raised by implicit bias and systemic racism is ludicrous, given her studies of the Shoah and her experiences of antisemitism. To render unimpeachable arguments about Arendt's covert racism, indifference to slavery and idealisation of colonialism scholars must – and, unfortunately do – dismiss her remarks about the debasement of persons of African descent in eighteenth-century America and discount criteria she set for alternative collectives to practise politics, specifically, the respect that citizen-statesmen must show for plurality. To become statesmen, citizens in her unconventional public realms must champion not only diversity but also equality.[53] European history (and especially Europeans' history in Africa) documented for Arendt how statists and elites deployed racist tropes. She seemed stunned by their insensitivity and wary about – although hardly insensitive to – the politicisation of race.[54]

Arendt chronicled the effects of prejudice on the persecuted, especially and dramatically in her *Origins of Totalitarianism*, which discussed parvenu and pariah Jewish communities in Europe. The precarious position of the parvenus in Germany ('assimilationists' known also as 'exception Jews') was abundantly clear to them. As a result, they were ever-apprehensive. Their 'messianic hope evaporated,' Arendt sensed, whereas the pariahs' messianism held – at great cost.[55] They were marginalised and maligned, then finally murdered. Antisemitism prevailed. To Arendt, it seemed to be incurable, an affliction she encountered in her studies and her universities during the late 1920s and early 1930s.[56] Racism would have seemed similar. Conventional politics afforded no significant protection. History relayed the corrosive effects of ordinary citizens' prejudices on even the best-intentioned politicians' determination. There seemed no reason, therefore, for Arendt to classify racism as anything other than the social blight it so irrefutably had been. But politicisation merely upped the stakes and ended with demonisation. And when politicians' prejudices (and ignorance) were factored, Arendt's conclusion appears even more comprehensible, that is, her conviction that inequities occasioned by racism were best resolved at some remove from conventional politics. Lasting solutions would depend on character formation and re-formation. Statutory and structural adjustments were likely to be negligible and ephemeral until prejudices against pluralism were addressed by change-agents. The conceit of this study is that Arendt realised as much. Disappointed with politics, as conventionally defined, she trusted that politics redefined could change citizens' character, reshape democratic practice and, ideally, compose inclusive democracies. Her disappointments with conventional political protocols and apparatuses – and with self-indulgent statists – remained in tension with the hopes she harboured that constituted powers might provisionally address inequities and bigotry. But her hopes do not excuse her for having inadequately appreciated the extent to which access to public discourse and fair hearings of their grievances had been denied persons of colour by the founders of the republic and by their heirs in the twentieth century. Confronted with African-Americans' strenuous efforts to acquire access and to find a voice, she miscalculated, construing 'the new trend of black power' in the late 1960s as rigorously separatist.[57] Furthermore, as often noted, defending the distinctions between the social and the political impaired her ability to identify ways that even the conventional approaches characteristic of the latter might usefully address injustices plaguing the former. She seems not to have consistently sensed the urgency of starting to remedy the effects of prejudice before – or while – working more assiduously on character re-formation in alternative public spaces.[58]

Her support for friends protesting racial discrimination went only so far. She was not about to march. She highly regarded civil disobedients opposing Americans' intervention in southeast Asia, as we learned, but she was also critical of the demonstrators' under-theorised campaigns. Arendt complained that the 'old left' and, in the 1960s, the so-called 'new left' had limitations. Vladimir Lenin, the paladin of many in the old and new, for example, learned lessons from the French revolutionaries, but, she recalled, he had failed to put in place conditions that prevented Stalinism.[59] Liberals disappointed her. Had she been haunted by failures of nerve in Germany during the Weimar Republic?[60] It had been powerless to cope with fascism. As for the leftists and liberals in the United States, they seemed to Arendt to have missed what was at stake when Joseph McCarthy's rancorous accusations gained traction. Liberals ostensibly forgot how fragile freedom was.[61] Had McCarthy's celebrity been sustainable, Arendt wrote to Robert Hutchins in 1957, the rabid senator and his cutthroat accomplices in congress and in the press would have hollowed out their country's political culture. She also told Hutchins that 'race hatred' looked terribly tenacious and confided that the awful jeopardy that the minorities faced might justify remedies that factored the 'interplay ... of the social, private and public realms.' So, at that moment, and to shape a new beginning, the distinctions between the social and political she defended the following year in her volume, *The Human Condition*, appeared to have been negotiable.[62]

During the next few years, as measures 'redressing relations of inequality' were tested and contested, Arendt, according to Seyla Benhabib, gathered that the 'walls' between 'the public and the private' and those between the social and the political were destined to come down.[63] But, as the letter to Hutchins attests, those 'walls' were arguably erected to protect the social from the conventionally political. As noted, Arendt failed to lower them consistently, yet she intermittently acknowledged the importance of having conventional politics penetrate realms where legitimate grievances festered. She issued stinging rebukes to her academic colleagues unwilling to denounce unfairness. They seemed spineless to her. And, when Mary McCarthy called out intellectuals' 'ritualistic doubting,' which she deemed responsible for the persistence of disinformation, racial prejudices and purges, Arendt replied with remarks about intellectuals' 'feebleminded thoughtfulness or thoughtful feeblemindedness.'[64] But, had they been otherwise, what difference would her academic colleagues have made? Her marking in the margins of Carl Schmitt's *Begriff des Politischen* suggest she may have concurred with the volume's concession that scholarly colleagues were powerless to stop the inevitable polarisation developing from the prejudices society deemed permissible.[65]

Scholars' coffers of concern were hardly empty, yet, as we contended, statists were successful keeping the concerns of the most critical out of play. Nonetheless, should the intellectuals and pundits on the left be blamed for the failures of conventional politics? Perhaps. Arendt pondered that question as she compared the social, cultural and political wreckage in the United States and central Europe with what had been left of the western Roman empire in the late fourth and fifth centuries. Something among the ruins gave her pause and cause for hope. Even then, there were new beginnings. The 'memorable continuity' of civilisation was preserved, but, from its decline and purported fall, fresh ideas emerged. Arendt dragged from Augustine – and dragged from its context – a remark she took to have been a proclamation to that effect, misappropriating it to introduce her doctrine of natality.[66] Still, notwithstanding her faith in new beginnings, she fit well with political realists, who, in the aftermath of the Second World War, were unimpressed with statists playing statesmen and pretending that Germans had foresworn fascism *en masse* or that Europeans would forever be deterred from genocide.[67] Fast forward from the early 1950s to her last public lecture, delivered in 1975, and one glimpses diminished confidence in humanity's resourcefulness moored alongside her anticipation of new beginnings but also in tension with the disappointments she accumulated during what she dubbed the intervening 'years of aberration.'[68]

## Nationalism, Capitalism and Freedom

The argument of the previous chapter and of the present one is that those years of aberrations took a toll. Despite her search for remedial measures and for leaders committed to regeneration, Arendt's disappointment with the effects on democratic practice of statists' salesmanship was palpable. She found that citizens were unable to agree on how to discuss what constituted their common good. Factions' struggles for domination put her off. When statists marketed capitalism and nationalism so effectively to attenuate citizens' political participation, there seemed to be no space to redefine and reintroduce it. She increasingly concentrated on statists' political behaviour and its influence on citizens' disinterest in politics and classified both as unambiguous betrayals of the founders of the American republic. Late in her career, she brooded about the proliferation of weapons of mass destruction. Decades before, Arendt was brooding about fascists' lurching for *lebensraum*. From the early 1950s, she fretted that nationalists' and capitalists' desires for influence and profit moved them to turn limited, local territorial conflicts into wars of annihilation. The stressful, conventional political climates in Europe and the United States appeared quite unfavourable for new departures and new beginnings. But she lectured on, and wrote about, contemporary crises as though she believed the 'incredible' might occur, that an assortment of collectives or 'counter-republics' (or 'oases') could be found or created and that citizens there might lay the cornerstones for a new politics. Although such collectives, as she imagined them, disavowed pretensions to perpetuity, she occasionally mused that they might exhibit an 'incredible, enduring tenacity.'[69]

But she was no fool. She never exaggerated the prospects for endurance. Yet endurance was what statists prized. She knew as much and, as Douglas Klusmeyer says, Arendt could never have overlooked or underestimated statists' abilities to capitalise on what he calls 'modernity's pathologies' and then turn them to their own and to the political elites' advantage. Facing them gave her 'thinking about politics and ethics' a 'strong tragic cast.'[70] Reflecting on nationalists' intrigues, which accounted for the conduct of American foreign policy and which, she judged, exponentially increased the risk of escalating foreign conflicts, as just noted, she concluded that statists' practice and 'policy of lying' captivated and captured ordinary citizens.[71] Arendt could not imagine historians or journalists successfully contesting the nationalism statists paraded as what is generally known as American exceptionalism. She would read the fawning, fallacious reports about and justifications for an American presence in southeast Asia. The few, reputedly 'best and brightest' – 'problem-solvers,' image-makers and 'decision-takers' – appeared to have misplaced both their analytical abilities and their consciences. So, it bears repeating that Arendt was living through a time when sovereign powers, statists and scholars in tow were resolved to pacify Vietnam and to salvage their country's self-image as a sensible world power, permitting 'no reality and no common sense [to] penetrate the[ir] minds.' 'None of them sensed that the "world" might get rather frightened of American friendship and commitment.' It seemed that they somehow had been airlifted out of the 'untold misery' their interventions and escalations, their sense of self-worth and their wretched exceptionalism occasioned?[72]

Both this chapter and the last have concentrated on the misery. The intention was to assist readers to see how prevailing political practices looked to Arendt and how looking at them affected her. Given her observations of the politically influential, she might have remembered Martin Heidegger disparaging politicians as mindlessly mediocre. A few of her indictments of leadership corresponded with his assessment. But she could not forget and was unforgiving of leaders' retainers, the statists who created and feasted on the incomprehension among ordinary citizens. Statists even became adept at leading leaders, but their merchandising was directed at citizens. They created what Arendt disdained as 'mass culture.' Lavish displays of nationalism turned individual citizens into masses. Yet Arendt, as we intimated, witnessed one significant failure, a president's predicament from which statists' *non sequiturs* and deceit could not save him. President Lyndon Johnson blundered into a war that his predecessors started in southeast Asia, Mary McCarthy argued, and further blundered by deferring to his cabinet's counsel, which left him 'act[ing] as if he has a mournful obligation to go on' sending soldiers to Vietnam 'until,' McCarthy surmised, 'somebody finds him an honorable exit.' Looking to leave honourably was ludicrous, however, for 'there can be no honorable exit from a shameful course of action.'[73] If Arendt had been sitting beside McCarthy while she was drafting her reports, she might have prevailed on the journalist to interpolate Plato's claim that the loss of moral compass could reasonably be attributed in many instances to politicians' near 'mystical adoration' of their missions.[74] Might Robert McNamara and his coterie of civilian and military statists, whose follies in 'the fog' of foreign wars have become legend – and to whom we have already been introduced – be cast as cultic, as devotees of American exceptionalism? To be sure, they could not have been called mindless and mediocre. For they were as learned as the 'highly cultured' killers who presided over Hitler's horrors. Nationalism made them all fools – and worse.[75]

What could be done? Arendt confided to Mary McCarthy in 1968 that she fatigued and frustrated – 'depressed.'[76] McCarthy's plan to call for strikes made no sense to her. 'We are too weak,' she warned: 'if we try' to strike, the powerful 'will see how weak we are.'[77] The platoons of campus protesters were admirable, Arendt conceded, though they had not deterred faculty colleagues from research serving nationalists' and capitalists' interests. Faculty colleagues studying the humanities parsed in their journals the rhetoric of exceptionalism but had little effect. Arendt conceivably thought of them as

*Formdenker*, borrowing a term from Ernst Troeltsch, who had compared scholars abstracted from life to others who were more attentive (*Lebens–Anschauer*).[78] Both nationalism and capitalism perversely affected life in ways that the statists preferred to hide but that Arendt wished to reveal and denounce. She alleged that the war in Vietnam was as much about capitalism as about nationalism; post-colonial control over commerce was at stake. Arendt was struck by the Canadian premier's revealing press release answering critics who objected to the country's arms sales to the United States for use in southeast Asia. His reply appealed to the unappealing choice Canada faced between 'dirty hands and empty bellies.'[79]

Nationalism and capitalism in the United States were nearly indistinguishable to Arendt. She feared that progressives had capitulated and let production and consumption dominate politics and the public realm. During the twentieth century's first decade, Henry Adams famously had referred to self-satisfaction as a typical 'Americanism,' but Arendt read American sensibilities differently. She associated satisfaction with the fulfilment of citizens' desires for possessions and profits. By the late 1940s, and consistently thereafter, she recorded the seismic shift in the ordinary citizen's attention. Preoccupations with political issues and arrangements gave way to obsessions with finance. She wrote disapprovingly of the change, which, she insisted, led nearly everyone to look 'for absolute value in the world of economics.'[80] Moreover, Adams's sense of fellow citizens' self-satisfaction, which comes across as swaggering self-congratulation, gave way to greed born of dissatisfaction. They wanted and grasped for more. Arendt accused her adopted country's image-makers and decision-takers of having permitted the shift to eclipse citizens' residual interests in civic affairs. It would not have been in statists' interest to coax citizens to be politically involved. Democracy was doing exceptionally well for elites without ordinary citizens' interest in its work. Best, therefore, to let statists handle publicity. Politicians gave only lip service to the unfinished business of securing citizens' rights while conspicuously and, to Arendt, ruinously competing with each other for rule. When, as a consequence, human rights were 'merely formulated' – that is, 'proclaimed' but not 'politically secured' – the first casualties were plurality and freedom. And, in the instances that she chronicled in her *Origins of Totalitarianism*, unpleasant outcomes followed for persons whom nationalist and capitalist elites 'denationalis[ed]' and 'put outside the protection of law.'[81]

From Arendt's perspective, as we repossessed it in the last chapter, what qualified as landmark achievements of the founders of the American republic were their statements promising political freedom. They agreed it was of inestimable value, yet they thought less, if at all, about freedoms denied to significant sectors of their new continent's population: indigenous tribes, the slaves of African descent and women. They retrieved what Cicero, Locke and others had written about government, but what they composed also showed they were clueless when it came to finding comprehensive, lasting ways to prevent tyrants' monopolisation of power. Their sources were unimpressive on those counts as well. But, arguably, the founders' most maddening oversight was their failure to make adequate provision to bridle 'the power of the many,' notwithstanding their awareness of the need for some aristocracy (of intellect, character or achievement).[82] Still worse, from Arendt's perspective, however, evidence from the eighteenth century suggests that revenue quickly came to dominate the early republicans' debates about – and to dictate their definitions of – freedom. By the twentieth century capitalism unchained was unchallenged. Arendt berated statists for having indefatigably marketed 'the monstrous falsehood' that political freedom and free enterprise were not just compatible but identical.[83] The political institutions that were supposed to be independent of economic forces were not. They were hostage to such forces. Assuming, as Arendt did, that 'what protects freedom is a division between political and economic power,' with the barricades between them down and with draconian measures protecting property well established, the practices that she identified as political were unsustainable on the large canvas – that is, in the conventional public realms.[84]

For that large canvas was covered and cluttered: prosperity, complacency, conformity, narrow-minded nationalism. No room was left for the political virtues Arendt treasured. She subscribed readily to one opinion that was circulating among many colleagues in Europe, the gist of which was that, as early as the last decades of the eighteenth century, abundance made citizens of the United States insatiable. Their 'land of plenty,' 'gargantuan appetites' and arrogance prompted incivility. What Arendt called 'the massive temptations of mass culture' should have been easy for committed artists and scholars to avoid, but they were not.[85] As for the poor, they were the symptoms of government failures to sustain freedom and to foster equality simultaneously. As we discovered, Arendt has been accused of having set off the destitute as a social rather than a political problem. But that accusation is patently unfair. For her, the poor were emblematic of capitalism's and nationalism's failures – a political embarrassment. Early, often and ably, she studied the effects of poverty on the rise of totalitarianisms, which transformed lower 'classes into masses' to be rallied or distracted or sedated by regimes' rituals and rhetoric as capitalists thought profitable and nationalists deemed necessary.[86] Arendt charged statists were monetising politics – with looking to secure their clients' rule but also looking to profit from rule by turning the masses into markets. Citizens were politically disempowered but, to some extent, held the power of the purse. Nonetheless, all but politically comatose populations in twentieth-century democracies attested tyrannies' efficiencies, which, for Arendt, led to 'the decay of culture in mass society.'[87]

'Mass culture" was a symptom of conventional political cultures' success. Statists and their accomplices in the marketplace and media succeeded in dulling what Arendt called citizens' 'taste for political freedom.' When not pushed into masses, persons withdrew to 'an inward domain,' 'the individual having gotten the better of the citizen.'[88] Under other and, for Arendt, more agreeable conditions – with their citizens' altered predispositions – leaders should surely have designed an infrastructure of voluntary associations and would have allowed public virtues (tolerance, lively curiosity, promise-keeping) to fill public spaces where the discussion of plural perspectives offered possibilities for new beginnings. Arendt imagined something on this order – her new beginnings, staging areas where citizens could become citizen-statesmen, practise a new politics and reimagine both citizenship and democracy. One may refer to this as the high ground, to which she sometimes climbed from the political realities that disappointed her. One may also think of this as her legacy, a more exhaustive discussion of which we postpone to this study's final chapters.[89]

But we are far from finished with her disappointment, which persisted. For her, conventional political practices that rewarded citizens' political somnolence with economic security were lamentable. From what she wrote, readers may be pardoned for thinking she condemned the practices and the statists managing them as treasonous. Conformity betrays democracy, she alleged, plumping for plurality, which conventional politics profaned, making politics about ruling, producing, possessing and consuming. And, Arendt observed, it was not ending at all well. 'The troubled balance between laboring and consumption' led, she said, to 'mass culture['s] … universal unhappiness.' The 'waste economy' democracy created in the United States 'quickly devoured or discarded' whatever citizens produced and possessed. Arendt saw little to choose between an uninspiring mass culture and a narcissistic 'me-generation,' with no authentic I's and no eyes – with no politically innovative vision. The results: civic irresponsibility as well as the aforesaid unhappiness. The protests against conspicuous consumption commonly suffered hits below the waterline and sunk before advancing very far. Or, ordinary citizens simply ignored dissidents' protests. The easier that life 'become[s] in a consumers' … society,' the more easily citizens lose perspective and, she averred, 'the more difficult it [is] to stay aware of the urges of necessity by which [that society] is driven.' Arendt volunteered that appraisal during the 1950s, but it still seems sound: 'no true public realm'; 'only private activities displayed in the open,' while citizens, 'dazzled by abundance,' become incapable of 'recognis[ing] its … futility.'[90]

Abundance, waste and citizens' conformity: Arendt held that the statists' orchestration of it all constituted a colossal betrayal of the *demos*. She was particularly upset measuring the distance between contemporary political behaviour and the conduct she expected of her citizen-statesmen. The political climate during the late stages of her career was wholly inhospitable to the latter in conventional political culture. The proliferation of disinformation there deeply discouraged her. Perhaps by intent, she was composing what Elisabeth Young-Bruehl calls her most 'unpolitical work,' lectures on thinking delivered in Scotland, just as one of the episodes that dramatically disclosed the extent of government impropriety made headlines, the burglary at the Watergate and the American president's retainers' efforts to cover it up. Both Arendt and her friend Mary McCarthy were distraught.[91] Arendt, however, was the more reserved of the two. Presumably, her lectures on thinking preoccupied her, but we may reasonably infer from her other remarks drawn into this study that she generally kept her distance from activism, as she had of all other *isms*, which were purposeful. Her evasive answers to persons who inquired about the endgame suggest that she usually put process before purpose. She explicitly endorsed Aristotle's high regard for 'activity that has its end in itself.' 'Wherever you have an end, and everything else becomes the means,' she told her colleagues at a conference in 1973, 'that is being depraved.'[92] To her, many activists resembled ideologues whose infatuation with 'the consistency of [their] fiction[s]' distanced them from 'verifiable experience' that statists deliberately misrepresented, composing rhapsodic statements about policy goals and achievements.[93]

So, although she was inspired by the collectives that disobedients formed in the 1960s and early 1970s, Arendt discountenanced their fixation on their protests' ends. It was not that she disagreed with their perceptions that something needed to be done to salvage what the statists were running aground. She thought that the protests were politically necessary, but they were not, in her terms, political. As we learned and as David Antonini succinctly states, for Arendt, 'political experience [was] something other than an instrumental endeavour.'[94] She used the term 'depraved,' claiming that the subordination of political performances to planning or to implementing outcomes would ordinarily undermine political practice, as she redefined it. Moreover, many of the outcomes she witnessed, before and after coming to the United States, qualified as the 'aberrations' we found her chronicling. In 1975, she disinterred the Watergate fiasco and commented on its aftermath, suggesting that both were standard political fare, as 'the political' was conventionally defined. She took that 'aberration' as an especially vivid example of what she persistently censured as the compromised, commodified mass culture, which betrayed the founders' ideals. President Richard Nixon's cabinet epitomized statist hypocrisy and treachery. Nixon himself personified a desire to dominate gone rancid. Arendt lived just long enough after his resignation to witness his sulking, but she predicted that he would reap tremendous rewards massaging the evidence of his crimes, becoming a commodity and selling his memoirs crammed with 'lies and fabrications.'[95] He had become a pariah yet, to her, a decadent one. Most pariahs crossed the threshold from insider to outsider, developing fresh perspective, as insiders could not, on what had gone wrong with the protocols and apparatuses statists laboured to keep in working disorder. Imposed on democracy, then deposed and sullen, Richard Nixon was what had gone wrong.[96]

The pariahs' critical perspective on politics-as-usual was tremendously valuable. Pariahs were ultrasensitive to the dangers of nationalism. Outsiders, for example, comprehended more clearly than insiders what was at stake in strident expressions of American exceptionalism. Pariahs also could discern the subtler, though still objectionable, symptoms of nationalist zealotry, according to Arendt – émigré and outsider – watching the traffic in myth and legend that coursed through the instruction American children were receiving about their republic's history. The instruction normally came clad in contempt for dissidents dedicated to resurrecting the revolutionary spirit of the founders. For what good could possibly come from shocking students with the news that the triumphalism embedded in their curricula could not stand careful inspection? Pariahs knew that 'even a great power is *limited* power.'[97] Arendt and her fellow émigrés learned in Europe and by following fascism's progress from a distance how swiftly nationalism could erode the pragmatists' willingness to search at a lower altitude for the suitable and sensible. The nearly cyclonic force of nationalism caught her unawares in 1948, when, lecturing in Massachusetts about prospects for a Jewish and Arab confederation in Palestine in 1948, Jewish nationalists shouted her down.[98]

But her faith in conferences and in conversation never flagged. Receptions at her other lectures and discussions during forums in which she participated seemed to have no effect on her belief that conferees committed to the discourses that sustain alternative public realms also sustain the values and develop the virtuosity shaping the behaviour of citizen-statesmen. She advised against underestimating the effects of such commitments and especially of the reciprocities that evolved from them, which, in turn, promoted self-discoveries, self-disclosures and new beginnings. The reciprocities reflected the interlocutors' respect for the differences enlivening and enriching the 'back, forth and up against' critical both for the political performances she commended and for the preservation of plurality fostering friendships and maintained by forgiveness. This emphasis on participation contrasted with prevailing definitions of citizenship that, as we often reiterated, placed premiums on conformity and obedience. But Arendt, as also noted, was not troubled by precarity, for, if freedom, equality, plurality, friendship and forgiveness lasted long enough to incubate citizen-statesmen, such alternative arrangements were worth whatever time they were given. Certainly during that time and, ideally, after adjournment, in more conventional political forums, to the extent that citizen-statesmanship proved infectious, the statists', nationalists' and capitalists' definitions of citizenship and of politics would seem less compelling.

The opposition between collectives promoting freedom and plurality, on the one hand, and conventional societies preferring participants' assimilation and conformity, on the other, had attracted Arendt's attention early in her career. Soon after finishing her doctoral dissertation in 1929, if not before, she started research for her *Habilitationsschrift*, the passport to a teaching post in German universities. Her study of salonnière Rahel Varnhagen circulated in German shortly after its completion in 1933 but was printed only after a revised version was translated into English and published decades later. Arendt must have been pleased by the attention. She responded favourably to an inquiry from a French publisher in 1966.[99] Varnhagen seemed to her an excellent specimen of the parvenu. An assimilated German Jewess in the late eighteenth and early nineteenth centuries, she embraced the patriotic sentiments in Fichte's famous *Reden an die deutsche Nation*.[100] Yet she also presided over a salon in Berlin that attracted poets, musicians, diplomats, courtiers, historians and philosophers. The resurgence of nationalism in the wake of Napoleon's conquests was likely responsible for the dispersion of Varnhagen's cosmopolitans, but salons such as hers generally were impermanent. Arendt was also profoundly interested in the salonnière's correspondence. Arendt exploited the revealing self-inventories to elaborate the differences between parvenu insecurities and pariah camaraderie, to which we shall return. What seems most telling at the moment, however, is the distinction between the urbane and ecumenical salon's freedom and the nationalists' efforts to patrol the frontiers of their territories and fraternal organisations so scrupulously. For a time, Arendt's Varnhagen relished her salon's and her own distance from such efforts, celebrating the unconventional and welcoming cultured friends who declined to 'shy [away] from appearing grotesque,' who were untethered, uninhibited prophets (*hemmingslos*).[101]

Arendt pondered pariah candour, insight and daring during the early 1930s, studying Varnhagen's correspondence, as the Nazis strutted to power and closed the universities to Jews. She may also have pondered the pariahs' plight as she became a pariah by daring to interrogate the canonical interpretations of the Shoah. Many of her Jewish friends and colleagues shunned her once they read or read about her reports of the Eichmann trial in Jerusalem. Also, at about that time, she incurred the ire of colleagues who had come to terms with the disturbing revelations about the Americans' involvement in southeast Asia and, to her vexation, with public officials' readiness 'to circumvent Constitutional guarantees' to intimidate their critics. In several essays composed during the chaotic 1960s and into the 1970s, she exposed the corroded plumbing that kept what passed as democracy (and civilisation) consuming abundance and producing waste. And what she exposed looked neither democratic nor civilised. The wars in Palestine and southeast Asia; disturbances in the schools and in the streets of her adopted country; government scandals and duplicity: there looked to be no end to disappointments. Having written controversially about much of it, she likely paused at times to ponder the pariah's fate and 'exemplary fortitude?'[102]

Colleagues at American universities continued to ask her to lecture, despite her searing examinations of conventional assumptions about American rectitude. She was acerbic, complaining about 'lying in politics.' She complained also about non-thinking citizens' indifference to the fate of what she called their 'common world.' At some point in her career, Arendt took notice of Hegel's criticism of political passion that concealed the special interests driving political practice. Those interests – material interests, which, in her time, corresponded with aspirations of capitalists and nationalists – displaced republican ideals that had inspired her. They survived 'splendidly in thought,' she said but conceded that 'a fearful distance separate[d]' twentieth-century statists from the founders. At some point, Arendt read and marked out Hegel's prediction that the time must come when partisan interest and self-promotion would govern how factions characterised the common good.[103] She predicted the consequences would be 'numbing' and 'paralysing,' yet they likely looked to be just over the horizon; Richard King gauges that her 'reservoir of hope was just about empty' by the early 1970s.[104]

She continued to speak and write. Her remarks about statists' marketing, nationalism and 'non-thinking' must have increasingly been disorienting, yet the evidence suggests that most auditors and readers were uninterested in radical criticisms of democratic practice. Scholars now, however, find her particularly fascinating. Her arguments for freedom, equality, plurality, friendship, forgiveness and natality seem particularly pertinent as political discourse and deliberations becomes more acrimonious and polarised. Rummaging for remedies among Arendt's summonses to monitor and, when possible, to attenuate statists' influence, admirers debate whether she was a post-war liberal or a political conservative who thought patching up conventional public realms in democratic republics sufficient. Yet such approaches obviously have a difficult time making sense of her call for citizens to make new beginning and enter the 'living flux of acting and speaking.'[105] But before we dismiss her as a mystic, a postscript to our discussion of her disappointments (that should serve as a preamble to our reimagining citizenship and democracy) will tempt us to take her as a radical or visionary by refocusing discussion of her contributions from structures and protocols. Ironically, broad and imprecisely defined political venues (that large canvas) appear to have made her claustrophobic. Her citizen-statesmen must break out for breathing room to become political agents, and it was agency and agents – and not structures or systems – that concerned her. Her citizen-statesmen must start apart, much as pariahs, to become part of that 'living flux' and, as change agents, to claim what Arendt called the 'proud privilege of beginners of something altogether new.'[106]

## Notes

1. Yael Tamir, *Why Nationalism* (Princeton: Princeton University Press, 2019), 164–5.
2. Hannah Arendt, 'Understanding and Politics,' EU, 320–2.
3. OT, 275. Also see Roberto Berlato, *Il buio del tunnel e la strada della libertà: Hannah Arendt e il XII secolo ronnovata epoca di fascino dei totalitarismi* (Bologna: Diogene Multimedia, 2022), 38–41.
4. MDT, 35. When Arendt was eleven years old, her mother took her to a demonstration in Königsberg supporting the *Spartakusbund*, for which see Young-Bruehl, *Hannah Arendt*, 25–9 and 124–6.
5. LKPP, 56–7.
6. CR, 214.
7. OT, 148.
8. MDT, 50–1.
9. Christopher Holman, *Politics as Radical Creation: Herbert Marcuse and Hannah Arendt on Political Performativity* (Toronto: University of Toronto Press, 2013), 123.
10. OR, 259.
11. Arendt, 'The Hungarian Revolution and Totalitarian Imperialism,' in TWB, 109, 127.
12. See Arendt's epistolary tribute printed in TWB, p. 156. She did not dedicate her essay on Hungary to Luxemburg, suspecting that readers would mistakenly think the tribute a brief for Marxism. Several years later,

however, she did honour Luxemburg with the extended essay, reprinted in MDT, 33–56, to which we have already referred.

13. PP, 110–11.
14. HC, 182–3.
15. Ibid., 301.
16. Katherine Arens, 'Hannah Arendt Translates Culture: *Men in Dark Times*,' *Monatshefte* 108, no. 4 (2016), 543.
17. Compare OT, 423–4 with Adut, *Reign of Appearances*, 152–3.
18. OT, 65–6.
19. Arendt, 'Home to Roost,' RJ, 269–70.
20. Arendt, 'Der Zionismus aus heutiger Sicht,' Speeches and Writings File, 50–2; 004033–5; USLC, advising the politically powerful to cope with, rather than to conceal, their world as it was, though it was far less lovely (*nicht allze schönen*) than statists would say.
21. CR, 13.
22. BPF, 247–8.
23. H. R. McMaster, *Dereliction of Duty: Lyndon Johnson, Robert McNamara, the Joint Chiefs of Staff, and the Lies that led to Vietnam* (New York: Harper, 1997), 317–18.
24. Ibid., 244.
25. Mary McCarthy, *The Seventeenth Degree* (New York: Harcourt, Brace Jovanovich, 1974), 431–2.
26. Arendt seems to have been fond of the characterization (*neuzeitliche Kraftmaschinentechnik*) she found and underscored in Martin Heidegger's *Der europäische Nihilismus* (Pfullingen: Neske, 1967), 141; BCSL.
27. BPF, 254. For the domino theory, see CR, 24–5.
28. CR, 27–30; for Arendt's take on Joseph McCarthy, see *Briefwechsel*, 248–52 and Young-Bruehl *Hannah Arendt*, 288–9.
29. LIOC, 123.
30. Villa, *Arendt*, 327.
31. Arendt, 'Thinking and Moral Considerations,' RJ, 178.
32. Arendt, 'Is America by Nature a Violent Society?' 2, 021596; USLC.
33. OR, 246.
34. For which, see David Arndt, *Arendt on the Political* (Cambridge: Cambridge University Press, 2019), 74–5.
35. Arendt, 'Home to Roost,' RJ, 263.
36. Adut, *Reign of Appearances*, 13–14, 84–5.
37. HC, 129.
38. Ibid., 132.
39. CR, 89.

40. Arendt, 'Authority in the Twentieth Century,' TWB, 73–5.
41. Arendt, 'Ideology and Propaganda,' Speeches and Writings File, 1923–1975), 9; USLC.
42. Arendt, 'Public Rights and Private Interests,' TWB, 509.
43. Arendt, 'Karl Marx and the Tradition of Western Political Thought,' TWB, 38–9.
44. Walter Lippmann, *Public Opinion* (New York: Macmillan, 1929), 114.
45. Ibid., 263–5.
46. Arendt, 'Reflections on Little Rock,' RJ, 211–13.
47. Ainsley LeSure, 'The White Mob (in) Equality Before the Law, and the Racial Common Sense: A Critical Race Reading of the Negro Question in [Arendt's] "Reflections on Little Rock"' *Political Theory* 49, no. 1 (2021), 4–5.
48. For which, see Massimiliano Tomba, *Insurgent Universality: An Alternative Legacy of Modernity* (Oxford: Oxford University Press, 2019), 58–60.
49. OR, 103–5, 231–5.
50. Richard J. Bernstein, *Why Read Hannah Arendt Now* (Cambridge: Polity, 2018), 48.
51. Arendt, 'The Deputy: Guilt by Silence,' RJ, 217. For the papacy's silence or complicity, consult Richard J. Evans, 'Why Did he not Speak Out?' *London Review of Books* 45 (October 19, 2023), 33–4.
52. Norma Claire Moruzzi, *Speaking through the Mask: Hannah Arendt and the Politics of Social Identity* (Ithaca: Cornell University Press, 2000), 106.
53. But see OR, 60, for remarks about the 'strange … absence of the social question' in the discourses of the founders of the American republic, who ignored the 'degrading misery in the form of slavery.'
54. But compare Moruzzi, *Speaking through the Mask*, 189; Owens, 'Racism in the Theory Canon,' 420–3; Dirk Moses, '*Das römische Gespräch* in a New Key: Hannah Arendt, Genocide and the Defense of Republican Civilization,' *The Journal of Modern History* 85, no. 4 (2013), 889–93; and Gail Presby, 'Critic of Boers or Africans? Arendt's Treatment of South Africa in *The Origins of Totalitarianism*,' in *Postcolonial African Philosophy: A Critical Reader*, ed. Emmanuel Chukwudi Eze (Oxford: Blackwell, 1997), 173–7.
55. OT, 74.
56. Arendt, 'Jewishness as a Social Phenomenon,' (1946), Outlines and Research Memoranda, Speeches and Writings File, 1923–1975 folder 1, 20–1; USLC.
57. She was far from alone; see Bayard Rustin's '"Black Power" and Coalition Politics,' *Commentary* 42 (September, 1966), 35–40.

58. *Between Friends*, 229–30.
59. König, *Die Gründung der Freiheit*, 201.
60. Judith Shklar, *Political Thought and Political Thinkers*, ed. Stanley Hoffman (Chicago: The University of Chicago Press, 1998), 371 suggests Arendt was 'unable to forget' Weimar.
61. Arendt's letter to Gershom Scholem in 1963 suggests that she regretted her distance from 'the German Left,' 'especially since the McCarthy era.' JW, 466.
62. Arendt's letter to Hutchins is reprinted in TWB; see especially 97, 102–3.
63. Seyla Benhabib, *The Reluctant Modernism of Hannah Arendt* (Lanham, MD: Rowman and Littlefield, 2003), 136.
64. *Between Friends*, 19–22.
65. Carl Schmitt, *Der Begriff des Politischen* (Hamburg: Hanseatische Verlagsanstalt, 1933), 10; BCSL.
66. Arendt, 'Understanding and Politics,' *Partisan Review* 20, no. 4 (1953), 390–1.
67. *Briefwechsel*, 120. Her letter to Jaspers was written in 1947, the year before Hans Morgenthau published his *Peace Among Nations*, political realism's most popular unmasking of the purported benevolence in international affairs.
68. Arendt, 'Home to Roost,' RJ, 275.
69. PP, 160–1.
70. Douglas Klusmeyer, 'Beyond Tragedy: Hannah Arendt and Hans Morgenthau on Responsibility, Evil, and Political Ethics,' *International Studies Review* 11, no. 2 (2009), 349.
71. CR, 14.
72. Ibid., 19.
73. Mary McCarthy, *Vietnam* (New York: Harcourt, 1967), 94, 101.
74. For which, see the passage underlined in Arendt's copy of Werner Jaegar's *Paideia: The Ideals of Greek Culture*, vol. 2, 243 BCSL.
75. Arendt, 'Some Questions of Moral Philosophy,' RJ, 96–7. Also, in this connection, see McMaster's discussion of President Johnson and his advisers in McMaster, *Dereliction of Duty*, 49–61 and 300–34.
76. *Between Friends*, 211.
77. Arendt's response is recorded in McCarthy, *Seventeenth Degree*, 39.
78. See the margins of Arendt's copy of Troeltsch's 'Die Logik des historischen Entwicklungs-begriffs,' in *Kant-Studien* 27 (1922), 283; BCSL.
79. Arendt, 'Home to Roost,' RJ, 273.
80. Compare OT, 188 with Henry Adams, *The Education of Henry Adams* (New York: Random House, 1996), 107.

81. OT, 446–7.
82. OR, 142.
83. Ibid., 209.
84. CR, 213; for courts, journalists, and universities, see *Between Friends*, 365.
85. Arendt, 'Europe's Image of America,' Speeches and Writings File, 1923–1975, 6; USLC. For 'gargantuan appetites' and for what follows about 'mass culture,' see BPF, 203–5.
86. OT, 460.
87. Arendt, 'Society and Culture,' *Daedalus* 89, no. 2 (1960), 284.
88. OR, 131.
89. HC, 178.
90. Ibid., 134–5.
91. *Between Friends*, 341 and 365.
92. Arendt, Remarks, American Society of Christian Ethics, Richmond, Speeches and Writings File, 1923–1975, 9; 011836; USLC.
93. OT, 362.
94. David Antonini, *Public Space and Political Experience: An Arendtian Interpretation* (Lanham, MD: Lexington, 2021), 7 and 147–8.
95. Arendt, 'Home to Roost,' RJ, 274. The memoir appeared three years after her death.
96. Arendt, 'We Refugees,' JW, 268.
97. CR, 38; italics in the original.
98. Young-Bruehl, *Hannah Arendt*, 233. The following chapters reconsider Arendt's experiences with leading German and American Zionists, reintroduce the proposals for a Palestinian confederation and explore Arendt's admiration for, and subsequent disappointment in, the Israeli kibbutzniks.
99. See Arendt's letter to Jean Gonthier; 'Contracts and Royalties;' 029075; USLC.
100. On Varnhagen and Fichte, see RV, 139.
101. Ibid., 161–2.
102. CR, 44–7.
103. See the passage Arendt underscored in Hegel's *Die Vernunft in der Geschichte: Einleitung in die Philosophie der Weltgeschichte* (Leipzig: Meiner, 1919), 62–3; BCSL.
104. Arendt, 'Home to Roost,' RJ, 257–60; Richard King, *Arendt in America* (Chicago: University of Chicago Press, 2015), 296.
105. HC, 187.
106. OR, 223–4.

# Interlude: 'The Onslaught of Modernity'

In March, 1955, Arendt confided her frustration to her journal. 'Why is it so hard to love the world?'[1] She left the question unanswered, provoking speculation. Several years earlier, the publication of her *Origins of Totalitarianism* gained her an enviable reputation, so she could hardly have been thinking about professional difficulties. Preparation of her colossal study of cruelties, however, constantly confronted her with the consequences of prejudice and political ambition. Capitalism but especially nationalism, she remarked, had 'foredoomed' 'republican fervor' that had been inspired by classical antiquity's 'example[s] of what politics could be and of [what] participation in public affairs would mean for the happiness' of citizens.[2] Conceivably, then, she was reflecting on that 'doom' as she accumulated material for her *Origins*: imperialism, slavery, antisemitism, fascist purges and related colonial atrocities. Or possibly she was referring to perfidious politics in her adopted country? For several years, the media had awarded a dubious celebrity to a malevolent demagogue, enabling him to commandeer public attention and to press forward with a campaign to criminalise political heterodoxy in universities, the entertainment industry, the military and government agencies. Episodes from Joseph McCarthy's campaign were still fresh, moreover, when white supremacist governors, accommodating the fears and anger of much of their electorates, barred classroom doors in the United States to African-American students. Those portions of Arendt's world surely have seemed hard to love?

Some of this ground has been covered in our chapters on Arendt's disappointments, which rehearsed as well her displeasure with statists' efforts to protect their political infrastructure, papering over the wars and scandals of the 1960s and 1970s. Still, Arendt was unprepared to countenance sealing off collectives from that sordid world, so hard to love. Instead, she pressed for political engagement, yet redefined 'political,' expecting the powerful to object. She agreed with Brecht, whom she quoted in her last interview. 'The ruling classes,' he claimed, permitted 'small crook[s]' and 'clown[s]' to wreak havoc and to become criminals of consequence. Their crooks and clowns, after all, served the *status quo*. Such servitude, however, robbed all citizens of their dignity, for, even when havoc was relatively inconspicuous, the reigning arrangements still disempowered them and would continue to do so, until they overcame statists' inducements to conform and until citizen-statesmen could pump 'lifeblood' into discourses and deliberations.[3]

Arendt's recoil from Brecht's crooks and clowns and from citizens either indifferent to, or fond of them, was perfectly understandable. After all, her studies of totalitarianism recovered crimes for which they were responsible. And while colleagues were still receiving review copies of her *Origins*, she was compiling fresh evidence of what she called a 'breakdown of authority,' which looked to be the prelude for more of the same. 'Our sense of a common world' seemed lost, she said, referring to the post-war settlements that, to her dissatisfaction, failed to protect ordinary Europeans from demagogues, crooks statists. The settlements simply reflect 'the onslaught of modernity,' sidelining would-be benefactors and leaving the underclasses exposed to statists' wiles. Her notes for a lecture in late 1953 repeated the terms 'broke down' and 'breakdown.' Before the next chapters use Arendt as a resource for building back up, therefore, we should attempt in this interlude to repossess what it meant for her, from the 1950s, to love the world during that onslaught.[4]

Arendt suspected that most lovers of the world loved select parts of it. She missed the early Brecht's exuberant or 'wild' love of life. It was hardly tribal, yet affections commonly were. Statists exploited citizens' susceptibilities to tribalism. Affection followed proclamations of affinities – racial, ethnic, ideological – that, in her judgement, were obstacles to inclusive new beginnings, which prioritise and preserve plurality. The love for the world Arendt commended maximised citizens' self-respect and mutual respect. It did not rule out rivalries, yet it deplored the 'exceptionally inhuman conditions prevailing during the early stages of capitalism.' Contests had their places, yet she thought that capitalists' competitiveness licensed cruelty. Entrepreneurs as well as statists apparently found consumers were more easily manipulated than citizens and, therefore the ruling elites represented conspicuous consumption as every person's prerogative and as the proper response to 'the devouring character of biological life.'[5] It appeared not to concern political and commercial elites that compulsions to produce and consume spawned resentment and envy or that civic responsibility precipitously declined. But that decline was predictable and unlamented, inasmuch as citizens' political intelligence was bottoming out.

It was one of the more conspicuous casualties left by modernity's onslaught. Moral judgement was another. Statists did not take morality seriously, and, one could argue, they had dissuaded Arendt from doing so. Their mission was to control the compasses – moral and political – and have the ships of state steer towards north stars of their own making. And, many boasted, their north stars – their visions of 'the good' – were as infallible as revealed truths. They defined that 'good' as what profited the elites they served. (Arendt's contemporary, C. Wright Mills, dubbed them 'power elites.') And we must remember that, retaining our metaphor here, jumping ship or disembarking was no option for Arendt. She believed that the unworldly were politically derelict. The rewards they reaped – stretches of solace apart from political turbulence – only attested their irresponsibility. They left the rest exposed to tyrants, to statists and the aforementioned clowns and 'crop[s] of criminals' who reached for 'the reins of world politics' and who found ways to 'justify the exaltation of brutality and unscrupulousness.'[6]

The unworldly were 'lovers of goodness,' but they were not lovers of the world – certainly, not on Arendt's terms – for they 'negate[d] its public part,' the portion that she reserved for testing evidence and opinions about such lovers' common world. She assumed such testing, correctly conducted, disclosed and discredited unjust regimes. Refusals to test were inexcusable. Still, Arendt acknowledged that philosophers and theologians who advocated withdrawal got one thing right: they knew 'goodness … as a consistent way of life' was 'impossible within the confines of the public realm,' as conventionally conceived. Directing her remarks to citizens buoyed by prospects to the contrary, she reintroduced the counsel in Machiavelli's *Principe*, which revealed the politically 'ruinous quality of doing good.' It directed would-be leaders to learn not to be good, inasmuch as sovereigns who were saddled with moralism were unlikely to prevail against immoral and amoral rivals. Machiavelli's prescriptions for political survival and success sanctioned pretence. Sovereign powers and statists only needed to seem to be moral, to be discreetly duplicitous. The Florentine was emblematic of the onslaught of modernity, of the political eclipse of morality. Arendt cited him to prove that conventional politics in his time – and in hers – was bruising business: coarse, corrupt and dehumanising. It bracketed law and order with manipulation and intimidation. Conceivably, Machiavelli assumed corruption was contagious. Did he worry, as Arendt did, about the fate of 'goodness that comes out of hiding and assumes a public role?' Perhaps, yet she emphatically warned that such goodness is then defiled, 'no longer good, but corrupt,' carrying 'its own corruption wherever it goes.'[7]

Might the sources of corruption be anticipated, attenuated, or eliminated? Arendt did not think citizens were helpless, but the onslaught of modernity left conventional political protocols and apparatuses to the statists. So, on that front, she was less sanguine about the progressives' and pragmatists' prospects. She could not turn a blind eye to statists' apparent resilience, their clever salesmanship but also ordinary citizens' susceptibilities to pretence and pressure. Her *Origins of Totalitarianism* documented how easily misguided pride and resentments congealed in tribalism, nationalism and imperialism. She studied how early twentieth-century statists' blathering about racial purity stirred indignation and fears of contamination. During and after the 1950s, Arendt found a somewhat modified, more subtle version of the same. And much the same ought to be said about conditions in twenty-first-century democratic republics where, as Arendt remarked about fascists and fellow travellers, statists have 'recoiled from the ideal of humanity.'[8]

But, truth be told, ideals of any sort generally troubled Arendt. For missions driven by ideals could be as destructive as fascists' fists. Political practices, she claimed, were best cleared of abstractions, ideologies and ideals to make room for realistic assessments of what she described as 'verifiable experiences' – as well as for new beginnings. On that count, she found a few allies among existentialists who seemed savvy, to a point. Facing up to the incoherence of the universe, they sought and found 'salvation from thought through action' and dissent. Yet, during the post-war period, they were politically ineffective, albeit culturally notorious. They found no way to 'give direction to political choice[s].'[9] Meanwhile, idealism persisted, as did many other, more pernicious *isms* that reinforced tribalism. Until discursive spaces were cleared of, and preserved from, persecutors' invidious *isms*, respect for plurality was unlikely to gain sufficient traction to overcome tribal prejudices.[10]

For such prejudices have had remarkable staying power. To some, they afford the comfort of belonging; to others, they result in exclusion and injury. From Arendt's perspective the prices paid for belonging were too great. Comfort and conformity robbed citizens of their freedoms, the cost for which, as pariahs learned, included uncertainty. But what made that 'price … for plurality and reality' worth paying, Arendt explained, was 'the joy of inhabiting together with others a world whose reality is guaranteed for each by the presence of all.' Yet, for each and all, plurality, freedom and joy could only be experienced 'under the condition of non-sovereignty.'[11] Citizens who saw nothing improper about making nationalists the trustees of popular sovereignty resembled Emperor Augustus's subjects, whom Arendt chided for having permitted him to grant the senate what little was left of the people's power over the regime. 'Public space' in Rome, she recalled, never recovered.[12]

'Public space' remains in contemporary democracies, though control has been ceded to statists who maintain the illusion of public participation at ballot boxes and in focus groups. Agonistic exchanges commended by Arendt are rare, save for candidates' forums, during which the polite gets confused with the political. Statists prepare or script candidates and often become them. In either case, the statists' principal task is to ensure that prevailing, conventional protocols and apparatuses – or, to be precise, citizens' faith in them and, Arendt quipped, their faith in 'the whole ground of the future' – remain sturdy. Statists sell predictability and pretend that their declarations determine destinies. By contrast, citizen-statesmen unreservedly embrace the 'incalculability of the future.' There were no wrap-ups, no closures.[13]

In her lectures on resolve, Arendt singled out John Duns Scotus, 'the only thinker for whom the word "contingent" ha[d] no derogatory associations.' To Scotus, the medieval realists, his rivals, were far from the mark, insisting that absolutes or abstractions superseded and gave meaning to what appeared independently real – to what Arendt called 'verifiable experience.' Absolutes guaranteed a purposeful universe. But, for Arendt and Scotus, set purposes and destinies were fictions, far less important than freedom. Arendt was impressed by Scotus's stamina. He had doggedly defended the superiority of humans' wills to intellects. But medieval realists relied exclusively on the latter for access to absolutes. But intellects, Arendt alleged, 'cannot save freedom in any way.' Her Scotus acknowledged that contingency was 'the price for freedom,' but her contemporaries were contemptuous of the contingent. Their realism and other *isms* – moralism, nationalism and the latter's cousin, exceptionalism – seemed rather medieval and intellectually unsustainable. They made their age (and hers) appear unrealistic.[14] Nonetheless, those contemporary realists and the statists who deferred to them controlled the narrative and kept citizens in awe of sovereign powers. To that end, they were scrupulously unscrupulous, vouching for the existence of abstractions and absolutes that awed ordinary citizens and giving a wide berth to what Arendt called 'disconcerting contingency.' They presided over the 'onslaught of modernity,' forgot Scotus, yet looked morosely medieval – but, to her, still menacing.[15]

She knew why their absolute truths were attractive. They were consoling, compact and orderly. For her, however, tidiness tended to tyranny. To her analysis of the appeal to – and of – order and conformity, she brought to bear her objection to Jean-Jacques Rousseau's anthems to 'the General Will.' While the American founders shaped their republic, the more tyrannical statists among them raved about Rousseau who prominently featured in their celebrations of modernity, conformity and solidarity, which stabilised the *status quo* by suppressing discourse and ordinary citizens' initiative.[16] Statists wed Rousseau's General Will to their own will to power, excusing the harassment of dissidents and justifying the will to submit as suitable to citizenship.[17]

From the 1930s into the early 1940s, Arendt witnessed that wedding of wills, blessed by the fascists. When friends later confided that the result made them ashamed to be German, she responded that, in any venue, the consequences of coupling sovereignty and statists' will to power with citizens' conformity made her 'ashamed of being human.'[18] Arguably, such shame drove her, spurring her to make political practices resistant to ideology. She started early, determined to make a career of campaigning to construe interpersonal performances as political only if and where they contributed to an effective redefinition of politics and citizenship. Location was hardly insignificant. As noted, distance from, and resistance to, the conventional were required. Change-agents (citizen-statesmen) required space to change, space protected from the onslaught of modernity. Concentrating on the structure of such spaces somewhat misses Arendt's emphasis on change and on agency as well as on the importance of interpersonal performances as a prerequisite for both and for the reimagination of citizenship. One can read her campaigning for all that – her commotion – in nearly every essay contesting the association of politics with contests for power and rule.[19]

But it bears repeating that the association she contested was fixed in citizens' minds. Arendt presumed that reorientations would not be easy. Nonetheless, she trusted that eventually, much as their forbears, citizens of the United States would come down-to-earth, realising that 'none of the country's institutions and constituted bodies could be traced back to the factual development of absolutism.'[20] True, the founders of their republic awarded the deity honourable mention for the successes of their revolution. Their muted secularism, as it happened, was sufficient to keep their more pious followers patriotic. Arendt's rehearsals of the republic's first few years made it seem so. Americans had avoided the 'semi-religious' expressions of trust in human nature that fed the fantasies of revolutionaries in late eighteenth-century France. Arendt celebrated American insurgents for having cultivated what she perceived as a uniquely 'American faith' in 'the possibility of checking' nearly all the disagreeable features of a flawed human nature with appeals to citizen's 'better angels' and to their 'common bonds and mutual promises.' She expected citizen-statesmen to rediscover that 'faith' and to rekindle the revolutionary spirit, sparing fellow citizens what she believed to have been the 'cheapest and most dangerous disguise an absolute ever assumed in a political realm, the disguise of the nation.'[21]

That modernity would welcome scepticism and secularism was hardly a given. Statists clearly recognised the power of religious imagery (and we shall soon see that Arendt did as well), but statists were particularly adept at such 'disguises.' When absolutes were imported from sacred literature, they endowed nationalist regimes with religious authority and 'force[d] people into a unanimous, uniform opinion.' That ruse was used for centuries, Arendt went on, alluding to the resourcefulness of twentieth-century statists and nationalists recycling theological motifs along with philosophical absolutes to keep citizens in tow or, she observed, to reinforce 'dictatorships of the most divergent kinds and provenances' and to tempt citizens 'to sacrifice actual political freedom.' To her, the nation-state's 'unsuitability for life in the modern world' was self-evident, but crafty statists could make it seem to be otherwise.[22]

For all the good the founders of the republic had done, they failed to make subsequent statists' appeals to divinity utterly implausible and their brand of 'hard' federalism or centralisation an unconscionable betrayal of the revolutionary spirit. Arendt all but accused the founders of accelerating the shift to bureaucracy and away from the local colonial assemblies that had learned valuable lessons about empowerment. The locals learned that sovereignty could be exchanged for new beginnings and for more dynamic ways to define and to build respect for democracy. But, as Sarah Hinchman points out, Arendt pardoned the founders because their reliance on 'intersubjective' tests for the validity of their causes gave posterity a foundation on which to build new staging areas for democracy. George Kateb, though, offers a different assessment. He sees improvidence where Hinchman sees prudence. Kateb suggests that Arendt was wrong to resurrect whatever intersubjective tests or protocols she extracted from the founders' repertoire to address what she ought to have seen as 'the great threat to authentic politics' in the twentieth century: citizens and statists' 'misguided attempt to act from intense moral distress.'[23]

Arendt's remarks about, and reliance on, the intersubjective or interactive drew from Immanuel Kant's work on practical reason and justice. Kant persuaded her to emphasise the importance of 'earthbound creatures,' who relied on 'each other's company, even for thinking.'[24] He appeared to have been following Aristotle, who presumed that 'man in the singular' was autonomous and 'cannot very well be trusted with what is good for others,' and, Arendt continued her exposition, should be trusted 'least of all with the common good.' 'Disastrous consequences,' she noted, 'for any community' ensued when the statists there appealed to 'ethical principles derived from man in the singular.' So, she proposed to revive interest in intersubjective tests for validity.[25] Prudent (Hinchman)? Or improvident (Kant)? With reference to conventional political cultures, the latter seems likelier, for statists determined the contours of (the political conversations within) them. But citizen-statesmen were advocates of change who understood that statists' *isms* made it hard to realise the 'good peace,' to which Arendt referred in her analysis of nationalism and which, she contended, could only result from 'negotiation and compromise.' Ardent nationalists and statists of their persuasion or in their service, however, equated obedience with morality and turned history into destiny. Both that equation and the deployment of destiny should now be classified along with the prevalence of dispositions that capitalism promotes – as well as the marketplace ascendant – as distinctive features of the onslaught of modernity.[26]

In the margins of her copy of James Harrington's seventeenth-century treatise on government, Arendt called attention to its indictment of indolence. Harrington assessed (and she apparently concurred) that 'where there is not a nobility to bolt out the people' (to chase them from their warrens), citizens would be 'slothful,' 'regardless of the world' and careless with their liberty. Those of 'nobility' in Arendt's century – though, in her estimation, ignoble – were politically powerful elites and the statists who served their interests and who preferred politically indolent citizens; they obviously made less trouble for governments than agitators. Nationalism as well as other *isms*, as often noted here, however, could be used to rein them in or to 'bolt [them] out' when the dexterous controlled the sedatives and stimuli. But complacent, listless citizens troubled her, as we learned, although Arendt was also wary of masses collected, 'bolted out' and directed or 'aimed' by statists. Yet, reading Harrington, she might have been thinking of citizen-statesmen as a new nobility and trusting them to inspire idlers.[27]

David Riesman was drafting his acclaimed study of crowds while corresponding with Arendt in 1948 and 1949, and she hastened to endorse his analysis: their century's crowds were brimming with complacent – Harrington's 'slothful'; Riesman's 'other-directed' – persons flush with faith in those shepherding them. Mistaking feigned rectitude for competence, citizens – sheep, in this application – were easily led by statists choreographing spectacles and drafting speeches to fire up the flock and to channel its grievances and allegiances. Equally serious, citizens in the herds mistook bluster and tirades for political discourse, assuming the accuracy of what they were told, which was, as often as not, concocted. What Arendt identified as a 'new type of man, who wants only to fit,' believes whatever governments conveyed.[28] And statists said whatever satisfied those who made politics their careers. But citizens, she remarked to Riesman 'transcend[ed]' self-interest. The implication was that they were positioned advantageously to make new beginnings.[29]

Jonathan Peter Schwartz aptly refers to Arendt's doctrine of natality and her interest in new beginnings as 'the rise of revolutionary politics.' Despite wariness about importing religious rhetoric into political declarations and deliberations, she apparently could not restrain herself when contemplating chances to redefine citizenship and politics and to match her convictions about new beginnings with a distinctive, memorable precedent. She invoked Jesus, exploiting advantages of what could be termed his incumbency in North American and European cultures. She asserted that biblical passages attributed to him confirmed his 'extraordinary understanding of freedom' and, she added, of the 'power inherent in human freedom.'[30] She could not have asked for a more compelling figure. Jesus and her doctrine of natality seemed made for each other. His advent still signals a new beginning on calendars in the West that jump from BCE to CE (or AD). And, as nonconformist and pariah, he would have been welcomed into Ralph Waldo Emerson's – and, presumably, Arendt's – pantheon of notable, if also somewhat reckless, 'sayers of no.'[31] Arendt also esteemed Jesus for having emphasised, as she did, the duty to forgive. But his novelty and nonconformity were more important to her than later doctrinal claims about his atonement. The pardons that interested her were those he told the faithful to offer as they set or reset themselves 'within a web of relations.' 'Trespasses' were 'everyday occurrence[s]' that made what she rehearsed as Jesus' radical brief for forgiveness both a 'founding event' and a timelessly timely reminder, for Arendt's Jesus suggested that the forgiving conspired with the forgiven in a 'constant mutual release' that related every absolution to the 'willingness to start again.'[32] New beginnings, in turn, revealed human dignity. So, according to Arendt's book of revelations, Jesus could well be registered as the precursor of nonconformists and enlightened insurgents everywhere, who believed in 'the grandeur' and dignity of free persons in societies that qualified, on her terms, as political and that were insurgents' 'most far-reaching results.'[33]

Arendt, then, conscripted Jesus into her company of revolutionaries, demonstrating what Samuel Moyn describes as 'the difficulty of overcoming political theology.' Others who learned from her and from whom she learned – respectively, Giorgio Agamben and Carl Schmitt – set forth finely manicured, although perhaps too tidy, arguments about secularism's debts to the Judeo-Christian traditions. Moyn characterises secularism in their texts as Christianity's subtle 'self-encryption' but puts Arendt in a different category, suggesting that she conscientiously policed the border between secular and sacred applications of biblical passages.[34] Indeed, she was miffed at critics of political behaviour who recruited sacred skeletons – the bones or reputations of famed ascetics and martyrs – to justify their own unworldliness. She reminded the otherworldly that Jesus only temporarily retired to the desert. His withdrawal should not be cited to countenance flights from the world. Stupendous, spiritual deaths to this world may be the 'only way of life that in earnest has renounced … all vanity in the biblical sense of the word,' Arendt admitted, but those 'deaths' led to bereavements on both sides of the divide:

losses of the contribution to political life that the pious might have made as well as the loss to the pious of a political life, free and full of new beginnings. She specified: 'insertion' into the *saeculum* 'stimulated by the presence of [a] company we may wish to join,' would be 'like a second birth,' the start 'of [a] somebody,' not simply the start of something.[35]

The significance of agency here is self-evident. Arendt's concerns with structures, statists' salesmanship and bloated bureaucracies pale before her interest in citizen-statesmen's self-discoveries – in somebodies. In her scheme, the collective 'migrate' and 'relocate,' as Seyla Benhabib suggests; they experiment with fresh forms of exchange when 'the public square is filled with the hollow signs of the regime's power.'[36] Arendt was never quite as explicit about such plasticity, though she expected something novel could come 'into being wherever [persons] are together in the manner of speech and action' – wherever 'organization … rises out of acting and speaking together.'[37] Still, she continued to fear that compassion could capsize whatever the collectives developed, inasmuch as 'human solidarization' (her term) invariably tempted citizens precipitately to lose themselves in others' suffering. Such losses (as well as the disappearance of *inter-ests*) prevented interpersonal performances that, for Arendt, defined politics.[38]

Yet are we dragging Arendt along (or has she been dragging us) on a fool's errand? There is every chance that, despite her assessments of the grim prospects in conventional public realms for freedom, plurality, reciprocities, political discourse and political activity – as she redefined the latter two – during 'the onslaught of modernity' in second half of the twentieth century, she might nonetheless be sceptical about the chance in the first half of the twenty-first to reimagine democracy. But recall that she left her doctrine of natality and the new beginnings, to which it referred, tantalisingly open to interpretation. Perhaps, then, she would have approved efforts to adapt her values and strategies to unconventional alternative venues to address what Marc Stears perceives as a 'need to preserve the parochial in a nationalising age' to contend with 'globalising tendencies' and with statists' persistent efforts to channel citizens' participation in contemporary nationalists' mock-ups of republican government.[39]

What follows asks what it might mean to find unconventional spaces where citizens resist pressures to conform.[40] Doing so requires that we propose defensibly faithful adaptations of Arendt's version of politics – or perhaps more accurately her vision for politics – and to stipulate conditions that could accommodate them. This requires that readers not only review expressions of her appreciation for pariah perspectives as early as the 1930s but also remember her instructions that we attend to 'situation-bound reality' but that we resist citizen capture and probe for places to make new beginnings.[41] Yet two complications should be noted at the start. First, as we learned, Arendt never underestimated how deftly statists incentivised their citizens' conformity. Discussing how, where and why one might locate alternatives, we cannot forget her observation that, as a result of the onslaught of modernity, 'reality and human reason have parted company.'[42] To imagine Arendtian alternatives, we must reintroduce those two, to be reasonable and realistic without renouncing Arendt's openness to ostensibly implausible outcomes when an experiment in unconventional venues proves unsustainable or when an appealing new beginning obliges interlocutors to adjourn the familiar. Second, Arendt is something of a complication; she was and still is an 'enigma,' as Martin Jay says, pointing out that her 'elusive and unpredictable mind' 'confound[s]' yet has managed 'to inspire and infuriate almost all sectors of the political spectrum.'[43] But, without discounting the enigmatic character of her expressions, what remains of this study explores how, where and why we ought to redefine politics and to reimagine both citizenship and democracy while continuing our reconnaissance of the routes other colleagues have followed from her remarks to contemporary political reforms.

## Notes

1. *Denktagebuch*, 522 (*Warum ist es so schwer die Welt zu lieben?*).
2. Arendt, 'The Freedom to Be Free,' TWB, 375.
3. LIOC, 130–1.
4. Quotes are taken from Arendt's notes for the lecture, 'Breakdown of Authority,' November 23, 1953; Speeches and Lectures File, 1923–1975; USLC.
5. HC, 131–2.
6. OT, 94.
7. HC, 75–8. Also review the underscoring in Arendt's copy of Friedrich von Oppeln-Bronikowski's German translation of Machiavelli's *Prince*, *Der Fürstenspiegel* (Jena: Eugen Diedrichs, 1912), 40, 52, 56; BCSL.
8. OT, 235.
9. Arendt, 'Concern with Politics in Recent European Philosophical Thought,' EU, 438.
10. Benhabib, *Reluctant Modernism*, 89 seems to be channelling Arendt on this point.
11. HC, 244.
12. For Emperor Augustus as a patron of the senate yet also a trustee of popular sovereignty (*Treuhänder der Volkssouveränität*), see the underscoring in

Arendt's copy of Karl Löwenstein, *Beiträge zur Staatssoziologie* (Tübingen: Mohr, 1961), 21; BCSL.

13. HC, 245.
14. LMW, 134–5.
15. CR, 12.
16. For which, see OR, 68.
17. CR, 139.
18. Arendt, 'Organized Guilt and Universal Responsibility,' in *The Jew as Pariah: Jewish Identity and Politics in the Modern Age*, ed. Ron H. Feldman (New York: Grove, 1978), 234–5.
19. For which, see Arndt, *Arendt on Politics*, 166–7.
20. OR, 187.
21. Ibid., 166–7, 186–7.
22. Arendt, 'Nation-State and Democracy,' TWB, 260–1.
23. See Hinchman, 'Common Sense,' 321 and George Kateb, 'Political Action: Its Nature and Advantages,' in *The Cambridge Companion to Hannah Arendt*, ed. Dana Villa (Cambridge: Cambridge University Press, 2000), 139–42.
24. LKPP, 27.
25. BPF, 240–1.
26. Arendt, 'Peace or Armistice in the Near East,' 60–3 discusses 'the closed framework[s]' of nationalist arguments in the context of the ongoing Palestinian crisis.
27. See the underlining in Arendt's copy of *The Political Writings of James Harrington: A Selection* (New York: Liberal Arts Press, 1955), 75; BCSL.
28. See Arendt's letter to Riesman, May 21, 1948, 009235–009236; Correspondence, 1947–1956; USLC.
29. Arendt's letter to Riesman, March 9, 1949, 009241; USLC.
30. Arendt, 'Freedom and Politics,' TWB, 239–40 and Schwartz, *Arendt's Judgment*, 81.
31. Arendt, 'Emerson – Thoreau Medal Lecture,' American Academy of Arts and Sciences (1969); Speeches and Lectures File 1923–1975, 2; USLC.
32. HC, 239–40.
33. Arendt, 'Revolution and Freedom,' TWB, 345.
34. But Samuel Moyn, 'Hannah Arendt on the Secular,' *New German Critique* 105 (Fall, 2008), 93–6 attributes to Arendt an emphasis on 'the difficulty of overcoming political theology' (96).
35. HC, 176–7.
36. Benhabib, *Reluctant Modernism*, 127–30.
37. HC, 198.
38. OR, 71.

39. Marc Stears, *Out of the Ordinary: How Everyday Life Inspired a Nation and How It Can Again* (Cambridge: Harvard University Press, 2021), 141.
40. Steve Buckler, *Hannah Arendt and Political Theory: Challenging the Tradition* (Edinburgh: Edinburgh University Press, 2011), 88 calls them 'homogenising imperatives.'
41. Arendt, 'Philosophy and Sociology,' EU, 31–3.
42. HC, 300.
43. Martin Jay, *Permanent Exiles: Essays on the Intellectual Migration from Germany to America* (New York: Columbia University Press, 1985), 238–9.

# 3

# Arendt's Hints at How to Begin

## Getting Past Mistakes

How to begin? First, take lessons from the past, to be precise, from what Arendt considered political philosophy's many missteps. She followed Nietzsche's lead. Knowing it would be impossible to run time backward and change the past, she resolved, as he had, to will the past into the present to reconceive and revise the latter and to do away with the obstacle the past had become.[1] Navigating from Nietzsche back to Plato, up to Hegel, and then further up, reengaging the philosophers with whom she had studied, she redeployed and exploited ideas she teased from the history of the human imagination. She trusted them to yield fresh perspectives on problems political theorists confronted. In the lecture she delivered at a meeting of the American Political Science Foundation in 1954, she inventoried what, to her mind, were political philosophers' most egregious errors, which enabled them cavalierly to 'live undisturbed' by 'the human condition of plurality.' Well into the twentieth century, their indifference to the 'realm of human affairs' kept political philosophy from making any meaningful contributions to a rehabilitation of prevailing political cultures. The more contemptuous philosophers flaunted their disrespect for colleagues interested in public life. And when some of the contemptuous condescended to offer principles for political behaviour, their offerings, Arendt complained, were impenetrable, and the little that could be comprehended seemed irreconcilable with the best political practices of their time. Had they read some of Arendt's favourite poets, they might have come to understand that freedom was not something to be theorised or buried under an avalanche of conjectures but something similar to 'air or food, the lack of which leaves a terrible void.'[2]

Instead, the philosophers who improvised to become politically relevant, wrote or spoke as if they were 'laying down rules for a lunatic asylum.'[3] Her mentor Martin Heidegger, announced that he was ready to 'leave the arrogance of all absolutes behind' but pondered political history as one would regard a farce with no serious implications for the history of Being. Arendt sensed that philosophers' 'old hostility' towards political culture coloured much of what he drafted as he occasionally climbed down into them.[4] Other colleagues made a show of scorning what passed as politics, although they rushed to rule over faculties and universities when the fascists asked. Others aspired to no such fiefdoms, heeding 'old Epicurus's exhortation' to 'live in hiding.'[5]

But we learned that Arendt found some exceptions in France. Whereas many of their colleagues, much as the German philosophers she knew well – past and present – pondered principles, which 'owe[d] their origin to altogether different experiences' from those derived by trial and error, the existentialists in France (and she bundled Karl Jaspers with them) felt 'obliged to take a stand on everyday issues.' Yet, as noted, she regretted that the principles making those stands intelligible were usually unarticulated. Existentialists preached courage with conviction but without giving their convictions and political choices much direction.[6] Still, Arendt was far more irritated with conventional philosophers who disparaged existentialism, as they disdained political theory; she acknowledged their prestige and agreed with them that philosophy was mother to all disciplines, but she thought the more traditional small-minded treating theorists who took political practices seriously as unworthy and unwanted 'stepchild[ren].'[7]

Sometimes Arendt appealed to colleagues in philosophy to indulge political theory that could influentially propose how, where and why political practice might enliven alternative public realms and might reimagine citizenship and democracy. She thought Hegel and Heidegger were among the prestigious philosophers who made mistakes and insufficiently reflected on political practices, yet she commended them for several of their contributions. She respected Hegel for having given the lie to philosophers' alibi, refusing to let them claim a higher calling, removed from the unremarkable and from what they took to be irrelevant. He held that public events were not the sources of truth but were where absolute truth lurked backstage – 'behind the back of the political actor.' Adapting his metaphor, one could say that, from Arendt's panoptical perspective, the foyer looked crowded with philosophers pondering precepts for politics without any sense of what playgoers saw from the stalls until Hegel endowed the quotidian with meaning. 'Living through the age of revolutions, witnessing devastation then liberation, Hegel proclaimed what she described as a 'glorious mental dawn.' He awarded what transpired onstage the dignity it deserved yet had never before enjoyed among conventional philosophers. He all but issued a manifesto for philosophy to restore the dignity to what people did daily – and to change.[8] No wonder, then, such dignity should come to depend on persons' actions 'making public' ideas that, according to Hegel, 'preceded' and 'shaped' them. He lured philosophers from the foyer into the theatre, and he persuaded them that ideas assumed 'tangible reality' onstage. Political theory's contributions should thereafter have been welcome there, redefining political practice. The discipline's deficiencies, however, kept philosophy from proceeding in that direction. But, thanks to Hegel, political activities and discourses might yet 'attract modern philosophy to the political realm' and invite analysis from those 'thrown from their ivory towers' on his orders.[9]

As for Heidegger, he told students to hunt for Being in beings. His instructions did not explicitly endorse philosophical reflection on political practice, yet Arendt suggested that his 'rejection' of philosophers' arrogance 'open[ed] the way [for] a re-examination of the whole realm of politics in the light of elementary human experiences;' yet, as mentioned, she thought him sluggish, slow to tug those experiences into political theory and slower to oppose those who identified the finite with the fallen. And he was manifestly hesitant to incorporate the contingent into his search for authenticity.[10] Arendt also thought Heidegger reluctant to deny consistently that absolutes could be politically useful. Despots, therefore, were free to rely on them. For a short time, he partnered with them, presiding as rector of the University of Freiburg over the expulsion of the Jews. But the democratic as well as the despotic trafficked in absolutes to win over citizens. Statists of all stripes deferred to divine laws. Insurgents did as well ('endowed by their creator with certain unalienable rights'). Absolutes ricocheted around all sorts of political discourse. But Arendt defended human dignity differently. For her, it was performative. Dignity was conditional, depending on how one used freedom in the 'back, forth and up against,' in the agonistic discourses and activities that created for others a common world.

Freedom was not freely available. Despots' and statists' demanded obedience. Arendt noted their successes in the Soviet Union where, from the 1930s through the 1950s, Stalinists – even without Stalin – looked to be exquisitely adept at suppression, at focusing their citizens' concentration on 'labouring and consuming,' which she classified as the 'lowliest of human activities … in which one is already subject to compulsion, although,' as she qualified, 'not of the political kind.' Yet Stalinist statists made it political. Their five-year plans were imperfect; their gulag penal system, terrifying. But, to Arendt, they were fine examples of what happened when statists and sovereign powers permitted *isms* and absolutes to shape policies that secured their authority.[11] Extorting compliance, they rendered their public realms wholly resistant to reform – or so they intended. Arendt reviewed the totalitarians' tactics yet noticed as well the dehumanising effects of most compliant citizens' obsessions with possessions (with production and consumption), even in republics where statist pressures in conventional public realms amounted to persuasion more often than coercion. So, precincts might well be reserved within capacious, conventional public realms for alternatives, for oases in the deserts. What creates, textures and, for a time, sustains them is Arendt's version of politics. That said, her controversial distinction between the social and political acquires fresh meaning. To be sure, as Tobias Albrecht confirms, this left her left flank open. Critics were quick to point out that any depoliticisation of social problems would make them more difficult to resolve, but Albrecht is wrong to take that as her purpose and to assume that Arendt devised her distinction to stave off political criticism of social conditions. Nonetheless, the distinction served to purge the precincts of Arendt's unconventional public spaces, of problems statists created when they confused political with economic planning.[12]

How, then, might one capitalize on, or create chances in democratic republics for, generative discourses and actions in public realms and, on doing so, address social inequities? Inequalities were the cause of many, so, we might inquire whether inequalities could possibly be overcome when conventional politics is based on discrepancies, notably on the distinction between rulers and ruled but also on the distinction among the ruled between elites (the affluent and influential) and ordinary citizens? Arendt found Plato's defence of such distinctions especially objectionable, inasmuch as his metaphors fixed frontiers between subjects and sovereign powers by comparing that pair to patients and physicians, sheep and shepherds, slaves and masters. The last signalled that commoners were, in effect, reduced to servility. Introduced into contemporary discussions about governance, such imagery would likely irritate and agitate, although Plato surely offered them to inspire submission. Yet statists resourcefully adapted his strategy to make inequalities seem natural, to present commercially and politically powerful elites' demands for deference as reasonable and often to enshrine them in laws.[13] Power then emanated from legislation, which, Daniela Bassi explains, obviated regimes' need to intervene irregularly.[14] Christian Volk takes up the issues of power, citizens' alienation and inequality in ostensibly democratic regimes and fixes on what seems to be a cyclical process by which, despite democratisation, ordinary citizens are actually removed from sources of power. Their removal or alienation exacerbates the effects of inequalities, leading to their mistrust of leadership and politics. Statists, however, adjust and develop 'a populist take on power,' pretending to level up or to equalise and empower citizens. Statists, that is, create a 'mass culture,' which, as we now know, Arendt found terribly wanting in power and culture.[15] Inequalities remained, but that was the point: to preserve them yet, with Plato as a model, to represent subordination and disempowerment as natural and logical. Arendt predictably saw that inequalities interfered with airing and sharing diverse perspectives. Getting past the many past mistakes that derived from Plato's distinctions required her to dethrone truth and to urge that conversations and camaraderie equalise interlocutors and encourage them to determine the relevance to their experiences of others' opinions.[16]

Arendt took Plato's metaphors as vindications of the disparities that sanctioned discrimination, which was the bedrock of conventional politics, but the doom of her enterprise. Yet a few of his dialogues tempted her to accept Socrates as an ally. After all, that ill-fated critic of conventional politicians was effective coaxing their *non sequiturs* into the open. Their circulation presumably prompted others' circumspection. On other grounds, Arendt had reservations. She thought that the self-styled gadfly was inclined to 'fall back on conversing with [him]self' too often.[17] And she complained that he too infrequently (and then only superficially) acknowledged the 'abyss between truth and opinion' that divided philosopher from citizen. So, Plato's Socrates was just as responsible as Plato for traditional philosophy's estrangement from political practice as well as from public opinion. And, to her mind, that estrangement was 'characteristic of all post-Platonic philosophy.' It accounted for 'suspicions and hostilities' that were responsible for 'the flight of philosophy from the sphere of human affairs.'[18]

A jarring judgment! Its validity is questionable, but Arendt formulated it, implying that the flight of philosophy left statists propping up regimes with platitudes that ideologues derived from what some philosophers left behind. Philosophy's return in the form of political theory, though, could well assist citizens looking to redefine political practice to play up plurality. To illustrate, return to Arendt's analysis of an American mantra, the Declaration of Independence, specifically, its phrase, 'we hold these truths to be self-evident.' Then amend the customary reading. Whereas philosophers, just as historians, tended to look for bookish sources of 'these truths,' presuming that the founders leveraged the foundation of the republic with received wisdom or self-evident truths, imagine, as they did (in Arendt's account) that their truths and the human rights inferred from them were less significant than the 'we' in the declaration's 'we hold.' That reading, then, makes the self-evident character of the founders' truths depend on the deliberating that preceded the holding. The truth that all were created equal was far from self-evident. In Arendtian politics, only colloquies and conversations could make them so. The discourses preceding the declaration made the founders' opinions – specifically, what they decided to 'hold' as 'truths' about freedom and equality – appear beyond dispute.[19]

Their freedom, therefore, was not inherent, but acquired. Their equality was not inherent, but acquired. Both freedom and equality were circumstantial and performative. The founders were free and equal because they assembled 'as a body of peers,' whose reciprocal respect dignified the declarations and documents they issued and equalised the interlocutors who signed them. Deliberations not only leavened the republic but also 'levelled' its founders and, in theory, citizens or constituents who trusted them. 'The equality of the Greek *polis*,' Arendt explained, 'was an attribute of the *polis*,' 'a body of peers' who were determined to fill a 'political space proper' and to practise a new form of politics there.[20]

Citizens were not political spectators in Arendt's universe. Looking on rather than engaging yielded power to tyrants, she said in another context, intimating that more engaged dissidents, during the 1920s and 1930s, might have stalled the Nazis' juggernaut.[21] Without agitation for what she characterised as 'limiting and protecting principles,' nationalists could do irreparable damage in her time. Admitting that there could 'never [be] entirely reliable safeguards against action from within the body politic,' Arendt nonetheless reckoned that 'the boundlessness of action' could possess 'a tremendous capacity for building relationships' that heal fractures in political cultures. Others worried about 'boundless' actions' 'unpredictability;' she was persuaded that the chances to retard statists' and reigning political elites' most damaging initiatives justified the risk.[22] In alternative, unconventional venues and wherever citizen-statesmanship was present, new beginnings might equalise interlocutors, giving each 'the greatest possible overview of all the possible standpoints ... from which an issue can be seen and judged.' For Arendt, the exchange of opinions and the enlargement of every participant's perspective ought to be the purpose of politics.[23] Would-be citizen-statesmen 'mak[ing] their appearance[s] explicitly,' engage with other interlocutors and, as a result, fill the in-betweens with better informed opinions. Such interpersonal performances or interactions made public spaces political.[24]

## On Closure and Overconfidence

To identify public, political realms as spaces for appearances suggests something insubstantial; appearances could be taken as apparitions. But Arendt never meant statements about alternative political spaces to be taken lightly or pejoratively. Quite the contrary, as Jerome Kohn confirms, she anticipated that what she termed participants' 'explicit' appearances made best political practices possible. And, Kohn continues, she trusted that political 'activity [was] inseparable from the activity of judging.' Judgement ordered 'appearances for the sake of the plurality of persons to whom they appear.' Kohn is correct, although there is a strong probability that his uncomplicated assessment could be misconstrued. 'Ordering' might be mistaken for sifting and selecting from appearances the most respectable or ostensibly incontestable either to encourage deference or to avoid defections. But he prominently parks in his sentence the phrase, 'for the sake of ... plurality,' alluding to Arendt's cogent commitments to candour. Interlocutors were urged to be open-minded and careful to keep from dominating discussions. Deference to others' opinions was an interim courtesy rather than an endpoint. Her expectations made her alternative to conventional public realms a training ground for citizen-statesmen.[25]

Kohn's 'for the sake of plurality' contains most of what we need to know to redefine politics and citizenship and to reimagine democracy. The phrase explains why Arendt preferred trafficking in opinions to dealing with tendentious presentations of truths, preferred equality to domination and preferred contingency to closure. She was annoyed by scientists who tenaciously held their truths and their ground, fending off critics and discouraging paradigm shifts. And she was equally irritated by theorists who avowed that scientific methods could reveal the laws of historical development. Such scientists as well as political and social theorists who exalted the methods and findings of the natural and social scientists – to be precise, her colleagues who trusted the sciences' 'general rules' to 'subsume occurrences of all times and types' – appeared sheltered from reality. Arendt objected because their 'formal and unhistorical categories' governed their questions as well as the questions asked and answered along the corridors of power and in the academy. In science, government and education terminology favoured the general and obscured the particular, tending, she argued, to universalise itself. How, then, to escape that tyranny of terminology, if only provisionally, when influential theorists leash all changes to laws and to patterns that diminish the political importance of 'verifiable experience'? 'The day will come,' Arendt prophesied, when history will give the lie to social and political scientists' laws, which will prove incapable of rendering political changes intelligible.[26]

Given what she advocated and what she prophesied, Kei Hiruta's classification of Arendt as a monist is perplexing. Hiruta's exposition of Isaiah Berlin's disagreements with Arendt relates them to Berlin's discomfort with the monism motivating Plato, Rousseau, Hegel and Marx to look for ideal social settings to 'implement' a 'final solution' to the political problems of their times.[27] Hiruta is aware of 'the multiple senses in which Arendt is a pluralist.'

'Pluralism,' he allows, 'highlights,' for her, the importance of a 'vibrant civil society and associational life for democratic politics.' Nonetheless, he maintains, her insistence that citizens 'can appropriately respond to the human conditions of natality and plurality' 'only in political action and speech' made her a 'monist.' She qualified as such, in Hiruta's book, because she denied or, at the very least, she minimised the significance of casting humans as 'choice-making creatures.' But when Arendt declared that citizen-statesmen are bound to make political 'appearances,' she was hardly denying or compromising their freedom to make choices.[28] Monists look for laws of nature or of history; Arendt did not. In fact, she excoriated statists for having done so and not only for having looked but for having pretended to find those laws. Then, they disempowered ordinary citizens whom they thought too obtuse to decode history and nature and to put current political theories and arrangements in the context of either. Statists, then, were the monists, presuming that what Darwin did for nature could be done for society. Purveyors of laws that supposedly determined the trajectories of social lives and political progress larded their expressions of confidence with promises to please the public. Citizens craving certainty become credulous. Arendt studied how and why their craving led ordinary citizens to trust totalitarian leaders who were convinced that elites and sovereign powers were 'servants of [benevolent] inhuman forces' thrusting towards some desirable destiny or denouement.[29] Governments' improvisations were taken as history 'arrang[ing] itself' ... conveniently and consistently under the category of challenge and response.' Citizens bowed before what Arendt dubbed 'secular religions,' because statists paraded proficiently, albeit preposterously, as priests and prophets.[30]

Improvisations, then, passed as history's or nature's laws working through challenges to some closure. Most political philosophers, statists and scientists, in Arendt's time, preferred closure. She prized openness. Max Scheler, widely known during the early twentieth century for efforts to integrate philosophy with anthropology, stunned Arendt by proposing that human nature was fixed 'morphologically,' not malleable. To her, Scheler seemed to have halted human evolution. Fondness for closure foreclosed options for new beginnings.[31] She was also struck by Niels Bohr's comments on the future of theoretical physics, specifically, by Bohr's confidence that scientists' latest laws would eventually correct misperceptions generated by the then current, though 'necessarily prejudiced, conceptual frame[s]' of reference. Bohr predicted that apparent anomalies would persist for a while, until any unexplained irregularities fell 'into place through an appropriate widening of the current conceptual framework.' He forecast that the future would only require adjustments. The paradigm might be refined but not significantly altered. Closure, again! Arendt was dismissive. Bohr's talk of 'widening' or 'adjusting,' allowed only for minor changes but not for new beginnings.[32]

Natural and behavioural scientists were thought to rely on reality checks, and even theoretical physicists were assumed to attend to slabs or slivers of fresh evidence. But, as Anya Topolski reminds us, evidence that mattered most to Arendt derived from interactions with others, which ostensibly did not figure into Scheler's or Bohr's calculations. Arendt trusted the evidence from interpersonal encounters to counter, to some extent, mendacious statists' pronouncements about citizenship and sovereignty as well as the inferences that political philosophies teased from their abstractions. She continued to depend on the interpersonal rather than the theoretical.[33]

Meanwhile, the increasing prestige of the natural sciences gave social sciences – and thereby political science – a formidable reputation. But Arendt claimed (and complained) that physicists possessed a fleet of public relations specialists who exaggerated sciences' accomplishments; the adjustments Bohr predicted were characterised as 'conquests.' Publicists immodestly attributed social as well as scientific progress to their clients' ingenuity, Arendt alleged, maintaining that both the natural and the social sciences were 'still beset by paradoxes and the most bewildering perplexities.' She also accused scientists and their publicists of having ignored technicians – the 'plumbers,' in her version of natural sciences' progress – who deserved recognition for bringing 'the results of the scientists down to earth.'[34] Yet scientists' publicists – the equivalent of elites' and sovereign powers' statists – had more experience selling fictions and more arrogance than those 'plumbers.' Publicists in science, as in politics, misled the public to believe an imminent overcoming of the unpredictable was in the offing. But, in an essay on the effects of space exploration on 'the stature of man,' Arendt tried to bring expectations 'down to earth.' She seconded Werner Heisenberg's restraint. Probability, she explained, would never morph into certainty. Still, optimism reigned; the public believed science was furlongs farther along than where it was. She was despondent upon hearing – even if not also believing – that computers would soon relieve humans of the need to think. Her essay on space explorations reads like a filibuster staged to put off popular enthusiasm until the allegedly 'glorious,' though 'baffling' achievements of the sciences begin to stir a recognition of finitude. She was encouraged after being told that 'paradoxes' had 'begun to worry the great scientists.'[35]

As both her despondence and encouragement suggest, the paradox that 'haunted' Arendt – and, she believed, haunted Heisenberg as well – revealed that, notwithstanding the popular acclaim, 'the more knowledge and the more power' scientists acquire, 'the less respect [they] can harbour for' themselves.

Undeniably, the natural scientists' findings 'enhanced enormously' the powers humans had over other parts of nature, but the enhancements, she feared, not only occasioned a 'decisive diminishment of man's self-respect' but also made it harder to reassert the importance of the interpersonal.[36] Ponder limits, she counselled, yet philosophers' overconfidence in their truths severely limited contributions to theory that experience might make. And the scientists' overconfidence in their 'conceptual frameworks' created cultures of closure that, in disciplines unrelated to their work and in government eclipsed the significance of new beginnings. Arendt believed that sustaining openness was critical if democracy were to be made politically new.[37]

To a point, of course, scientists and statists were interested in novelty, though, for both sets, except for the former who accepted Werner Heisenberg's corrosive effects on confidence in precise measurement, uncertainties were troublesome. But resistance to paradigm shifts and resistance to political innovations were rife among scientists and statists, respectively. Statists were content with what time and their regimes proved to be sustaining, with whatever enabled them to manage their citizens and to preoccupy them with production and consumption that supposedly 'enrich[ed] the world.'[38] But Arendt's volume on *The Human Condition* looked askance at such enrichment and at 'labouring activity' inasmuch as it 'concentrated exclusively on life and its maintenance' and thereby distracted citizens from civic maintenance – from civic activity. Labourers, she lamented, were 'oblivious of the world to the point of worldlessness.'[39] But when labour became work, something 'durable' was added to the world, some 'fabricated thing,' fixed and with sufficient 'durability to remain in the world as an independent entity.' Closure, yet again; but Arendt acknowledged that, until it was consumed, razed or felled, whatever was made 'added to the human artifice' – often advantageously. The 'fabricated,' however, was also fixed, incontestably transforming process into product. For that reason, process was distinct from what she denoted as an activity creating a common world and dignifying interpersonal performances as political.[40]

Arendt's distinction between labour and work (or fabrication) continues to intrigue scholars, although what is more significant for our purpose, as we consider how to encourage political discourse and activity, is the distinction that Arendt ventured between performative political activities, on the one hand, and labour and work, on the other. As she sets the contrast, the latter two submerge personality in productivity, whereas political action and discourse enable citizen-statesmen to emerge. At labour and at work, citizens are reduced to aggregates of achievements. Only political participation (interpersonal performances) gives them a right to have rights; only participation in politics, as she redefined it, gives them the dignity that depends on their (and on their collectives') promotion of plurality, freedom, equality and natality. Arendt contrasted such virtues with qualities engendered by competitions for rule in conventional public realms where action amounted to pandering and speech was insincere and often mendacious. To win mattered more than self-discovery, self-disclosure and self-improvement (or, as Arendt, after Kant, would have it 'enlargement'). Challenges to create alternative public venues and therein to be politically present, though, are staggering, for statists' conventions, competitions and closure are pervasive. How, then, should we start? We cannot 'unbecome' producers and consumers, but we can stop judging ourselves and others by what we and they produce and consume. We can look to sift different opinions, avoid both overconfidence and closure and begin to redefine citizenship, statesmanship and politics, caring less for statists' determinations of what will pass as civic responsibility but, in reality, is fashionably irresponsible – obeisance devoid of initiative.[41]

But statists were nearly impossible to disregard. They held the helm. Their influence with the media and in the marketplace, as we and Arendt noted, was considerable. When they sensed the need, they turned to other truthtellers to dress up their own practice as political philosophy. Even before hearing it from Adolf Eichmann, Arendt knew that Immanuel Kant was a favourite among the fascists whose statists justified subservience to the government. They improvised what she caustically called an 'approximately correct definition of the categorical imperative' that would have them behave as though their behaviour should become 'the principle of general laws,' as if obedience could be lifted from the conduct of one to become what each expects of every other. Eichmann normalised his conduct that way, for who would want all citizens to disobey orders that had the force of law?[42] This extension of Kant seemed odious to her, although she faulted Kant himself. 'The inhumanity of [his] moral philosophy,' she wrote, [was] undeniable.' Kant imposed an absolute duty on an 'interhuman realm' of ever-changing relationships, she claimed in an address she delivered in Hamburg in 1959, after receiving that city's Lessing prize. Arendt contrasted Gotthold Lessing's 'openness to the world,' which, she said, terribly 'distressed other philosophers, with Kant's devotion to, and dissemination of, 'a single truth.' She contended that Lessing had no interest in unfettered access to some dossier of truths, on which philosophers or governments had based their demands for acquiescence. Arendt's Lessing trusted that societies were in no way harmed by their erudite citizens 'who take more trouble to make clouds than to scatter them.' He knew, she went on, that civilisations 'incur … harm from those who wish to subject all men's thinking to the yoke of their own.' The ambiguities – Lessing's clouds – were indispensable. They invited interlocutors to share opinions, whereas the imposition of truths did not. Nothing ought to 'stand ... above men' and be 'decisive in all human affairs and cannot be infringed even for the sake of humanity.' To Arendt and apparently to Lessing, the 'death of all disputes' comes upon collectives whenever the interlocutors' fondness for closure obscures the importance of agonistic engagement. Hence, her Lessing lecture made a case for clouds and appended a caveat to truthtellers whose skies were characteristically yet unrealistically clear: 'there cannot be one single [extrinsic] truth within the human world.'[43]

We begin, then, by contesting statists' truths and extrinsic ends, by disputing the preeminence awarded sovereignty in political theory. Withdrawal may be tempting but it is not contestation. Arendt, as we know, was critical of ascetic impulses in late antiquity. Acting on them, walling oneself off from the world's untidiness finally rather than provisionally, depleted the supply of sincere, informed, thoughtful citizens.[44] Perhaps equally regrettable to her, Augustine and his prelatical colleagues in late antiquity organised their alternative collectives (congregations and convents) hierarchically, prohibiting the laity from interpreting Christianity's *credenda*, which were to be defined by a few, then uncritically accepted by all. Opinions were heresies. Finally, what made early Christianity so objectionable to Arendt, in addition to its overconfidence and certainties, was the virtue that, along with humility, became one of the faith's two mainstays, compassion that paid God's love for creation forward in love for others.[45] Her quarrel with compassion, which we encountered earlier, bears repeating, as we discuss how to maintain alternative public realms, for the 'fusion[s]' she attributed to compassion scuttled *inter-ests*, those in betweens required for interlocutors' amicably agonistic confrontations, the give-and-take-and-up-against, which, for Arendt, made conversations political. She figured that fusions kept plural perspectives from developing and encouraged conformity.[46] Her reservations about yielding compassion a prominent place in redefinitions of politics – in what Eric Gregory calls 'an ethics of citizenship' – leads him to frown on her 'misamorism.'[47] But because bonding was central to her redefined politics and her preferred poleis, she replaced the fusions she feared with forgiveness and friendship. Friends become 'equal partners in a common world' without limiting 'the ever-increasing differentiation of citizens' Arendt required for the 'agonal life,' to which she often referred. And, if not for forgiveness, interlocutors risked colleagues' rancour by engaging in lively exchanges of opinions, specifically, the *Wider* or 'up against' that went along with the *Hin und Her*, the Arendtian 'back-and-forth.'[48]

Arendt apparently trusted that friendship and forgiveness could replace consolations normally given by conventional collectives' confidence in closures.

Assurances of both forgiveness and friendship, moreover, encouraged interlocutors to 'take ... part in what is common' and thereby to contribute to new beginnings.[49] A synopsis of what she required is our study's constant refrain and suggests how she might have proceeded (and how we may proceed) to create and sustain the alternative public spaces where freedom, plurality and equality inspire citizens (us) to reimagine citizenship and democracy. Arendt called for (1) emotional distance from cultures dominated by production and consumption, that is, some adaptation of the pariahs' perspective; (2) freedom to sift multiple opinions; (3) interlocutors' eagerness to speak and act (and, as she said, to 'appear'); and (4) notwithstanding her warning against fusion, the realization that too much distance courts miscommunication, which argues for the cultivation of friendships and for a readiness to forgive and be forgiven. Arendt's alternatives to conventional public realms were, she reckoned, 'oases' in the desert but not of it. They were places to contemplate what went wrong in desert politics and to make new beginnings.[50]

## How to Be 'in Conflict with the World': Arendt, Heidegger and Nietzsche

We have looked to repossess Arendt's assessments of how much had gone wrong. Her undated lecture on war and politics suggests that statists coupled the two as contests for domination that demanded citizens' cringing conformity.[51] Such demands and the belligerence proved to Arendt that 'the public realm lost the power of illumination' in the twentieth century. In her Lessing lecture, she recalled that her subject 'never felt at home in the world' and, she said, 'probably never wanted to.' Her Lessing and her experiences of politics and wars convinced Arendt that 'genius' (and the same may be said of citizen-statesmanship) can only 'develop ... in conflict with the world and the public realm,' as conventionally conceived. Lessing did not withdraw, however, and, as we now know, Arendt would not have citizen-statesmen withdraw, for, she explained, 'with each ... retreat, an almost demonstrable loss to the world takes place.' Her lecture's Lessing was 'radically critical' of the 'public realm of his time.' He was 'completely revolutionary,' relishing chances to 'challeng[e] prejudice.' She relished the lesson and urged readers to renounce the 'extreme of sentimental utopianism' without ceasing to oppose statist advocates of *Realpolitik* passing off conformity as solidarity. When citizens find or found the oases and especially when, as citizen-statesmen, they venture from them into the desert, they must persuade others of the importance of exercising their own freedoms to form, alter and exchange opinions.[52] That responsibility summons them to be invasive and to make spaces for 'web[s] of human relationships' that invariably accommodate 'conflicting wills and intentions.' Politics of that (potentially subversive) sort clearly poses problems for those who measure the success of political endeavours by policy formulation and implementation.[53]

Arendt measured political success differently, in terms of disclosures. Her oases, for example, were where citizen-statesmen learned to disclose who they were and who they would become. Embarking from there, they encouraged others' disclosures, in part, by creating conditions that rewarded transparency with freedom and friendships. Or, by undoing the harm done by statists, who confused conformity with solidarity to suppress individuality, citizen-statesmen changed existing 'webs of relations.' But she cautioned readers that disclosures in political action and discourse revealed who citizens were and not necessarily who they thought they were. Along with their 'qualities, gift, and talents,' citizens exhibited 'shortcomings' that otherwise might have been hidden from them, as the *daimōn* in Greek religion accompanying persons, always 'looking over [their] shoulder[s] from behind and thus visible only to' persons who encounter them.[54]

Perhaps how successfully citizens form alternative communities depends on how judiciously they assess themselves. Yet Arendt found that supposedly secure self-assessments were not only capsized during collectives' conversations, as above, but also by disorienting experiences. Exile was traumatic. Among émigrés' during the early 1940s, many radicals wrote as reactionaries.[55] Yet, in different situations, what Arendt identified as the enviable 'warmth' of 'pariah peoples' prompted a 'cheerful unconcern' for the world among those who had joined them. From having studied refugee communities and from having been with and then around émigrés, she concluded that 'human relationships assume' a 'weird irreality' as relationships develop therein and 'in absolute worldlessness.' But their worldlessness prompted an admirable spontaneity distinct from philosophers' detachment.[56]

To illustrate the distinction, so critical to our reimagining citizenship and to underscore the contrast between what developed from the pariahs and émigrés' 'weird irreality,' we should revisit her vexed relationship with Martin Heidegger's formulations. She initially commended them. They constituted what she called 'the first absolutely and uncompromisingly this-worldly philosophy.' Yet, as we know, she could not abide the accusations of inauthenticity with which Heidegger pelted other philosophers who were more attentive to the world's political dilemmas. He was known to advise devotees to zip up against the rough weather in political cultures and to resign themselves to the alienation that would follow – to reconcile themselves to 'not-being-at-home in the world;' '*Dasein* could be truly itself,' Arendt paraphrased, 'only if it could pull back from being-in-the-world.' But because 'that is what its nature can never permit it to do,' being in the world must always be inauthentic. Being's plummeting into politics was a 'falling away from itself,' for Heidegger, for whom 'unconcern' was a principal characteristic of authenticity; for him, it seemed incomprehensible that philosophy should assist with the incubation of political virtue. Arendt shared his critics' displeasure with inferences he would have his devotees draw from *Dasein*'s predicament, namely, that persons should become neither world-berating nor 'world-creating being[s].'[57]

To the extent that Heidegger made what Arendt considered 'absolute isolation' and reflections on death's door (or mortality rather than natality) the condition for experiencing Being, he was no help to her. For him, the 'essential character of the Self' was 'radical separation from all its fellows.' She recalled his lectures' 'mythologizing and muddled concepts.' So, it came as no surprise to her that the Nazis found him – and he, them – agreeable. Nazism's idealisation of blood and soil were muddled myths that its statists laid as the foundation of their government's fictions. Arendt suspected Heidegger's insistence on experiencing Being as 'not-being-at-home-in-the-world' explained why, pursuing Being, he became oblivious to the swells of emotion that carried his countrymen to horrifying extremes?[58] Her rejoinder: existence, 'is, by its very nature, never isolated. It exists only in communication and in awareness of others' existence.' Heidegger was aware of those others. They were 'structurally necessary' elements of existence, although, to her regret, he saw them as 'impediment[s] to the Being of the self.'[59] He disdained conformity as she did, yet, unlike her mentor, Arendt held that alternative public spaces need not reinforce it. Heidegger's mistake, Richard Bernstein says, was that he had 'fail[ed] to distinguish authentic public life from the degenerate mode of publicness ... manifested when there is no plurality.'[60]

Encountering Heidegger's views on alienation was fortuitous. They schooled Arendt. She learned about feelings of personal isolation that contributed to statists' and totalitarianism's successes and that stiffened her resolve to overcome them in alternative public spaces.[61] After trudging through Heidegger's two-volume interpretation of Nietzsche, she made clear that her disagreement with him persisted late in her career. She was as impressed as Heidegger was by the adrenaline fix Nietzsche provided the human will, but whereas Heidegger concentrated on the will empowered to rule, dominate and destroy, her marginalia call attention to passages in Nietzsche's *Wille zur Macht* that allude to the misery that the efforts to dominate leave in their wake. Nietzsche's text refers to 'the wretched history' of domination (*jammervolle Geschichte*). Arendt must have figured that Heidegger missed the innuendo and went on to explain that even promising insurgencies, given insurgents' ulterior motives – that inescapable *Wille zur Macht* – could never redeem political enterprises.[62] Undeniably, diabolical 'destructiveness,' as Arendt admitted, was closely associated with what Nietzsche wrote about both personal and political ambitions. Heidegger's reading emphasized as much. But, for Arendt, Nietzsche's 'last word' concerned the will's 'creativity and superabundance.' Unlike Heidegger, she was disposed to work with what was basically biological and only accidentally political for Nietzsche, though, when political, defiant, 'in conflict with the world.' She was prepared as Heidegger would not have been to stress the importance of challenging conventional political prejudices with power generated at first in interpersonal performances in alternate, unconventional venues.[63]

Political power, for Arendt, did not reside in offices or office-holders but in relations between persons. Obviously, some persons retained the power and cunning to manipulate others. There was not much to choose between that craft and the shaping and reshaping of things that *homo faber*, any maker of artifacts, undertook. Statists were makers in that respect, but, according to Arendt's definition, their power was not political. True, they turned the individual citizens they ruled into masses and mobs, collecting citizens and selling conformity as critical to citizenship. One could justifiably conclude, therefore, that they thereby made citizens. Citizen-statesmen – Arendt's reimagined citizens were made differently, generated in interpersonal performances. Arendtian politics located power relationally, between free persons, who were made equal by that process.[64] Of course, relations involved risks. The freedom to act, to speak and to define political practice, first in alternative public realms then, conceivably, within public realms as conventionally conceived, required courage as well as creativity. As Bonnie Honig says, the route to citizen-statesmanship on Arendt's map passes from 'risk-aversiveness' to 'courageous competitiveness.'[65] Along the way, temptations to dominate must be snuffed out. Arendt put it this way: 'to reestablish contact between knowledge and understanding' 'obsessions with rule,' and 'the lust for conquest' (along with political prejudices that appeared to legitimise urges to manipulate) would have to be left behind with *isms* and ideologies that long provided cover or rationale for such prejudices and political lusts.[66] She once compared the latter to masturbation, insinuating that statists and elites were self-indulgent, that self-gratification mattered more than public service.[67]

Statists' self-indulgence was hardly beside the point, inasmuch as a measure of selflessness was required for plurality and equality to survive in unconventional public spaces. The desire to veer off and become 'remote and uninvolved,' just as the lust or urge to dominate, must be overcome if citizen-statesmen are to be responsive to 'the multitude and variety' of what Arendt called the 'concrete' and 'verifiable experience[s]' that ought to inform political practices and outcomes.[68] Such experiences corrected political prejudices proffered by statists and dramatized as well as reinforced by spectacles (and enforced by soldiers). In democracies, distractions were dazzling, but intimidation was more subtle. The upshot: citizens deferred to, rather than conferred with, leadership that built up bureaucratic apparatuses to keep the *demos* at a distance. Unchallenged, political prejudices prospered. During Arendt's stay in the United States, therefore, there seemed no need for draconian, dystopian political protocols. Meaningful political deliberations were all but extinct. She feared for the future of democracy. Fifty years after her death, the fear has not dissipated, neither in the old democracies of Europe and the Americas nor in newer experiments with democracy elsewhere. Professed democrats display authoritarian impulses. They still talk at, rather than with, citizens. Meanwhile statists, who profess to be democratic, tend to trivialise what Arendt idealised, what she posted as 'the back, forth and against' of agonistic discourses. Conventional political practice reflects the prejudices she anticipated and challenged, and her challenge bears on this chapter's inquiry: how might one reimagine citizenship as well as being in the world, and how might one reconceive political practice and reimagine democracy. 'True understanding,' she wrote, 'does not tire of interminable dialogue' because discussions that air and evaluate plural perspectives help interlocutors 'take [their] bearings in the world' and fire up their imaginations. Borrowing from Wordsworth, she then reminded readers that 'imagination' was 'but another name for … Reason in her more exalted mood.'[69]

But can citizens ever be free from the seemingly pervasive, powerful influence of statists, many of whom appear to be untroubled as the fallout from fascism rains down on twenty-first-century democracies? Notwithstanding Arendt's unequivocal support for being in the world, which was evident in her criticism of Heidegger, and her insistence on engagement with, rather than flight from or philosophical detachment from, 'verifiable experiences' and issues prompting political controversy, one may nonetheless make a case that she conceded provisional withdrawals were permissible. One may even construe her alternative collectives, her oases, as retreats of a sort. Her Lessing lecture seemed to sanction an exodus 'from public life to anonymity.' Yet Arendt declared almost immediately that reality was not to be ignored. Her readers and auditors, who were as yet unconvinced, must learn that statists' *Realpolitik* had no unassailable claims on reality and that their political 'reality [was] actually expressed by [their] escape' and by their defiance of, or conflict with, the world.[70] Perhaps had Arendt been less opaque in her Lessing lecture about provisional withdrawal, we could see more clearly the relationship between her remarks there – in 1959 – and the worries she expressed several years later that alternative political spaces for freedom, equality, plurality, forgiveness, friendship and natality were 'disastrous[ly]' shrinking. As we now know, the 1960s terribly disappointed her. Statists in democracies proceeded unimpeded to 'transform government into administration' and their 'republics into bureaucracies.' Arendt thought that opportunities 'to embark on something [politically] new' were diminishing, as citizens' longing to be 'political being[s]' abated.[71]

Being political, in Arendt's sense, required settings conducive for interpersonal performances that incubated the virtues she valued. What she elsewhere depicted as a 'lofty freedom' among pariahs required more than conventional regimes were ready to give ordinary citizens. In Franz Kafka's last novel, *The Castle*, Arendt came across 'plain villagers, controlled to the last detail by the ruling class.' 'Slaves in their thoughts to … all-powerful officials,' Kafka's characters could serve as stand-ins for citizens whom statists captivated and captured and who, therefore, would not have appreciated the reciprocities that, for Arendt, only developed in opposition to assimilation.[72] Kafka's pessimism was infectious. In what looks to have been a retrospective, Arendt acknowledged that 'something very tangible' might never 'come … out from anything' she had written.[73] Had she come to believe that democracies were unsalvageable and would be remembered as cynical charades? Our chapters on her disappointments suggest that she was not far from concluding as much. But dealing with her disappointment, she left a legacy from which we should draw to work through our disappointments to new beginnings very much in, yet also in conflict with, the world.

How? By challenging conventional political prejudices but also by lowering the horizon of our political expectations. Arendt's reference to oases indicates that the challenges she articulated were intended to develop into a 'more satisfying and dignified' politics – but on a small scale. Arguably, that was precisely her project. She was reconciled to beginning with 'small, well-defined' sections of an otherwise 'unmanageable' mass society.[74] The next chapter finds her thinking along those lines, but we must not forget her assurances that 'constant interchange of talk,' especially discourses that sift plural perspectives, 'unite[s] citizens in a polis,' whereby the 'things of the world, however deeply they may stir' individual interlocutors become 'human' and, Arendt added, 'humane' only when they discuss them together.[75]

## Making Space

Yet how might one make space for Arendt's 'constant interchange[s]'? Her friendliest critics suggest she was cavalier – the less friendly say careless – inasmuch as she provided no clear instructions on governance. Seyla Benhabib thinks nearly all her comments about forgiveness, friendship, freedom, plurality, equality and natality were made in a 'phenomenological register' rather than an 'institutional register.' Benhabib believes Arendt meant to address a 'diminution of the person' and an 'increasing sense of unreality' that attended the loss (or statists' theft) of conventional public realms once conducive to democratic deliberation. When Arendt mentioned realms, she referred to 'space[s] of appearances' where 'the human condition unfolds' as persons 'act, speak, and interact.'[76] We return to locate places for those spaces, to ask, in the chapter that follows, where appetites for new beginnings and for agonistic discourses might be satisfied. But, as this chapter concludes, we must recall her disappointments in order to assess the difficulties and to introduce the need for new spaces. Rehabilitating the old would not do. Arendt was not seeking a truce with sovereign powers but an alternative to sovereignty. She was uninterested in patching up representative democracies and, in effect, she licenses us to reimagine politics from the bottom up. To that end, we will recall why she unambiguously professed that 'the reality of politicians' *Realpolitik*' casts too powerful a spell to overcome with the right adjustment or with the right candidate. What statists and political elites seemed bent on creating, in her time and in ours, was a 'monster that could only urge' the exclusions of unwanted others.[77]

Christian Volk suggests Arendt concentrated on what statists expected of exclusions, namely, that they would stabilise the status quo. She likely sensed statists' fears that the excluded would be radicalised and could destabilise established apparatuses and protocols.[78] Many statists could well have seen pariahs as powder kegs. Unless regimes kept lids tightly fastened, the excluded could offer answers to our question: how do we make space for alternatives to debased democracies as new beginnings rather than as rafts of new regulations? Hence, statists were inclined to depend on the included and indoctrinated instead of on those whom Arendt designated as 'authentically political talents,' prepared in those spaces encouraging them 'to survive the petty maneuvers of party politics with its demands for salesmanship.'[79]

One might imagine massive humiliations would prompt regimes to allow those 'talents' to participate more extensively in deliberations, but Arendt was sceptical. Nation-states that had been reduced in size by military setbacks were prone to revive stories of past glory. She feared Germany had reached that point and feared as well for Jaspers's safety. He angered nationalists by publishing an exposition of their country's leaders reprehensible conduct before and during the war. Predictably, those revelations were unpopular in 1966, as a few unrepentant Auschwitz guards were put on trial. But the danger to Jaspers, she guessed, would come from the 'parasites and profiteers' holding influential positions in government and industry, notwithstanding their prominent roles years before turning 'the extermination of millions' into 'a legal duty.' Making spaces for circulating diverse opinions would be problematic with such statists and many others like them in nations of every size, with histories as different as their climates, working to ensure that conventional public realms were unalterably inhospitable to alternatives.[80]

It bears repeating that Arendt contemplated making such spaces, as her disappointments with conventional democratic politics increased, as Joseph McCarthy's celebrity, for example, had proven how easily an unscrupulous, intimidating impresario's 'fraudulent, stupid and dangerous farce' could capture citizens' attention and create a fresh set of excluded others.[81] Many statists could be subtly divisive. But there was nothing subtle about Senator McCarthy's grandstanding, which illustrated a second trait that, for Arendt, made conventionally democratic public realms impossible to reupholster. To be sure, what she depicted as McCarthy's 'farce' was no slight tremor. It terribly scuffed the reputation of the United States Congress, which has further deteriorated during the twenty-first century, thanks to the polarisation caused by fractious political parties and to the grotesque burlesque that passes as deliberations or interrogations. Parliaments elsewhere have fared little better. But Arendt's consideration of political psychology in her studies of totalitarianism and citizen capture also concentrated on citizens' contributions to the mayhem, specifically, on their exuberance for ideologically freighted displays and for ethnic homogeneity. Looking to impress citizens with their truths, ideologues believed that they were justified misleading citizens, rewriting history until ideology came to represent reality.

Ideological consistency was purchased at the expense of accuracy. Making spaces to challenge statists' preferences for consistency and homogeneity could be dangerous. Nonconformists and ethnic others attested the limits of statists' powers, and statists as well as the elites they served could ill afford to appear anaemic or indecisive. The suppression of dissidents and differences followed. Deviating discourses were embargoed. Arendt chronicled the effects in her *Origins*, then revisited them when she reported on the Eichmann trial for *The New Yorker*, as we now know, and her engrossing conclusions, though they have not yielded consensus, amount to a warning of sorts for twenty-first-century efforts to make space to reimagine citizenship and statesmanship, politics and democracy. She ascertained that statists had learned during the twentieth century that lecturing about and libelling nonconformity were insufficient. Better, therefore, to isolate or extradite critics – and best to cancel them. Citizens came to expect it. Sharing the regime's prejudices, they construed statists' inability to complete such tasks and purge pariahs as an embarrassment. And governments' failures to hide or erase evidence of impotence stokes what Arendt described as citizens' and statists' 'dumb hatred.' The odds against changing or overcoming commonly held, illiberal dispositions in conventional regimes were and are overwhelming.[82] Statists, citizens and elites responsible for the obstinacy of such prejudice were probably that 'something' Ken Krimstein had in mind when he drafted Arendt's lament that 'there is something at work in the world' causing 'people to cannibalise their own freedom, and ... turn other people into landfill.'[83]

For her part, as we shall see, Arendt continued thinking about alternative venues where the actions and discourses she identified as political would be encouraged. She lost faith in the congresses where elected representatives deliberated, as Winfried Thaa reminds us, but not because representatives were removed from their constituents until elections loomed. Arendt's complaint was that elections had become occasions for voters to subordinate public policies to private interests. And, Thaa continues, those interests were economic, self-serving and corrupt. Representative democracy, therefore, was not Arendt's way forward.[84] As we learned, jurors impressed her as impartial and collegial. She averred that the only place a person 'could still function as a citizen' was 'as a member of a jury.'[85] She was keen on seminar conversations. Consoling herself when her reports on Eichmann's trial stirred abusive criticism from friends, she recalled parlour conferences with Karl Jaspers, some of his former and current students and their friends. For four decades, this company, with some additions and subtractions met to talk. Rival opinions were shared and compared. Interlocutors of various ages and attainments were treated as equals. Candour was treasured.[86] Participants amiably clawed their way to clarity, though not necessarily to consensus. To Arendt, the sessions seemed to be what 'was left of *humanitas* in Germany.' Jaspers saw to it, she reported, that their often-changing collective 'live[d] in that luminosity in which oneself and everything one thinks is tested.'[87]

Arendt's references to Jaspers's aura of his circle's 'luminosity,' should not screen us from what she believed was at the epicentre of his work: his devotion to draw philosophy into the give-and-take of human communication and to have it bind persons together and bind them to the pursuit of an authentic existence. That was how discourses and action should work in alternative public spaces. Pursuits of authenticity, though always fertile, were always unfinished, and the 'passion to be subjective' made each inquiry personal. Yet the inquiries Jaspers and Arendt countenanced, unlike those commended by several others heralded as psychologically astute philosophers – she specified those associated with Søren Kierkegaard's preferences – did not suggest solitude was a privileged setting and that persons' passions were elicited by lonely confrontations with ultimacy or mortality.[88] Reason was 'neither entirely within, nor necessarily above' interlocutors but came to life and resided 'between' them. For Arendt, as we noted, making alternative public places required an ardent interest in clearing space for in-betweens (*inter-ests*). Preserving spaces in between was how political deliberations preserved reciprocities. And, in Arendt's judgement, making those spaces in between afforded Jaspers' political psychology and political philosophy, considerable advantages over those of contemporaries who sent students scurrying for subtleties or prowling for truth supposedly hidden behind the political practices and, to them, peripheral to philosophy.[89]

On occasion, during the 1960s, she and Jaspers expressed hope that philosophy in the United States might colonise psychology, acknowledge the drawbacks of deploying abstractions, and concentrate on political communication. Jaspers let on that he would have been pleased to join Arendt in her adopted country but conceded that German history had an indelible effect on his sentiments and sensibility. He was not about to emigrate. Still, he read with interest (yet, he confided, with some difficulty) sections on the founding of the American republic in Arendt's *On Revolution*, which she dedicated to his wife and to him. He seems to have shared her book's excitement about the founders' initiatives, but he detected, as have we, her disappointment with what occurred as their interests in community and in the quality of communications were lost.[90] In Europe, both Arendt and Jaspers had witnessed the perversion of those interests, particularly the ease with which central Europeans fell for the fascists. Her anxiety about 'the trends of modern political life' must have been conditioned by what occurred during the 1930s. She 'shared strong affinities with many intellectuals in the European resistance movements during the Second World War,' as Douglas Klusmeyer notices, but, with the benefits of hindsight and foresight, she also took Nazism's ethnocentrism and insatiable thirst for power as symptomatic of 'a broader, generic crisis of the modern nation-state' 'inextricably bound to the triumph of sovereignty as a flawed foundational model for organizing political life.'[91]

How, then to contest the sovereignty of sovereignty both in political philosophy and in statists' practice and, simultaneously, to repudiate 'theories of the whole' that allegedly made *isms* and ideologies intelligible? Asking precisely those questions is how alternative public spaces could develop, how citizen-statesmen might learn to reimagine citizenship and democracy, sharing opinions as suggestions, 'always experimental and never rigidly fixed.' The optimal result: interlocutors form bonds that sustain collectives' unity without uniformity.[92]

Here, then, is how; admittedly, references to in-betweens are imprecise, therefore, this section about making space, requires greater elaboration before we ask where spaces ought to be made possible. To clarify, then, we ought to note that Arendt's debts to Jaspers were as unambiguous as her summons to discourse, self-disclosure, action and interaction. Equally clear and clarifying, of course, were her disagreements with Heidegger, which are often overstated yet tell against any wavering in her opinion that his *Being and Time*'s ultra-subjectivity had accelerated philosophy's estrangement from politics.[93] She preferred that politically informed and engaged students draw philosophy close to political practice. In that respect, Arendt may have been pleased to hear from Jaspers that students who submitted questions for the colloquy scheduled to follow his lecture in Heidelberg in 1951 inquired only about political psychology. '*Wie anders*,' how different things were! Ideologies no longer seemed to interest students.[94] The behavioural sciences reigned. Many philosophers still dismissed psychology and political interactions as too messy to be rendered rational. Yet Arendt held that their dismissals were only partly responsible for the 'antipolitical element' in 'the modern notion of free will.' Political circumstances contributed. 'Communal life' looked to be unravelling. Yet she held that, if philosophy failed to take political sentiments and political practice seriously, casualties of their neglect would mount. Freedom would be the first.[95] Second would be ordinary citizens' political literacy, the loss of which would enable statists to classify politics even more compellingly as a means to three ends: sovereignty and security along with capital accumulation.[96]

Watching such developments Arendt considered the reimagination of democracy all the more urgent. For 'the ideal of freedom' had already 'ceased to correspond with the liberty to act in concert with others.' It had become associated with 'sovereignty' – with 'independence from others' – and with the prowess, when necessary, 'to prevail against them.' Reconceiving public realms and taking up the challenges just mentioned, contesting theories of the whole as well as denying the sovereignty of sovereignty, afforded citizen-statesmen opportunities to resituate freedom as the alpha and omega of political practice.[97] Arendt liked the way her friend Glenn Gray phrased their tasks. Citizen-statesmen were to inspire 'nomadic thinking,' which ranged widely, 'cherish[ed] practical wisdom' and, therefore, 'liv[ed] close to' and routinely referred critically to a 'miscellany of political practices.'[98]

Arendt's presentations of citizens' challenges, as noted, pose problems for interpreters. Consistency was not her strong suit. Complaints about her reluctance to specify how alternatives might be organized are not unwarranted. But we find her hesitation generative. Collectives were free to find strategies that suited interlocutors as long as they resisted standard statist definitions of citizenship and developed virtues required for, and conditions conducive to, citizen-statesmanship. But most readers would agree that Arendt's disinclination to structure an alternative organisation and her interest in preserving plurality and in reorienting politics from rule to reciprocities (that is, from sovereignty to communication) constituted an indictment of statist salesmanship. Her reading of 'the pathos of parvenus' and her emphasis on the wisdom and 'warmth' of pariahs, may be read as her arraignment of reigning regimes. Arendt was known for the scorn she heaped on statists' pretentious pieties. But she left for others details about the workaround required to make space to begin trading opinions about alternatives.[99]

Yet statists' pretentions were not altogether unfounded. They made things: declarations, contracts and resolutions, which, in liberal democracies, ostensibly made spaces for dissent. Nearly all those spaces, though, became staging areas for the celebration of what they made rather than for critical examinations of the subversion of meaningful dissent. Meanwhile, stoic acceptance of the statists' marketing and of most media's marginalisation of radical innovation that manages to build momentum tend to discourage just that. To make any new spaces, citizen-statesmen face strong headwinds: statists' opposition as well as ordinary citizens' indifference. One reason for the latter, we alleged, is statists' successes convincing constituents of sovereign powers' rectitude. We have already noted Arendt's objections to that conceit, however, to make space for freedom, plurality and natality, her disappointments and criticisms must become those of citizen-statesmen seeking alternatives. Her opposition to the 'instrumentalisation' of politics must become theirs. The principal obstacle on that course, the quasi-canonical status of utility among pragmatists, has become especially difficult to scale because statists, when not relying on absolutes and abstractions, have adapted pragmatism to establish justifications for their political protocols and apparatuses and for promoting the greater good in material terms. But, for Arendt, instrumentalisation defiled politics, having reduced citizens to statistics or poll numbers used to document the popularity of conventional policies and the unpopularity of the unconventional. Statists polled rather than related to citizens.[100]

One might date her distaste for instrumentalism to her work on Augustine. Her dissertation scolded the prelate for having made love for neighbours a way to express one's love for God, which, arguably, reduced neighbours as means to an end.[101] Still, Arendt had done something similar. Other interlocutors constituting the plurality so critical to her redefinition of politics become means to all the objectives she set for her alternative venues, including transformations of citizens into change agents, into citizen-statesmen. Other participants were the means to self-discoveries and self-disclosures, critical for the incubation of virtues as well as for the virtuosity required of them.[102] Notwithstanding her opposition to instrumentalism, Arendt's campaign to reassert the importance of speech and action in public realms looked to make space, to discuss opinions and – more generally – to promote a new concept of politics as means to worthy ends. That one might do the same in the twenty-first century remains possible. Ordinary citizens may yet become catalysts, citizen-statesmen affecting radical reorientation, whereby their neighbours might no longer be content to possess rather than to assess rules that made them 'superfluous.' Apparently, Arendt would have had it so.[103] She anticipated that citizen-statesmen as catalysts required a substantial sense of self (*Einer-seins*). But she also understood that, to acquire it, 'a surrounding presence of others' (*Gemeinschaft*) would be necessary.[104]

This chapter considered how to make space for that surrounding presence as well as what to resist enroute. For Arendt, the formation of that presence or collective was necessary to inspire unsparing criticism of the statists' status quo, to preserve plurality and political freedom and to refine political judgement. All the above depended on how well interlocutors attended to the arts of communication – or, to borrow her words, how well they stayed 'in constant contact with the web of ... words of other[s].'[105] Having done so, they developed greater appreciation for the intersubjective as well as a new grammar and syntax of citizenship, avoiding sanctimonious nonsense and what she called the 'stupid invectives' that contaminated conventional political discourses.[106] Having done so in that surrounding presence of others, citizens filled what she perceived as the need created by a dearth of lively, intermediary, voluntary associations in democratic republics. But another problem she looked to address, commending alternative, unconventional public spaces and agonistic exchanges therein was pundits' appeal to silent majorities. She referred to them as 'inarticulate' and refused to value them as statists did.[107] Silence, for her, was anti-political. Words were important. In Arendt's collectives – and, as citizen-statesmen become effective change agents, in political discourse beyond them – the words 'establish relations [that] create new realities.'[108]

Could this be done in traditional poleis? One might say that Socrates had tried and failed. With Plato's help, Arendt conceived of Socrates endeavouring 'to make everybody around him, and first of all himself, more truthful.' Contrary to his intent, opinions went unexamined; philosophy became irrelevant for politics. Omens for another outcome were inauspicious, Arendt explained, because leading citizens were impatient with 'the inconclusiveness' that remained after Socrates 'destroy[ed]' their truths; when conversations ended without closure, citizens retired, 'not with a more truthful opinion, but with no opinion at all.'[109] Arendt's Socrates floundered where, ideally, citizen-statesmen would succeed, fashioning public spaces where interlocutors embraced what she described as a 'universal relativity.' Athenians wanted secure moorings; she wanted citizens to discover satisfaction, a measure of security and the meaning of freedom found in conversation. Truth was not wired into one opinion exalted over others. 'Within the existential realm,' truth and communication,' she wrote, 'are the same.'[110]

Within that existential realm, what had elsewhere been taken as truths lost their irrefutability, reemerging as opinions, and Arendt made the exchange of opinions (communication) her truth, the mainstay of her politics.[111] With truth demoted, judgement was promoted. Both opinion and judgement held privileged positions whenever she reeled off requirements for political practice. Goodness did not. Arendt endorsed social critic Dwight MacDonald's conclusion that ethical codes, though widely assumed, were 'no longer experienced.'[112] Hence, she could see off the good as long as goodwill was present, particularly, a 'good will to reveal and listen.' Goodness as a 'consistent way of life,' she reckoned, was 'not only impossible' in what passed as politics, but it would be 'destructive,' if ever it survived the myriad attempts to corrupt it. Machiavelli's position was sound: no matter how agile or acrobatic the politically influential were, whatever remained of their goodness would keep them from compromising their integrity to exploit the means necessary to overturn the ways of the wicked.[113] The unprincipled were formidable. In Arendt's journal, one entry puts it bluntly: statists did not care for society, save to dominate it.[114] So, she seemed pleased to see truth and goodness gone. Their disappearance, in effect, licensed her to emphasize the need for opinions, candour and judgement to replace the first – truth – and to foreground friendship and forgiveness to replace standards that statists and elites set for the second – goodness. She imagined that, in the absence of both goodness and truth, what she valued could sustain agonistic discourse and collective action.

It should be clear now how forgiveness and friendships fit with Arendt's focus on natality and how all three fit with strategies to make new spaces and to redefine and to perform politics there. Furthermore, her perception of statists' influence in conventional politics and what we described as citizen capture – statists' stranglehold over the very definition of citizenship – led her to leave as a legacy the insights one might exploit to develop and implement a workaround. Her insights could be characterised as navigational aids. They suggest how to begin anew rather than how to work through the prevailing protocols and apparatuses. They emphasise agency, not structures. True, when asked how to start, Arendt answered evasively, though we can already guess her preference for starting close to the ground, to 'verifiable experience.' She did not expect much would come from battling philosophies or ideologies.

She thought them relatively unimportant, awarding political theories little more than walk-on roles and criticising colleagues who valued them highly. Freedom, for Arendt, survived as the revolutionary spirit that outlasted revolutions and acquired traction in alternative public spaces. It survived there only as long as conversations or colloquies came only to provisional conclusions, then moved on to challenge them.[115] Without challenges, cognitive processes seized up. Thoughts lost their proximity to experiences, which she thought crucial for communication and interpretation to be plural and political. She gave experience and discourse the upper hand; 'that I cannot resolve reality into thought,' she declared, 'becomes the triumph of my potential freedom.'[116]

Access to that reality is required for making spaces for the practice of political virtues and virtuosity, as Arendt defined them. The spaces are not enclaves without exits, because citizen-statesmen have missions extending beyond the collectives where their judgement develops and where freedom, plurality, equality, magnanimity and eagerness to contemplate new beginnings shape political practice. But, ironically, the new practice of politics Arendt envisioned could be construed as anti-democratic. Given statists' and capitalists' effectiveness, most citizens in what she called 'mass society,' preferred entertainment to enlightenment.[117] As disempowering as the outcomes seemed to Arendt (and may seem to us), statists' democracies, after having structured citizens' desires – dictating what they liked and loathed – gave them what they liked. Arendt's 'democratic breakthrough' breaks with typical democratic dogma; she once admitted as much, intimating that making spaces might 'diminish,' as did civil disobedients' caucuses, 'the moral power of the majority.'[118] Still, citizen-statesmen must be prepared to reimagine citizenship as well as democracy in alternative venues and beyond. But first they 'move in[to] a network of errors,' then, with exertion and exhilaration, they make spaces for 'new beginning[s], where beginnings seemed to have become no longer possible.'[119]

## Notes

1. *Denktagebuch*, 804–5.
2. See the marginal marks in Arendt's copy of Stephen Spender, *The Year of the Young* (New York: Random House, 1969), 66; BCSL.
3. Arendt, 'Concern with Politics in Recent European Political Thought,' EU, 428–9.
4. Ibid., 432–3.
5. Arendt, 'Prologue,' RJ, 8.
6. EU, 'Concern with Politics,' 438–9.

7. Ibid., p. 430.
8. Arendt, 'The Great Tradition,' EU, 49; LMW, 45–6.
9. Arendt, 'Concern with Politics,' EU, 431.
10. Ibid., 432; *Denktagebuch*, 195–6 (*Wir haben die Anmassung alles Unbedingten hinter uns lassen*) and Benhabib, *Reluctant Modernism*, 110–11.
11. Arendt, 'The Hungarian Revolution and Totalitarian Imperialism,' TWB, 141.
12. Compare Tobias Albrecht, 'Arendt und Adorno: Ein Forschungsprogramm,' *Zeitschrift für Politikwissenschaft* 31, no. 3 (2021), 496.
13. BPF, 108–9.
14. Bassi, 'Verso una politica del limite,' 81.
15. See Volk, 'Hannah Arendt und die Kritik der Macht,' 519–20, for mistrust (or *Politikerverdrossenheit*).
16. Nordmann, 'Fremdsein,' 203 attributes Arendt's recommendations to her 'pluralistic understanding of truth.'
17. LIOC, 58.
18. Arendt, 'Philosophy and Politics,' 443.
19. BPF, 242.
20. OR, 20–1.
21. CR, 141.
22. HC, 191.
23. PP, 168.
24. HC, 198–9.
25. Jerome Kohn, 'Freedom: The Priority of the Political,' in *The Cambridge Companion to Hannah Arendt*, ed. Dana Villa (Cambridge: Cambridge University Press, 2000), 127.
26. Arendt, 'Religion and Politics,' EU, 377–8.
27. Kei Hiruta, *Hannah Arendt and Isaiah Berlin: Freedom, Politics, and Humanity* (Princeton: Princeton University Press, 2021), 114–15.
28. Ibid., 79–80.
29. For Arendt's take on the 'illusion' of such certainty, see Canovan, *Hannah Arendt*, 149–50.
30. Arendt, 'Religion and Politics,' in EU, 378.
31. See the underscoring in Arendt's copy of Max Scheler, *Philosophische Weltanschaung* (Bonn: Friedrich Cohen, 1929), 51; BCSL.
32. BPF, 266.
33. Anya Topolski, *Arendt, Levinas, and a Politics of Relationality* (London: Rowman and Littlefield, 2015), 49.
34. BPF, 268.
35. Ibid., 264.

36. Arendt, 'The Archimedean Point,' TWB, 412–13.
37. BPF, 273–4.
38. HC, 86.
39. Ibid., 118.
40. Ibid., 143.
41. See OT, 296–7, for conditions that bestow 'a right to have rights.' The discussion of submergence and emergence draws from Passerin d'Entreve, *Political Philosophy*, 46–7.
42. EI, 135–6.
43. MDT, 26–7.
44. Arendt discounted the political aims of Augustine's monumental *City of God* and of his other political treatises, as well as interventions commended and discountenanced in his politically charged correspondence and sermons, some of which are collected and translated in *Augustine: Political Writings*, ed. Robert Dodaro (Cambridge: Cambridge University Press, 2001).
45. HC, 53–4.
46. Ibid., 182–3.
47. Eric Gregory, *Politics and the Order of Love: An Augustinian Ethic of Democratic Citizenship* (Chicago: The University of Chicago Press, 2008), 204. But compare Liesbeth Schoonheim, 'Among Lovers,' *Arendt Studies* 2 (2018), 122–3.
48. See HC, 240–1 and Arendt, 'Philosophy and Politics,' *Social Research* 57, no. 1 (1990), 83. Suzanne Jacobitti, 'Thinking about the Self,' in *Hannah Arendt: Twenty Years Later*, eds. Larry May and Jerome Kohn (Cambridge: MIT Press, 1992), 211 refers to forgiveness as the 'constant mutual release' that would have made Arendt's new politics possible.
49. Arendt, 'Public Rights and Private Interests,' TWB, 511.
50. Arendt, 'Epilogue,' PP, 202.
51. Arendt, 'Krieg und Revolution,' Speeches and Writings File, 1923–1975, 5, 022749; USLC.
52. MDT, 4–6.
53. HC, 184.
54. Ibid., 179–80.
55. Arendt, 'French Political Literature in Exile,' JW, 186–7.
56. MDT, 16.
57. Arendt, 'What is Existential Philosophy,' EU, 177–9.
58. Ibid., 181. Also consult Roger Kimball, 'Heidegger at Freiburg,' *The New Criterion* 3 (June, 1985), 9–13.

59. Arendt, 'What is Existential Philosophy,' EU, 186.
60. Richard J. Bernstein, 'Provocation and Appropriation: Hannah Arendt's Response to Martin Heidegger,' *Constellations* 4, no. 2 (1997), 68–9.
61. Dana Villa, *Arendt and Heidegger: The Fate of the Political* (Princeton: Princeton University, 1995), 213.
62. See her copy of Friedrich Nietzsche's *Der Wille zur Macht: Versuch einer Unwertung aller Werte* (Leipzig: Kröner, 1930), 321; BCSL.
63. LMW, 177–8.
64. Bassi, 'Verso una politica del limite,' 83–4, referring to the location of power *tra gli uomini*, discusses the difference between statists' supposedly misshapen politics and Arendt's alternative.
65. Honig, *Political Theory*, 82.
66. Arendt, 'Understanding and Politics,' EU, 311–13.
67. *Denktagebuch*, 510 (*Lust als politisches Prinzip ist wie Onanie*).
68. HC, 266–7. Also consult Gerome Truc, *Assumer l'humanité: Hannah Arendt, la responsabilité face â la pluralité* (Brussels: Editions de l'université de Bruxelles, 2008), 93.
69. Arendt, 'Understanding and Politics,' EU, 322–3.
70. MDT, 22.
71. CR, 178–9.
72. Arendt, 'The Jew as Pariah: A Hidden Tradition,' JW, 293–4.
73. Arendt, 'Hannah Arendt on Hannah Arendt,' TWB, 468.
74. CR, 180–1. But Kateb, *Arendt*, 41 suggests the reduction in scale is a betrayal of Arendt's project.
75. MDT, 24–5.
76. Seyla Benhabib, *Exile, Statelessness, and Migration: Playing Chess with History from Hannah Arendt to Isaiah Berlin* (Princeton: Princeton University Press, 2018), 110–11.
77. Arendt, 'Dedication to Karl Jaspers,' EU, 215.
78. Consult Volk, 'Hannah Arendt und die Kritik der Macht,' 523.
79. OR, 269–70.
80. Arendt, 'Auschwitz on Trial,' RJ, 227–8.
81. See the *nota bene* in Arendt's copy of Hans Morgenthau, *The Purpose of American Politics* (New York: Knopf, 1960), 145, which reports citizens' approval of McCarthy. BCSL.
82. OT, 301.
83. Ken Krimstein's *The Three Escapes of Hannah Arendt* (New York: Bloomsbury, 2018) is a graphic 'novella' with lines drafted for – rather than drawn from the work of – his protagonist. For the 'lament,' see page 163.

84. Winfried Thaa, *Politisches Handeln: Demokratietheoretische Überlegungen im Anschluss an Hannah Arendt* (Baden-Baden: Nomos, 2011), 165–6 (*wirtschaftlichen Privatinteressen und korrumpieren*).
85. Arendt, 'Public Rights and Private Interests,' TWB, 507.
86. *Briefwechsel*, 545.
87. MDT, 75–6.
88. See Arendt, 'What is Existential Philosophy,' EU, 174 and Arendt, 'Concern with Politics,' 441–2. ('Jaspers, as far as I know, is the only philosopher who ever protested against solitude, to whom solitude appears "pernicious," and who even wants to examine "every thought, every experience, every subject" as to what they signify for communication.')
89. MDT, 93; Arendt, 'Concern with Politics,' EU, 442.
90. For Jaspers's admiration, see Young-Bruehl, *Hannah Arendt*, 403–4.
91. See Douglas Klusmeyer, 'Hannah Arendt's Case for Federalism,' *Publius: The Journal of Federalism* 40, no. 1 (2010), 31, citing Arendt's 'Approaches to "The German Problem",' EU, 106–9.
92. Arendt, 'What is Existential Philosophy,' EU, 183.
93. *Denktagebuch*, 723.
94. *Briefwechsel*, 199.
95. Arendt, 'Freedom and Politics,' TWB, 229.
96. PP, 148.
97. Arendt, 'Freedom and Politics,' TWB, 232.
98. See the underlining in Arendt's copy of J. Glenn Gray, *On Understanding Violence Philosophically* (New York: Harper and Row, 1970), 66; BCSL.
99. For that reputation, consult Jeremy Adelman, 'Pariah: Can Hannah Arendt Help us Rethink our Global Refugee Crisis,' *Wilson Quarterly* 40, no. 2 (2016), 5–6.
100. *Denktagebuch*, 695.
101. *Liebesbegriff*, 69–72.
102. Roger Berkowitz, 'Protest and Democracy: Hannah Arendt and the Foundation of Freedom,' *Stasis* 6, no. 1 (2018), 41–7 rightly places Arendt in the company of several other advocates of a 'politics of … resistance and protest.'
103. LMT, 177.
104. *Denktagebuch*, 263–4.
105. HC, 188.
106. See *Between Friends*, 156, where Arendt referred Mary McCarthy to Norman Mailer's rhetoric.
107. CR, 98.
108. HC, 200–1.

109. PP, 25–6.
110. MDT, 84–5. In 1951, before she articulated this sameness, Arendt selected Jaspers' mantra for the existential as an epigraph for her *Origins of Totalitarianism* (*Weder dem Vergangenen anheimfallen noch dem Zukünftigen. Es kommt darauf an, ganz gegenwärtig zu sein*; it is important to be unencumbered by the past and future and to be wholly in the present). OT, vii.
111. For which, see Ronald Beiner, 'Hannah Arendt on Judgment,' in LKPP, 108–9.
112. Arendt, 'He's All Dwight,' TWB, 401.
113. HC, 77. Thierry Ternisien d'Ouville, *Réinventer la politique avec Hannah Arendt* (Paris: Utopia, 2010), 114 agrees that Arendt was referring to statists' strategies to distract and intimidate citizens.
114. *Denktagebuch*, 23 (*Politik = die Fürsorge für die ganze menschliche Gesellschaft = die Kunst der Herrschaft über alle Menschen*).
115. For which, see König, 'Gründung der Freiheit,' 208.
116. Arendt, 'What is Existential Philosophy,' EU, 184.
117. Arendt, 'Society and Culture,' 284.
118. CR, 96. For 'democratic breakthrough, see Stefan Auer and Kurt Burdach, 'Der verlorene Schatz der Revolution: Hannah Arendt und die Revolutionen 1956, 1968, und 1989,' *Osteuropa* 56, no. 9 (2006), 90.
119. PP, 56–8.

# 4

# Arendt Suggests Where and Where not to Begin

## A Legacy Lost

Hans-Jörg Sigwart suggests that 'deviating discourses' and agonistic deliberations, which were so critical for Arendt, are most likely to originate and to be sustained among scholars relatively isolated from each other. That was not what she intended. She assumed interlocutors needed to share space to maintain the momentum of their enterprise.[1] She regretted conventional political practices made it impossible for citizens to find their 'way by … common sense' in what she once described as a 'topsy turvy world,' where, she brooded, a legacy left by early Americans had been lost and where new beginnings seemed 'no longer possible.' For public forums had become sites for self-assertion.[2] Hence, other places were needed for plurality – places where interlocutors were free to take up the pariahs' perspective to see as outsiders and to offer generative critique. Arendt allowed that seclusion, for some, might be useful to start them thinking circumspectly.[3] But asylums ought to be temporary. Participation in interpersonal performances were necessary if what she called 'the sheer capacity to begin' were to 'inspire' and 'animate' politics in 'public spaces' where opinions are valued more than outcomes. There, citizen-statesmen's versatility and virtuosity mature, demonstrating a 'sheer capacity to begin.'[4]

But Arendt's new beginnings, which restored that lost legacy, interrupted activities statists had come to identify with democracies, creating the problem Lelio La Porta describes as 'a vicious circle.' Democracy, he explains, functions satisfactorily only when citizens have been 'educated in democracy.' To educate them, however, one must already have a democracy in place working properly. La Porta recalls Machiavelli's solution. Absolute monarchs must break that 'circle' to set the conditions for a democratic republic.[5] Yet could guarantees be put in place to ensure that absolutists would accede to democratic reforms? Probably not. For her part, Arendt thought less about leveraging authority than about making space to practise what she redefined as politics. In those alternative spaces (or incubators) optimal conditions were maintained for the development of virtues and the virtuosity that would enable interlocutors not only to practise them but also to present them as more attractive than current, conventional democratic practice. In effect, Arendt became La Porta's absolute monarch. Recovering the legacy of the founders of the democratic republic in the United States, she set conditions for its new beginning.

For Arendt, what made discourses and practices in unconventional collectives attractive and political were interlocutors acutely attendant to each other and to circumstance.[6] We learned to expect that and to presume Heidegger and his devotees disagreed. The latter snubbed her when she lectured at the university in Freiburg in 1961. She told Jaspers, who was unsurprised. To find Arendt fascinating would have amounted to mutiny among her former mentor's mentees. Jaspers scolded his ill-mannered colleagues who returned the disfavour.[7] Yet it would hardly count as an overstatement to say that he and Arendt were seen in some quarters as evangelists for political psychology looking to make clear the importance of the interpersonal for political theory. She believed thinking critically about political circumstance and political communication required clarity. And, as noted, it also required space, for the 'communicability' of experiences and opinions, she added, 'implies a community' of others 'listening and … listened to.'[8]

Yet interlocutors must manage and carefully monitor spaces for listening and learning. For, if what some hear is so riveting, no rival perspectives will seem relevant, and the collectives, for Arendt's purposes, become as dysfunctional as prevailing, conventional spaces where opinions parading as truths and purveyors of those opinions, pretending to be 'in alliance with the secret forces of history,' were nearly insurmountable obstacles.[9] So, places had to be found or created where truthtellers, who imagined they had 'rise[n] above the realm of the plural,' were muzzled. The criticism mentioned earlier – that Arendt's pluralism is somewhat parochial – therefore, is valid, although her intolerance is understandable. It stiffened as a result of her experiences with fascism during the 1930s and 1940s. She professed an inability to name a 'single organization or institution in Germany … that [had] not become involved in criminal transactions.' Oblivious to 'the moral and political meaning of reality,' citizens thought in clichés, which basically undercut thinking and degraded communication.[10]

Nowhere, then, could qualify as what Peter Fuss calls the 'domain of the relative.'[11] Arendt probably never intended to let insensitivity and cliché-littered communication stand as the sole charges against the fascists. Yet Gideon Hausner, who prosecuted Adolf Eichmann in Jerusalem, complained that she compiled excuses for Nazism's inexcusable atrocities and that she presented a bogus, 'bizarre' vindication of their regime.[12] But she was not out to exonerate. She considered fascism's successes in benumbing citizens' consciences reprehensible. Consciences and morality in politics as Arendt defined it, however, were beside the point. They could too easily be turned against her new version or variant of the political. Trying to 'transcend the plural conditions of the public realm' (the 'domain of the relative') consciences internalised absolutes, and wherever absolutes govern thinking and suppress opinion, they discourage agonistic exchanges that prompt the self-discoveries and self-disclosures she advocated.[13] Admittedly, Arendt's redefined politics was discomforting to citizens who were accustomed to conventional politics (and particularly to statists who presided over it). But it also promoted friction within alternative collectives. And to keep the agonistic from becoming antagonistic, she advocated reciprocities there, sustained by friendships and forgiveness, which, along with plurality, freedom and equality resurrected the revolutionary spirit that had generated excitement about new beginnings. On her reading of history, spaces were found (though too soon lost) for all such ingredients in colonial and early republican New England. She recalled that covenants composed to encourage reciprocities (in Arendt's lexicon, 'mutual promises') refortified the revolutionary spirit responsible for what she called the 'world-building capacity' of a new sort of participatory politics, whereby 'binding and promising' were the 'means by which power [was] kept in existence' in spaces and in assemblies where such power to restore 'hope for man in his singularity lay in the fact that not man but men inhabit the earth and form a world between them.'[14]

But the power, to which Arendt referred, had been insufficient in conventional public realms to retain the respect for plurality she found among the continent's colonists. The problem surfaced early in the history of the republic. In her version of its origins, frustrations and deterioration, some founders came to mistrust their more egalitarian colleagues' faith in the intelligence of ordinary citizens. But, to Arendt, the mistrustful were injudicious, and their eventual triumph, betraying the early settlers' participatory politics, left nowhere that the 'binding' and 'promising' could thereafter ennoble political speech and action. Talk of 'rulership' displaced assertions that power 'resides in the people.' The mistrustful favoured 'federalisation' that, in effect, kept in place the feudal prohibitions that had long prevented European serfs and craftspersons from working among the supposedly noble to shape their collective political destinies. 'Federalisation' all but snuffed out what Arendt treasured as 'the eagerness for experimentation' she found among the founders, whose interests in sustaining reciprocities mastered their fear of their fellow citizens. She reported that the passions for a more inclusive democracy of the few she admired complicated the federalists' 'betrayal,' but only for a time. The public realm was soon given over to statists and bureaucrats. Federalists' caution, she protested, guaranteed that the republic they brought forth on their new continent did not offer citizens the quality of political participation that enlarged commoners' minds. Where something different survived, Arendt's history held, a 'novel form of community' elicited and parsed opinions in local councils. Where might that occur again? She knew that some settlers along with a few founders were inspired by trust in a deity that seemed to breed confidence in local conversations but that had far less traction among secular citizens. She became jaded by the indifference to politics that followed. The settlers left a legacy, although not ready-made places for meaningful political performances. So, their heirs must forage for their wheres elsewhere than in their regime's apparatuses.[15]

The legacy was lost. It took Arendt several years to discover that plurality and promises had come to matter little in the public realm of her adopted country. Various, often irreconcilable opinions about politics were aired, then ignored by statists expecting historians to stay in their lanes and out of the government's way. What developed as representative democracy could be presented as the founders' design and rebranded as the American republic's contribution to the progress of popular sovereignty.[16] Statists, as noted, conceived of citizens' conformity as a test for loyalty. Still, on her arrival in 1941, Arendt was tremendously impressed by the Americans' celebration of their freedom. Joseph McCarthy had not yet won over his supply of sycophants; stubborn segregationists had yet to boost the political careers of white supremacists.[17] That lay years ahead when, in 1946, Arendt wrote to Jaspers, apparently confident that the legacy of the founders of the American republic and, before them, of the settlers' assemblies had not been lost. She trusted that the pluriformity of the population in her adopted country and immigrants' ethnic pride might torpedo even well-intentioned efforts to homogenise. She celebrated the uniqueness of what was called the American melting pot, in which some differences did not melt, for most Americans still seemed to her to think that denying the freed to differ from their fellow citizens was unthinkable.[18] Nonetheless, having lived through major changes in central Europe, she may also have suspected that the political climate might chill in North America. Change was constant. Marginal marks in her copy of Daniel Boorstin's *Lost World of Thomas Jefferson* suggest that the former president's judgement, 'no society can make a perpetual … law,' seemed sound to her. One could hardly argue that the prerogatives of what Jefferson called 'the living generation' ought to be privileged.[19] Boorstin's book was published in 1948, and there is no telling how long afterward Arendt flagged that passage. Would it be unfair to say, however, that not long after the turmoil during the early 1950s, her hopes for her 'living generation' surfaced in tension with her disappointments? For the pursuit of what Jefferson called 'public freedom' (and the chances to rekindle the revolutionary spirit) in the country's conventional public realms, as McCarthy and the white supremacists came onstage, must have appeared remote.[20] Furthermore, among the crises swirling about McCarthy, white supremacy and American involvement in the Korean conflict, Arendt witnessed what Dana Villa describes as an increasingly pervasive 'technocratic or bureaucratic approach to government.' To her, it could only have seemed that citizens would only capitalise on their chances for a different sort of democracy – and recover that lost legacy – if some made spaces apart from conventional political forums.[21]

Earlier in the letter to Jaspers that commented on the possibilities for that legacy's recovery, Arendt identified the hurdles that would have to be cleared to achieve it. The highest among them, according to her measurements, were the 'pervasive social conformism' and the 'social oppression' casting shadows across the United States.[22] The contentions that she was relatively oblivious to oppression and that she scarcely noticed (or cared about) racism bear repeating and repudiating here. Five years later, in 1951, her *Origins of Totalitarianism* was published and, as we learned, still occasions criticism that she was insufficiently critical of European imperialists' racism in Africa. What most offends seems to be her sense that skin colour had less to do with the Boers' enslavement of indigenous Africans than the latter's behaviour. Kathryn Gines argues that Arendt all but excused colonial practice in Africa as 'fathomable response[s]' to unfathomable cultures. Susan Owens also complains of Arendt's insensitivity and 'refus[al] to place African American struggles in a colonial frame.'[23]

We have already proposed alternative explanations, yet at this stage we should reemphasise Arendt's reactions to state-sponsored prejudice, because it dissuaded her from presuming that she could promote alternatives to conventional politics unless they occupied spaces free from statists' interference. Moreover, Arendt's general responses to the racism in the United States now seems sibylline, inasmuch as her doubts that politics could offer lasting solutions to social prejudices have proven prescient. Three generations after progressives' legislative wins during the mid-1960s – specifically, explicit statutory protection of voting rights and civil rights – racism remains an all but insurmountable obstacle to achieving both. The courts' injunctions have made some, but not a substantial, difference, largely because justices still have difficulty gauging what equal opportunity and what equality mean in the

Unites States. As migration to Europe makes its countries racially more diverse and politically more divided, the same applies there. But Arendt was clear, if not emphatic, about the importance of equality for interpersonal political performances in the alternative public spaces she commended. Before we address that issue – and rehearse her appeals on behalf of the Palestinians – however, we should also respond to the indictment that was drawn from her *Origins*. For we must not overlook that, writing about colonialism, she deplored officials' accommodations to, and their acceptance of, 'the mob's race standards,' to the disadvantage of indigenous civilisations.[24] Arguably, one ought to expect more from an outspoken proponent of plurality, although an agitated Arendt often warned of treachery and tyranny whenever social conformism became the 'substitute for national homogeneity.' Because she saw it occur so frequently in the 1950s in the United States, she was intent on finding alternative venues to reimagine citizenship, reconceive democracy and recover her adopted country's lost legacy.[25]

Admittedly, even then, she narrowly defined equality. Tackling prejudice and poverty were daunting challenges. But in alternative public realms the small scale of agonistic exchanges increased the possibilities for equalising interlocutors. And, ideally, citizen-statesmen would contribute to overcoming inequitable arrangements based on racial, religious, socio-economic and ethnic differences by advocating conditions that had accomplished such transcendence in alternative venues where plurality and equality were valued. Arendt's aversion to incorporating the objectives of conventional politics – the prioritisation and preservation of sovereignty – into her redefinitions of political performances did not forbid discussions of bias. In effect, plurality as a precondition for politics guaranteed that prejudice would be aired, discussed and overcome within her unconventional political spaces, within her new wheres. Confronting the decline and ostensible discreditation of democracy in public realms as conventionally conceived – in courts, legislatures, cabinets and ministries – could hardly be attempted without confronting inequities prevalent in most republics. Arendt appears to have had no sense of the difficulties involved in devising strategies to manage social forces, but she conceded at one point that the solutions to 'very grave social problems' would be hard to achieve.[26] She was concerned with prejudices, problems and cruelties perpetuated by statists' deception and by political polarisation, which, apparently, both caused and resulted from them. And, as we continue to find that fraud in the twenty-first century, which has come to be called 'fake news,' exacerbates resentments along with the injustices produced by them, we might concur that Arendt has been justifiably blamed for having failed to write more consistently and pointedly about racial prejudice. Yet, that said, she should also be praised for having called conventional political practices and partisanship to account for institutionalising injustices. Of course, there is no telling what might have evolved, had Arendt been successful finding and founding venues where citizens were able to 'interact without compulsion, force and rule over one another, as equals among equals.' Perhaps the freedom, equality and reciprocities they created could have been among – and would still be among or could yet be among – citizen-statesmen's deliverables helping others discover what Arendt professed, namely, that to 'speak in the form of commanding and to hear in the form of obeying' never become 'actual speech and hearing.' Rule, obedience and conformity appear to be political only to those who possess a warped (yet conventional) sense of what is political.[27]

The ample yet growing supply of commentary on democratic decline suggests that Arendt had not exaggerated when she berated statists for directing the affairs of state to benefit loyal elites and, despite intermittent interest in human rights and disinterested public service, citizens have acquiesced. But, generally, her insights and indictments apply to the behaviour of statists, elites and relatively docile citizens in twenty-first-century democracies.[28] Developments tell against prospects for renovating democratic structures without attending directly to the dispositions of the *demos*, to the intelligence and goodwill of citizens. Yet the prospects for that are diminishing as the popularity of virtual communication grows. Many progressives anticipated that democratic regimes would capitalise on the advances in technology to encourage widespread participation in political conversations. Some political scientists looked forward to a revival of direct democracy, inasmuch as information could be piped into citizens' hand-held devices and their preferences could be recorded with clicks and then swiftly tabulated. But statists generally collaborate with impresarios of a more conservative bent in the mainstream media and in social media to humor or to distract or, when it serves their purposes, to arouse citizens. And those arousals ordinarily lead to surges of polarised and polarising speech and action. Impresarios in conventional public realms have come to count on citizens' indifference or complacency rather than honourably and ably to solicit citizens' participation. Statists adapt their sales pitches, which become more sophisticated or crude, as occasions require. They measure their successes in pluralities that conform rather than in the promotion of plurality. Nonconformity is anathema, but when it is unavoidable, the regimes concentrate on building majorities, settling for the lion's share of the electorate every few years. For her part, Arendt discounted counting. She doubted that majorities could be relied upon to work to the advantage of the whole. Majority rule, she generalised, tended 'to end in tyranny.'[29]

Little could be done about such tyrannies, but Arendt was enthusiastic about protests calling attention to oppression, especially since statists, to her mind, were clever at keeping citizens shuttered against unpleasant reality. During the late 1960s and into the 1970s, civil disobedience at American universities encouraged her, as we learned, particularly protests against government efforts to cover up the wreckage in southeast Asia associated with its military interventions. The demonstrators' 'concerted action,' to her mind, challenged 'unjust ordinances' and made spaces where the political practices she admired inspired righteous defiance.[30] Kati Genel refers to the disobedients' demonstrations as 'a concrete manifestation of the Arendtian concept of power as collective action.'[31] Might that lost legacy have passed to them? Arendt imagined demonstrators assembling to plan and coordinate. She imagined their assemblies were specimens of alternative venues where interlocutors initiated what she called 'a sequence to forge a new chain,' making new beginnings.[32] Surely, she knew that prospects for repositioning the universities reliant on government funding and tax exemptions were remote. Conceivably, as Dana Villa speculates, she figured that the disobedients could get otherwise complacent citizens thinking and inspire them to draw out the 'implications of unexamined opinions enthusiastically held' and to correct misperceptions.[33] But such expectations or ambitions might not have been Arendt's. She would undoubtedly have been gratified if citizens who had been dining on lies the government baked into its reports became wiser. Yet she was likely satisfied at the sight of the disobedients who, for a time and from her perch, appeared to have revived the revolutionary spirit she missed elsewhere in the republic.

The disobedients' protests at several universities persisted, but during the intervals between demonstrations most students returned to classes. Teach-ins convened for a day or for a few hours, but the regular curriculum summoned students back to their studies. Longevity of the alternative, unconventional associations, however, mattered less to Arendt than their intensity. As we now know, for her, public realms 'arise' when and where 'acting and speaking together' create in-betweens (*inter-ests*) that invite interlocutors' self-discoveries and self-disclosures as they sift multiple views and contemplate new beginnings.[34] Disobedients who decided to stand down and return to their other responsibilities intermittently still documented what politics might become when faith was restored in 'we the people.' Her interest in that continuity – in a recovery of the lost legacy of the founders of the republic and, before them, of the settlers who gathered in local assemblies, should not to be construed to prevent conversations and collective actions from pausing. Other wheres or elsewheres would assuredly have surfaced as long as the respect for plurality and for the binding power of interlocutors' contributions and friendships lasted.[35]

Longevity, security and sovereignty mattered more, of course, to those orchestrating the affairs of conventional public realms. The price for the first two was too steep for Arendt, who thought citizens willing to pay it with their freedom because statists' salesmanship had been so effective, marketing what she called 'the modern prejudice,' a broad definition of politics popular in the United States and in Europe. It stipulated that politics was 'an ineluctable necessity,' that it had existed 'always and everywhere.' Such claims to ubiquity encouraged citizens' satisfaction with the *status quo*. They were content to be acted upon; they lost any desire to be politically active. Arendt grew disappointed with their lethargy, and, as we discovered, she censured them along with statists for the circulation of dissimulation in conventional politics that she designated a 'desert.' There, salesmanship prevailed over statesmanship. There, political deliberations that counted were conducted along the corridors of power, to which few had access. The results of those conversations were then compressed for consumption at campaign rallies and in campaign rhetoric or at anniversaries commemorating the legacy that had been lost. There, citizens become consumers. But there, in deserts where democracies go to die, but 'where the realm of material necessities ... end,' Arendt located 'oases,' other venues, other wheres.[36]

## A Lesson from Palestine

Where might they be? Arendt looked for places and for models. Thomas Jefferson's elementary republics (or wards) appealed to her, as we know, but they were ideas, not concrete collectives. We learned that she liked what she knew of the early American settlers' town hall meetings in New England. Other models were attached to protests and rebellions, and, for a time she raved about kibbutzniks who had settled in Palestine. Arendt found their 'vehemently anti-nationalist, anti-state sentiments' compelling. They were something of a throwback to the eccentrics, whom she remembered as 'anti-Zionist die-hards.'[37] But the kibbutzniks were different, experimenting with 'new way[s] of family life and child education' and with a 'new form of ownership.' Their settlements, kibbutzim, presented Palestine and, more generally, history with a new beginning. They were unbureaucratic. The kibbutzniks proposed to create 'a society based on justice;' they knew that their experiments were as yet incomplete, but they and Arendt had great expectations. Might they 'keep Zionism within the highest tradition of Judaism' calling for justice and mercy? Might these 'new farmers' (Arendt also referred to them as a 'new elite') turn out to be effective counters to the competitive and acquisitive cultures, which, ever-apprehensive, she described as terribly seductive and destructive of human dignity?[38]

It was too much to ask. Kibbutzniks were soon in the slipstream of Israeli nationalism. Zionist statists defended Israeli territory from neighbouring states in 1948 then rejected proposals for an integrated bi-national regime in Palestine. Zionism, fortified with a determination born of recent immigrants' desperation, which, Arendt explained, developed from Jews' experiences in central and eastern Europe during the 1930s and 1940s, had come to subscribe to the maxim that Might made Right.[39] She expected that victimisation during the previous decades would have inspired greater understanding for outliers, a different mission, an indictment of bigotry, a more inclusive politics. But she was wrong and disappointed. Driven by arguments that made 'sense only in the closed framework of [their] own people and history,' Zionists became obsessed with identifying their safety and the future of their faith with what Arendt took to be a skewed, ultra-nationalist view of sovereignty. Zionist statists claimed national defence as a justification for their project, which she construed as the homogenisation of their homeland as well as documentation that Zionism had 'outgrown the sporadic sinfulness' of a benign nationalism and had entered a 'new stage of criminality.'[40] The Zionist statists turned the kibbutzim ('the most magnificent part' of the Israeli experiment) into armed camps, proving Palestine's political climate routinely suffered from extremist nationalist 'aggressiveness,' 'tribal thinking' and 'fanaticism.'[41] Behind all three, she perceived fear and arrogance that predated Nazi atrocities, the same fear and arrogance that moved the late nineteenth-century Austro-Hungarian Zionist, Theodor Herzl to declare he was prepared to deal with devils (authorities in 'nationality-states based on oppression') to marshal support for an as-yet-unformed Jewish state. Arendt argued that more than fifty years before the state of Israel realized Herzl's dream, he and fellow Zionists had forfeited Jews' 'solidarity with other oppressed peoples.' Zionism's strident, sectarian rhetoric preyed on Jewish citizens' fears, describing Palestinian Arab neighbours as feudal and feral. She accused Zionism of transforming the kibbutzniks, along with other Israelis, from pioneers and pariahs into persecutors.[42]

Arendt's assessments of the kibbutzniks' innovations and fate are obviously relevant to this chapter's efforts to locate places she would have found suitable as alternative public spaces. Kibbutzniks appeared to have reimagined democracy. For a time, they were free from statists' influence. For a time, the one weapon in statists' arsenals that was nearly always successful in pitting civic solidarity against reciprocities that ecumenically embraced differences seemed to her ineffective in the kibbutzim. But statists' successes were attributable to their skills at selling national solidarity, not necessarily to their intelligence but to their determination or will. And the latter, in Arendt's estimation, overpowered the resistance of her 'new farmers' or 'new elite.' Her aforementioned discussion of Scotus' efforts to reconcile necessity and freedom may shed some light on Zionist statists' conquest. Arendt assessed differences between will and intellect, much as Scotus had, concluding that intellects were powerless when confronted with steely, tenacious determination. Intellect was circumspect, deliberate, slow to evaluate plausible options. But, overwhelmed by statists' (or, in this application, the Zionists') will to power, intellects were tempted to defer to the will and to 'fabricate a story to make the data fall into place.' Intellect supplied necessity to the direction that will intended to take. Rather than direct or restrain the will, intelligence or analysis capitulated and furnished nationalists with the rationale for their pursuit of power. Long before she cited Scotus, she witnessed the wedding of will to intellect that led to the kibbutzniks' capture. Zionist statists overwhelmed them with what she called an 'assumption of necessity,' a mythical manifest destiny, a return home, a divinely choreographed reacquisition of a homeland. Until Zionist statists added to their imaginary an inevitability, their will to power, Arendt added, their 'story lack[ed] all coherence.'[43]

Having imported coherence, Israeli statists managed to capture kibbutzniks, much as statists elsewhere fed citizens a steady diet of promises and prospects that made it difficult for citizen-statesmen to attract them to democratic practices, as Arendt defined them. Statists 'dissolve[ed] every statement of fact into a declaration of purpose' that served their purposes and reinforced 'the spell of infallibility' enabling them to rule and to rule out nonconformity.[44] But infallibility and inevitability were foreign to Arendt's take on politics. Claims to both admittedly captivated and captured citizens, yet claims of that sort were viruses that eventually destroy the health of any body politic. She held that Zionist statists endangered the homeland they were devoted to protecting. The Zionists' embrace suffocated what the pioneering, revolutionary spirit of the kibbutzim – Israel's alternative public spaces – and, she warned, the Zionists' triumph – the triumph of the will – inched Israel and specifically Jewish nationalism dangerously close to 'racist chauvinism' and the fanaticism that 'screen[ed]' all *isms* 'against reality.'[45]

Arendt's repudiation of Zionism was cut from the same cloth as her condemnations of other statists' exploitations of what she called a 'presumed sameness' to problematise the plurality necessary for meaningful political discourse.[46] Before she arrived in the United States in 1941, she worked alongside the Zionists in Germany and France. She recalled that their objections to prejudice had been strangely muted, yet they seemed sympathetic to others' ordeals. But when parts of Palestine became the new state of Israel and when statists appealed to Jews in diaspora to approve militant Zionist nationalism, she was surprised by the many favourable responses that confused patriotism with religious piety. She was startled by the speed with which a large fraction of the faithful abroad became territorial, desperate for coreligionists to occupy and defend a stretch of land they had never seen. She learned that what mattered to Jews in the United States 'was really Israel.' It became their 'main thing.' 'I was a Zionist' when Zionists were stateless pariahs, she confided, but, even then, she continued, her Jewish coworkers were 'much more nationalistic than I ever was.' Israel's battles against its Arab neighbours and Israeli Jews' tensions with Muslims within the new state of Israel inspired Jews elsewhere to embrace Zionist nationalism with what Arendt characterised as 'the fervor of new converts.'[47]

By the early 1950s, she stopped referring to the kibbutzim. Yet thinking of the Kibbutzniks' capture probably put her in a foul mood. Had it not been for a cobweb of circumstances – the Israeli regime's need to rehabilitate its reputation after it participated in attacks on Egypt during the Suez crisis in 1956, the new nation's dispossession of Arab Palestinians and its shabby record protecting the rights of those remaining within its borders – Arendt presumably would have been inattentive to the Middle East, despite news media constantly combing through the evidence of conflict in what was, to some, a promised homeland and, to others, stolen property. But Israeli officials thought it timely to recall Nazi atrocities and to remind the world of the *raison d'être* for the sanctuary state over which they presided. Looking to reclaim the nearly unqualified support that their new state enjoyed after the European Jews' victimisation, the authorities ordered one of the notorious victimisers, Adolf Eichmann, kidnapped from Argentina and brought to Jerusalem. Arendt was assigned by *The New Yorker* magazine to cover his trial. Subsequently, she described it as a 'show trial.'[48] And, unsurprisingly, her characterisation angered not only Zionists but, as we now know, her friends who complained that she was insufficiently sympathetic with the victims of the Shoah and insufficiently outraged by the defendant.[49] The issues and identities at stake and the intensity with which partisans staked claims at the time foreshadowed the intensity and intractability of early twenty-first century belligerents in the Middle East. The lesson from Palestine was, and still is, that places within conventional political spaces will not be receptive to the reimagination of citizenship and the reinvention of democracy. Statists manage affairs and citizens in their public realms to serve interests of the state, which correspond with their own interests. Where, then? To contemplate, re-evaluate and reimagine, we must carve out the spaces to practise unconventional, Arendtian politics.

## Pariahs' Perspectives

Elisabeth Young-Bruehl refers to Arendt as 'a pariah within the *Pariahvolk*,' although 'within' suggests an embedded presence – a person who seems stuck.[50] Plus, 'within' does not suggest estrangement. 'Among' corresponds more closely to Arendt's sense that the 'cultural value' of the pariahs' arts as well as their political passions 'transcend[ed] the boundaries of [their] own nationality.' She was pleased that, with secularisation, possibilities existed in the United States for Jews to cross frontiers without abandoning Jewish culture or their pariah status. In 1947, in an essay on pariahs' 'cultural atmosphere,' she celebrated what she took as their transcendence. But the next year, soon after the state of Israel was recognised, she regretted that the Zionists so effectively pitched nationalism to Jews in diaspora that their secularisation and transcendence gave way to what has come to be called 'identity politics.'[51]

The consequences were unfortunate. But, with secularisation and transcendence, came some measure of relief from the race hatred that pariahs experienced for centuries. Even before she chronicled the antipathy during the nineteenth and early twentieth centuries in her *Origins of Totalitarianism*, she probed an earlier Jewish response to marginalisation (*Draussenstehen*).[52] After finishing her doctoral dissertation on Augustine in 1929, she prepared to submit as her *Habilitationsschrift* a study of salonnière Rahel Varnhagen, whose choices during the late eighteenth and early nineteenth centuries illustrated both pariah virtues and the pressure to assimilate (as parvenus) to host cultures. Varnhagen's correspondence revealed her wish to overcome prejudice and to fit in, but her conduct attested her readiness to create alternative spaces, her salons, where the learned could become critics of cultural accommodation. The Varnhagen study, as we shall soon see, had much to say about persons who accepted or even welcomed their status as outcasts, about others who did not, and about Arendt's protagonist's struggle with the choice. Years later, however, Arendt came across splendid specimens of the pariahs' virtues and trotted out the cinema personae created by Charlie Chaplin. They always seemed to be 'clashing with the law' but managed to 'slip through' and to exhibit what Arendt featured as an incompatibility between the law's formidable presence and pariahs' compulsive friskiness, ingenuity and innocence, enabling them – unrepentant – 'to get away with a great deal.'[53]

That 'great deal,' in theory, exceeded expectations imposed on and accepted by citizens who chose to assimilate. Chaplin's characters' nonconformity and non-compliance were emblematic statements for Arendt. They conveyed possibilities for pariah dissent, which signalled the survival of the revolutionary spirit she so admired. After much of Palestine became the state of Israel with 'openly discriminatory' edicts enforced there against Arabs, she thought Zionism bereft of pariah virtues. And what she heralded as the 'strong feeling of a definite beginning' found no further expression.[54] When she praised Chaplin's characters' knack for 'getting away with a great deal,' she had no intention of including persecution in that 'great deal.' Defiance and innovation were on the list, as we intimated earlier, so, John Lechte and Saul Newman, were right to pair Arendt with contemporary cultural critic Giorgio Agamben, for the latter two cast pariahs as innovators, whose 'exodus' from conventional political cultures constituted 'an engaged withdrawal' that eventually ushered in 'new form[s] of life.'[55] Pariahs' positions 'on the fringe' or even farther beyond the pale, in effect, amounted to a witness against conformity and for freedom. Chaplin donned a jester's cap to lay claim to the pariahs' prerogative to bear witness to the inadequacies of the normative – to both politics and policing. Arendt believed others on the 'fringe,' in their alternative wheres, were also positioned to cultivate freedoms, equality and respect for plurality that parvenus and assimilated others envied. Pariahs on the 'fringe' she added, cultivate an acute sensitivity to injustice as part of the preparation of citizen-statesmen that served them well upon their return to become agents or catalysts looking to make a difference in the desert.[56]

Conditions in alternative political spaces, as Arendt envisioned them, were dramatically different from those that, to her mind, made conventional democracies such deserts. The pariah collectives could conceivably inspire the 'broadmindedness' and forbearance that, to her mind, religions had preached but seldom practised.[57] But the reasons why such benevolent dispositions could not be transferred from the pariahs' fringes to the centre had little to do with truculent theologians and imams defending rival confessions of faith. The desert was a desert, for Arendt, because statists and elites had a lock on conventional political cultures. Anyone bent on reimagining citizenship and democracy would have to reckon with that. Hence, we should add another attribute Arendt found among pariahs and would have had citizen-statesmen cultivate as they prepared to coach others to overcome the daunting challenge of incorporating the pariahs' perspective, sensitivities and readiness for new beginnings into their redefinitions of democratic politics. And challenges have become especially complicated in the twenty first-century, when what one pseudonymous pundit calls 'piñata politics' prevails, that is, when, with or without statists orchestrating their expressions of anger or envy, citizens vent and vote their rage.[58]

Confronting rage called for courage. While reflecting on her internment in Vichy controlled France, Arendt recalled her fellow internees' fortitude. What she called their 'violent courage' developed and was displayed, she said, 'next door to despair.'[59] She admitted that the wardens' cruelty had been less virulent than what Jews experienced to the east. The French 'home-grown fascists' were unlike their German masters. In France, delirious, rabid antisemites, she went on, were taken as 'charlatan[s] and crackpot[s]' looking to persuade citizens that 'extermination of the Jews would' resolve all their problems.[60] Still, when Vichy and senescent Marshall Pétain bowed to the Germans' will and pressed on more ruthlessly with persecution, one can hardly exaggerate the courage of the Jews remaining. But, by then, Arendt had escaped. Years later, safely in the United States, she wrote James Baldwin, the acclaimed novelist and civil rights activist, alluding to the 'proud possessions' of pariah communities. Prejudice and persecution, she suggested, were the causes; courage and the other pariah attributes were the effects. Arendt, though, included a caveat: the pariahs' courage, forbearance and sensitivity to injustice appeared 'never [to] survive [their] hour of liberation,' which returned them to the desert and desiccated their enthusiasms for new beginnings.[61]

Might such returns temper citizen-statesmen's commitments and limit their influence? Arendt's letter to Baldwin suggests as much. It displayed her disenchantment with conventional political cultures intertwined with her dwindling hope that the values and virtuosity she would have had alternative public realms incubate might make an other-than-personal difference. We shall have to address that odd coupling and tension between hope and despair shortly, for many Arendtians, although they interpret her politics differently from the way we have, believe it has a bearing on the restructuring of political culture. If it had none, the virtues that she promoted – ranging from plurality to equality, freedom, forgiveness and natality – would simply be niche phenomena, suitable only for small sectarian collectives. Elsewhere, little would change.

But Ned O'Gorman thinks representative democracies can be rehabilitated following Arendt's prescriptions, though without alternative poleis.[62] The obstacle, he says, is citizens' helplessness. They feel powerless, having ceded their authority to the elites. And the dominance of technology contributes to their sense of obsolescence, sparing them the responsibility of making something of history.[63] O'Gorman's remedy: an Arendtian makeover of the public realm. 'What [her] politics calls for,' is 'debating and discussing matters as equals.' True, but getting there and restoring citizens' political agency require statesmanship that, as we argue, can only develop apart from, and in opposition to, statists' apparatuses and protocols.[64] And, contemplating that development and the places from which citizen-statesmanship might emerge, Arendt expected difficulties, which O'Gorman minimises. Statists were threatened by citizens' political agency. Parvenus, 'ready to pay any price in order to be accepted by society,' served statists' purposes quite well. But pariahs, set apart for a spell and emerging as citizen-statesmen, refused to cede custody of their consciences to officials in government and commerce, who, Arendt explained, exploited parvenus 'inferiority complexes' and 'political stupidity.'[65]

Unlike Arendt, O'Gorman underestimates statists' resourcefulness and tyrannies' efficiencies. His bibliography suggests Arendt's study of Varnhagen and early modern salon culture might not have figured in his inventory of Arendt's political preferences. Yet the Varnhagen volume documents how difficult it had been to maintain 'space[s] of persuasion' while others – in the salonnière's' time, nationalists – claimed the sole right to persuade citizens and, should that fail, to compel them to comply with the regimes' sense of civic responsibility. Varnhagen created an alternative space, to which Arendt referred as something of a refuge, 'a carefree and lively other world' set apart from the 'mass cultures.'[66] The salonnière created a 'center for cultivated social intercourse' where interlocutors experienced 'an unbelievable freedom from all conventions.'[67] They were 'a stark contrast' to that other world, where, according to Varnhagen, perspectives were 'poisoned.'[68] No doubt, many who had visited her salon and those of others accepted the validity of much of that other world's wisdom. They scavenged for miscellaneous evidence that augured well for its improvement. Varnhagen, however, urged those closest to her to reconsider their affections for the orderly and the precise that tethered them to that other world, to embrace uncertainty and to luxuriate in 'the liveliness of life' (*lebendige Spiel des Lebens*).[69]

But Varnhagen was tugged back to that 'other world' and intermittently tried to accommodate expectations of the arbiters of social orthodoxy. She married well and converted to Christianity. Arendt finished the initial draft of her study of Varnhagen by 1933, when, conceivably, she was considering accommodation. Conversion was not on the docket. Nonetheless, as a Jewess on the threshold of an academic career, she was likely looking to negotiate between two distinct worlds. Twenty years later, resettled in the United States, an émigré, outsider and sought-after lecturer, she was both pariah and parvenu, though the former, as noted, shaped many of her ideas about politics. But she then contemplated publishing her Varnhagen. She wrote to Jaspers for advice. He discouraged her; the narrative's remarks on nonconformity, he thought, would not appeal to publishers or readers in the 1950s.[70] At first, she agreed, but her reply insinuated that, if she had circulated the salonnière's dilemmas, its criticisms of Jews' assimilation during the 1930s could have retarded the development of Zionism's strident demands for conformity. No doubt, Arendt overstated the likely influence of biography. In any event, by the 1950s, she figured that Zionist totalitarianism was entrenched.[71] Some years later, though, she reconsidered publication, revised her Varnhagen and saw to its nearly simultaneous appearances in German and English. Perhaps she suspected that readers might benefit from learning about Varnhagen's 'basic method' of juxtaposing pariah and parvenu, 'correcting' the latter's conformity with pariahs' virtues and 'standards.' Did publication also signal Arendt's accelerated search for models for alternative public spaces?[72] She represented her study of the salonnière and her salon as a psychological supplement to criticisms of assimilation registered in her *Origins of Totalitarianism*. Both her Varnhagen and *Origins* discountenanced the conventional. Parvenus, she declared, traded too much for the respectability that rendered them deaf to derision and antisemitism. During the early twentieth century, therefore, parvenus were utterly unprepared for persecution.[73]

Arendt's study quoted Varnhagen extensively, allowing its protagonist to distinguish between pariah and parvenu and to reveal how close she came to assimilating while attempting to retain her 'pariah qualities.'[74] The salonnière berated parvenus, including herself, for having imagined they had 'arrived.' But she hosted the salon for years as a refuge of sorts where guests discussed conventional culture. One could make a case that her gathering was a forerunner of Arendt's alternative public spaces – her oases. Salons and oases were 'spaces of sociability,' Seyla Benhabib says, 'social experiments' where the interlocutors' desires 'for difference and distinctness could assume an intersubjective reality.'[75]

But most salons had short shelf lives. Collective expressions of 'pariah standards' were precarious. Even if alternative spaces were fated to be fugitive, however, values and skills acquired there by citizen-statesmen were sustainable. Notwithstanding statists' dominance, citizen-statesmen might find places to practise politics according to Arendt's specifications, but impermanence troubles progressives, who favour constitutions suggesting that prerogatives and rights inscribed therein are imperishable. Yet declarations referring to natural laws or to a donor deity only seem to provide hefty assurances of permanence by pairing sanctity with sovereignty and stability.[76] Arendt knew history attested such deference to deities. After all, her founders of the democratic republic in the United States embellished, pronouncing their citizens 'endowed by their creator with inalienable rights.'[77] But what she deplored were statists deployment of absolutes to defend sovereign powers' calls for ethnic, racial or religious homogeneity or for ideological conformity. She imagined that American citizens would 'annul' their Constitution before they let it be interpreted as a recipe for repression.[78] But relatively recent history proves her confidence misplaced. What is significant for our purposes, however, is that her respect for constitutions and other political 'origin' documents went only so far. Far more dependable were interpersonal relationships established through discourses and actions. They were impermanent, yet they created and sustained for a time an alternative politics that promoted plurality, equality and freedom. Still, citizens instructed by statists were likelier to see unconventional collectives as sideshows – probably as nuisances – far removed from 'the great deeds and words of which mortals are capable' because they do not 'do violence to nature.'[79] Arendt's cynical statement thinly disguises her dissatisfaction with historians who relished and reported such disturbances. To set her 'spaces of sociability' and version of politics against what 'made glory possible' in most citizens' imaginations, therefore, she would have to plane against the grain.[80]

Rosa Luxemburg likely had a profound effect on Arendt's disposition, as Ruggero D'Alessandro suggests, alleging that, for both, the success of forthcoming revolutions depended upon creating space for freedoms unimaginable to citizens caught or captured by statists.[81] But the trajectories of freedom and new beginnings that follow, as we remarked, are unforeseeable. As interlocutors recalibrate their positions in light of others' opinions – then assess those opinions alongside their own, digressions and reversals were likely. Arendt's unconventional politics relied upon citizens' friendships, forgiveness and statesmanship to weather whatever crises a back-forth-and-against occasioned. Ideally, agonistic discourses and exchanges never allowed disagreements to develop and cause festering resentments. But statists have an advantage. They rely on intimidation and salesmanship. If the former fails to ensure citizens' acquiescence, they count on a profusion of promises, assurances, spectacles, evasions and distractions. They use the proverbial sticks and carrots. The latter constitutes a charm offensive resourced to continue until citizens' disinterest returns.[82]

To counter, Arendt lined up examples of citizen interest in governance and empowerment. But whereas she was confident listing virtues that would-be citizen-statemen ought to acquire and promote, she could only be tentative locating compelling concrete alternative collectives. Her exposition of workers' councils' dedication to agonistic conversations, as we discovered, was unconvincing. She assumed the civil disobedients got resistance right but had no information about conferences preceding or following their demonstrations. The protestors at some universities were not known to have been keen on plurality and only intermittently invited dissident opinions before letting an outspoken colleague take the gavel and prepare the next intervention. And Arendt's introduction of Hungarian insurgents' cells, as noted, neglected to emphasise the statists' manipulation of factions that ultimately tore the fabric of the new order that appeared to be emerging. Her *Origins of Totalitarianism* offered yet another problematic example, a set of eccentric exiles from polite society in South Africa. She referred to them as Bohemians. To her, they seemed superb specimens of the 'superfluous men' and women any totalitarian regime preferred to lively, engaged citizens. Superfluous Bohemians were pariahs facing grim conditions, digging for gold on the frontier. Nonetheless, on their own terms, they made 'their way back into a world of fellowship and purpose,' Arendt claimed, underscoring their dignity and assuming that their 'countersociet[ies]' somehow became 'witnesses' to the 'absurdity of [other] human institutions.' But she proffered no evidence of their fondness for democratic practice or for their preferences for plurality.[83]

Given her interest in her 'energetic' Bohemians' countersocieties, it is surprising, that Arendt missed the chance to introduce into *Origins* (or in later discussions of American experiments with democracy) Frederick Jackson Turner's frontier thesis. It featured pioneer protagonists' individualism but also their collaboration, what Turner described as 'the steady influence of democracy. Moreover, with every wilderness they settled, they shied from statists' meddling.[84] But Arendt was content to probe democratic impulses among Athenians, Romans, bohemians and founders of the American republic. Did she think Turner's pioneers too individualistic? Or did she suspect that their interests, pressed with a sense of urgency, would be incompatible with an 'interest [in] the common world'?[85] Or perhaps deliberations on the American frontier seemed apolitical to her because they placed ends and needs – safety, timbering, farming, herding and housing – above communication. She may have classified such necessities as social, assuming they would eclipse the importance of interpersonal political discourses and performances and, therefore, impair interlocutors' abilities to create 'nonspurious public [and political] spaces.'[86]

Turner's frontier democracies solved problems. Arendt's democracies processed people. She wanted to prepare them to keep alive the revolutionary spirit and a thirst for new beginnings. 'Council systems,' she believed, came closest to preserving the 'revolutionary tenet' that held 'all inhabitants of a given territory were entitled to be interlocutors in a political realm.' With some justification, statists would object that all who are entitled to inhabit were not capable of deliberating productively. But as argued here, statists were and are largely responsible for that incapacity. Arendt kept looking to refute them, misappropriating collectives or councils, as we have suggested, though without doubting that 'spontaneous organs of action and order,' could reorganise political and social life, 'contradict[ing] sharply the old adage [that] … "natural" inclinations of a people left without [the] constraint of its government' had every chance of incorruptibly advancing citizens' and civilisation's interests.[87]

That was Arendt's point. Her wheres are instructive, but workers' councils, revolutionaries' cells and South African Bohemians gave her less than she thought. Her idealistic rendering of colonial New England townhall meetings may be the best specimen on offer. She generously ladled out praise for the assemblies, which, she said, 'regenerated' direct democracy. She thought the federalists and other founders of the republic blundered when they decided to establish representative government as the new normal for their new nation.[88] Those earlier settlers' conferences and consultations, during which freedom was synonymous with politics (rather than with results political cultures and conversations were intended to achieve) proved that the Athenians' experiments with direct democracy had taken root on American soil. Those local New England councils, according to Arendt's reconstruction, cleared space where persons 'manage … affairs by speaking with and persuading one another.'[89] In her account of clearings of that sort, James Madison played the villain. Knowing that citizens were 'men not angels,' he volunteered reservations about incorporating local councils in the founders' final designs. In effect, she lamented, he gave government over to 'the state.' From there, statists materialised, determining 'provisions for human existence.'[90] Citizens of the republic, deprived of their where, 'constituted by acting together,' 'retreat[ed] into their freedom of thought.'[91]

## Oases

It was no easy task to recall citizens in Arendt's time. And the recall was made more difficult because she would have them adapt a pariah's perspective to criticise precisely the conditions that led to Madison's reservations about direct participation. Many of her scholarly predecessors and colleagues studying philosophy, in her estimation, were no help. They preferred to stay clear of politics and political theory. But Friedrich Nietzsche, to a point, was useful. He ridiculed the conceit that in his time – and, Arendt noticed, in hers – socialisation and secularisation furthered citizens' interests far more than the superstitions of earlier ages. Arendt quoted Nietzsche in her journal, mocking along with him the confidence that modernity had 'conquered' fantasy.[92] For the fantasies that were marketed by statists made conventional public realms inhospitable to nonconformity and inimical, in most instances, to plurality and to citizens' freedom. Statist salesmanship along with political practices they sold made those realms deserts where the longing to rule and to be ruled was the rule.[93] Oases were places to prepare citizen-statesmen, agents of change, purveyors of new beginnings. But, for their resistance to statist 'frame[s] of reference' to be formidable and for their imaginary to compete with statists' interpretations of reality and of *Realpolitik* in what she assumed would be a 'far from untroubled' future, Arendt advised that proponents of plurality, freedom, equality, forgiveness and new beginnings should consult some of their radical forbears: Jefferson, Rosa Luxemburg and the early Brecht.[94]

Statists' counsel was (and is) different. Arendt found those of her generation guilty of having conspired with the media and marketplace to ensure that citizens 'lose the faculty to judge' and 'think ... something [is] wrong with [them] if [they] cannot live under the conditions of desert life.' The regime's ruses were largely successful. Citizens adjusted, assuming the fashionable was factual. And, Arendt went on, statists took 'away our only hope, namely that we, who are not of the desert though we live in it, are able to transform it.'[95] Her new politics was something of an escape from the pressures to adjust. She wrote about oases and about pariahs' perspectives distinct from, and defiant of, political conditions in the desert. Perhaps the dichotomy between oasis and desert came to mind as Arendt contemplated the kibbutzniks before so many of them became impassioned Zionists. Or possibly, she politicised the dichotomy after having read her friend Mary McCarthy's novel, *The Oasis*, which she said she liked.[96] Or, conceivably, the term 'oasis' came to mind when she confronted Augustine's remarks about Christians' part as pariahs in late Roman, residually pagan society. Arendt's doctoral dissertation on his understandings of love concluded that he had attributed his congregations' alienation (*Entfremdung*) to their place and purpose, *neben und gegen*, alongside and opposed to the dominant political culture with its emphasis on domination. Whatever the dichotomy's provenance, 'oasis' and 'desert' tell Arendt's readers that they ought to make space for new beginnings where the influence of conventional politics and of nationalism is negligible.[97]

Yet one of the best-informed Arendt scholars, Jerome Kohn, disagrees. He suggests that her statements about oases refer to psychic retreats. He infers that estrangement tended to drive pariahs inward. Arendt's oases, he says, can be found there. Kohn allows that Arendt's signature interests in, and her advocacy of, freedom as well as her criticisms of political practices in public realms led her to introduce alternative 'web[s] of relations.' But he believes her oases were never political and that what she alluded to as 'activities' at those oases would 'not require the presence of others.'[98] Contrary to Kohn, Judith Butler explains that Arendt's emphasis on *inter-ests* – on spaces in-between, 'space[s] of appearance' – required the presence of others. They were places for 'alliances' and 'plural action.'[99] We learned that introspection was also important for Arendt. We may presume that it preceded what Butler calls plural action. Introspection, then, became an 'internal check' that was undertaken to counter interlocutors' temptations either to be complicit in, or to be seduced by, statists' endeavours – or to remain reclusive. Resistance to the latter (to seclusion) was critical, Butler asserted, inasmuch as Arendt expected performative politics to ensure that citizens enroute to citizen-statesmanship join 'others in a ... struggle for social transformation.'[100]

Neither Kohn's psychic retreat nor Butler's emphasis on 'political agency' follows Augustine's script.[101] But Arendt did. She understood the apostle Paul's exhortations placed great importance on the presence of others (*eine so grosse Rolle*).[102] The faithful must pay forward God's love for creation by loving others. When she wrote about Augustine's interpretations of this obligation, Arendt foreshadowed her commitment to define natality in terms of collectives. The faithful were to see themselves as pariahs passing through this world as pilgrims creating alternative spaces with and for one another (*Miteinander und Füreinander*), alternatives to worldly citizens' selfish pursuit of glory.[103] Arendt set much of Augustine aside. He had stressed compassion; she feared compassion led to fusions that would obliterate the spaces in between interlocutors. What Augustine advocated seemed too otherworldly to be taken as models for her collectives. She was only partly right, however, to pounce on the prelate as the principal source for 'the well-known antagonism between early Christianity and the *res publica*.' In effect, it made political practice irrelevant for theology. But she followed him partway by commending alternatives to prevalent public realms, although she was convinced Augustine would never have warmed to her mission to reimagine citizenship there.[104]

But she returned to Augustine late in her career, contemplated revising her dissertation for publication in an English translation yet never completed the work. Nonetheless, she hauled a passage from his treatise on free choice into essays and lectures that appeared as her *Life of the Mind*. She caught Augustine acidly addressing contemporaries, who had censured their deity for having created an imperfect world. His rejoinder: even the most brackish and barren parts of the world (*salsissimam et infecundissimam*) were just as they ought to be. Creation and redemption, the culmination of God's craftsmanship, were perfectly ordered.[105] In what Arendt designated a 'strictly Christian context,' that response made sense, but she questioned how deserts passing as conventional public realms where creatures had little or no experience of freedom or of political responsibility could have been ordered by a benevolent deity? To be sure, Arendt's invectives against deceit in politics-as-usual are reminiscent of Augustine's complaints about the lust for domination common in late Roman political culture. Late in her career, she even conceded that he had not coached withdrawal from the world, that he might supply 'refutation[s]' to Stoics in her time who had grown disinterested in public affairs. Arendt was stretching the point, yet she reprised and redeployed one challenge that Augustine used strategically to silence his critics, and she turned it into an imperative that starts to address the question why one must locate (or to steal her term, must 'grow') alternative wheres. Augustine taunted and Arendt echoed: 'if you dare to find fault with a desert, do so only because you can compare it with what is better.'[106]

But we have discovered how hard it is to find that something better with which to compare conventional public cultures where statists' and elites' interests determine for citizens what citizenship means. The conclusion of Arendt's study *On Revolution* introduced readers to René Char as he was pondering that difficulty. Char enters just as Arendt finished her analysis of the early Americans' loss of their revolutionary spirit. The Second World War in Europe had been winding down for months, and the French were poised to expel the Nazis from their territory, however, Char grew apprehensive. He wondered whether the freedom and solidarity, which he and his comrades in the French resistance experienced during combat, would survive peace and 'liberation.' Or might the 'curse' that had 'hung over everything' before the war return? Would selfish pursuits prevail as they had before a common enemy forced those 'too self-centered' to care for their neighbours? Might '*ce sont leurs affaires*' (their business, [not mine]) become the routine response to neighbours' needs? Conflict with occupying forces had united the partisans. Would peace divide them? Frightening confrontations prompted camaraderie and what Char called sincerity. He confided that he had learned to 'appear' decisively, 'without equivocation,' and wondered, if anything short of war, would keep that sort of learning alive. Arendt answered, intimating, as we should suspect by now, that resolve was what created collectives, encouraging candour, self-discovery, self-disclosure, respect for plurality and, above all, freedom, friendship and forgiveness. But the final paragraph of *On Revolution* pivots from Char to Athens and to its legendary founder, Theseus, who was reputed to have urged citizens to 'endow life with splendour' by finding places where they could perform citizenship, speak freely, behave unpretentiously and act in concert. There, they create 'a polis' or jurisdiction of sorts that becomes political as the 'space of men's free deeds and living words' where, Arendt trusts, citizenship and democratic politics are reimagined, where citizen-statesmen have their oases.[107]

On another occasion, Arendt discussed the chances for oases' survival among pariahs. She echoed the encouragement supposedly offered Athenians in exile. Inasmuch as they were well acquainted with democratic practice, they were told that 'wherever [they] may be [they would] constitute a polis.'[108] Her repetition of that line likely prompted Judith Shklar to reckon that 'no one ever had a worse case of Athens worship than Arendt.'[109] Adding Athens to Arendt's list of models, of course, is hardly controversial, though what she excavated from accounts of classical antiquity should not be taken as a wholly accurate representation of Greek democracy. Athenians engaged in lively conversations, she alleged, imagining their enjoyment of the give-and-take (*das Hin und Her und Wider*), which, to her mind, made the prospect of sifting and debating multiple perspectives so exhilarating.[110] Yet she suspected readers could forget how often contrariness – the *Wider* or agonistic posturing – upset authorities. They needed reminding that Socrates was silenced and how slyly statists defended their political practices, prerogatives, and preferences. That last shifted from democracy to oligarchy and back to democracy during Socrates' tenure teaching. But her confidence in the Greeks never wavered, despite Athenians' wreckage of and return to democracy. Strangely, practices came to mean considerably less than theories, when Arendt invoked Aristotle's notion of *energia*, a term that could signify efficiency, vigour or actuality. For her, all three 'exhaust their full meaning in the performance itself.' Hence, 'the performance is the work,' she added, alluding to 'the art of politics,' the 'greatness' of which 'lie[s] only in the performance.'[111]

The performances she expected depended on citizens' willingness provisionally to see issues as others see them, then to enlarge or revise their own perspectives. She expected, perhaps naively, that, during this give-and-take, differences would be put to use in the service of self-discoveries as well as in the self-disclosures that followed. Ideally, such revelations reinforced citizens' commitments to their collectives and the collectives' commitments to plurality. Conceivably, Arendt was following what she took to have been the Athenians' lead, imagining, as Guillermo Zapata suspects, that they fashioned roles to perform publicly, to have staged vigorous, amicable debates and to have accommodated and then integrated as many of their city's citizens' different perspectives as possible.[112]

But Zapata and Arendt seem to have minimised the turbulence that led to Plato's conspicuous aversion to democratic practices. Ever since, piñata politics has seemed too pugnacious to his many acolytes. Lecturing on Walter Benjamin, Arendt insinuated that Plato's progeny were as responsible as statists and the elites they served for having so disdained political discourse that citizens discredit what she called 'palpable' perspectives on governance, perspectives Arendt's pariahs developed in collectives enlivened by political performances rather than enervated by political philosophy.[113] Much as the aforementioned Athenian exiles, who carried democratic practices with them, although without the 'tangible' organisation they left behind, her pariahs gathered in diaspora. But what they did there, in their various associations, was politics. And where they did it, their oases, became public realms.

## Notes

1. Sigwart, *Wandering Thought*, 130.
2. Arendt, 'The Difficulties of Understanding,' Speeches and Writings File, 1923–1975), 9a; USLC.
3. Arendt, 'Heidegger at Eighty,' TWB, 426.
4. BPF, 167.
5. Lelio La Porta, *Hannah Arendt: Il problema storico della libertà* (Milan: Unicopli, 2017), 105.
6. For which, see, *inter alia*, Richard Bernstein, *Why Read Hannah Arendt Now* (Cambridge: Polity, 2018), 88–9.
7. *Briefwechsel*, 484.
8. LKPP, 40.
9. For example, OT, 221.
10. EJ, 159.
11. Peter Fuss, 'Hannah Arendt's Concept of the Political Community,' *Idealistic Studies* 3, no. 3 (1973), 264–5.
12. Hausner is quoted in La Porta, *Arendt*, 167.
13. For which, see Buckler, *Hannah Arendt and Political Theory*, 127.
14. OR, 166.
15. Ibid., 163.
16. Linda Zerilli, *Democratic Theory of Judgment*, 137, 187–8.
17. For which, consult, respectively, Louis Menand, 'Joseph McCarthy and the Force of Political Falsehoods,' *The New Yorker* (August 3 and 10, 2020), 71–5 and Michael J. Klarman, 'How Brown Changed Race Relations: The Backlash Thesis,' *The Journal of American History* 81, no. 1 (1994), 81–118.
18. *Briefwechsel*, 66 ('*Über Amerika wäre überhaupt viel zu sagen. Es gibt hier wirklich so etwas wie Freiheit und ein starkes Gefühl bei vielen Menschen, dass man ohne Freiheit nicht leben kann*').
19. See Arendt's copy of Daniel Boorstin, *The Lost World of Thomas Jefferson* (Boston: Beacon, 1948), 210; BCSL.
20. For Arendt's adaptation of Jefferson's take on 'public freedom' and for her remarks on his 'halfhearted' desire for a revolution in each new generation, see Arendt, 'Action and the Pursuit of Happiness,' TWB, 216–17.
21. Villa, *Arendt*, 147.
22. *Briefwechsel*, 67.
23. Kathryn Gines, 'Race Thinking and Racism in Hannah Arendt's *The Origins of Totalitarianism*,' in *Hannah Arendt and the Uses of History: Imperialism, Nation, Race, Genocide*, eds. Richard H. King and Dan Stone (New York: Berghahn, 2007), 49–50; Owens, 'Racism in the Theory Canon,' 418.

24. OT, 217.
25. Compare Arendt, 'Reflections on Little Rock,' RJ, 206.
26. Arendt, 'Hannah Arendt on Hannah Arendt,' TWB, 456.
27. PP, 117–18.
28. See, for example, David M. Levy and Sandra J. Peart, *Escape from Democracy: The Role of Experts and the Public in Economic Policy* (Cambridge: Cambridge University Press, 2017), David Runciman, *How Democracy Ends* (New York: Basic Books, 2018), especially its section on 'Further Reading'; and Applebaum, *Twilight of Democracy: The Seductive Lure of Authoritarianism* (New York: Doubleday, 2020).
29. Arendt, 'The Great Tradition,' TWB, 53.
30. CR, 56.
31. Katia Genel, *Arendt: L'expérience de la liberté* (Paris: Belin), 256.
32. PP, 126.
33. Villa, *Arendt*, 332.
34. HC, 198.
35. CR, 95.
36. PP, 119.
37. Arendt, 'To Save the Jewish Homeland,' JW, 389–90.
38. Arendt, 'Peace or Armistice in the Near East?' JW, 443.
39. Ibid., 428–9; the capitalisation is Arendt's.
40. Arendt, 'Peace or Armistice,' JW, 445.
41. Ibid., 437.
42. Arendt, 'Zionism Reconsidered,' JW, 362–3.
43. LMW, 139–40.
44. OT, 385–7.
45. Arendt, 'To Save the Jewish Homeland,' JW, 393; Scholem, 48.
46. For this connection, see Benhabib, 'Political Geographies,' 559.
47. LIOC, 127–8.
48. EJ, 4–9.
49. Young-Bruehl, *Hannah Arendt*, 398 mentions the temerity of one journalist who collected letters critical of Arendt's coverage of the trial and published them in France under the title 'Hannah Arendt: est-elle une Nazi?'
50. Ibid., 168.
51. Arendt, 'Creating a Cultural Atmosphere,' JW, 301.
52. RV, 183 (also see 186–90).
53. Arendt, 'The Jew as Pariah,' JW, 287.
54. For 'strong feeling,' see Arendt, 'Revolutions: Spurious and Genuine,' Speeches and Writings File, 1923–1975, (023447); USLC.

55. John Lechte and Saul Newman, *Agamben and the Politics of Human Rights: Statelessness, Images, Violence* (Edinburgh: Edinburgh University Press, 2013), 126. Also consult Peter Iver Kaufman, *On Agamben, Arendt, Christianity and the Dark Arts of Civilisation* (London: Bloomsbury, 2020), 134–6.
56. OT, 66.
57. Arendt, 'Creating a Cultural Atmosphere,' JW, 299.
58. Bagehot, 'The Politics of Punishment,' *The Economist* 451, no. 9399 (June 1–7, 2024), 48.
59. Arendt, 'We Refugees,' JW, 266–8.
60. OT, 49.
61. The letter is reprinted in *Zeitschrift für politische Denkens* (2006), accessed from *Hannaharendt.net*, at http://www.hannaharendt.net/index.php/han/article/view/95/156-, July 31, 2020.
62. O'Gorman, *Politics for Everybody*, 19. For pervasive cynicism, see 53–4.
63. Ibid., 40–2.
64. Ibid., compare 99 and 140–1.
65. Arendt, 'We Refugees,' JW, 273–4.
66. RV, p. 141 (*eine andere leichte und lebendige Welt*).
67. Ibid., 71–2.
68. Ibid., 214.
69. Ibid., 88.
70. *Briefwechsel*, 230.
71. Ibid., 233.
72. Ibid., 236.
73. Ibid., 237; OT, 17–19, 38–45. Also see Benjamin Aldes Wurghaft, *Thinking in Public: Strauss, Levinas, Arendt* (Philadelphia: University of Pennsylvania Press, 2016), 177–9.
74. RV, 224 (*Pariaqualitäten ... hinüberzuretten*).
75. RV, 218 (*zum Mittel des Aufstiegs*); Benhabib, *Reluctant Modernism*, 16–17, 29.
76. For which, see Fina Birulés, *Hannah Arendt: Liberdad politica y totalitarismo* (Barcelona: Gedisa, 2019), 88–9.
77. LIOC, 112.
78. Hannah Arendt, 'Creating a Cultural Atmosphere,' JW, 302.
79. BPF, 42.
80. Ibid., 47–8.
81. Ruggero D'Alessandro, *La communità possible: la democrazia consiliare in Rosa Luxemburg e Hannah Arendt* (Milan: Mimesis, 2011), 98–102.
82. HC, 52.
83. OT, 188–9.

84. Frederick Jackson Turner, *The Frontier in American History* (New York: Holt, 1921), 247.
85. For which, see Arendt, 'Public Rights and Private Interests,' TWB, 508.
86. Arendt, 'Hannah Arendt on Hannah Arendt,' TWB, 457.
87. OR, 263.
88. Ibid., 255.
89. PP, 117.
90. Ibid., 115.
91. MDT, 9.
92. *Denktagebuch*, 952–3.
93. Arendt, 'Authority in the Twentieth Century,' TWB, 69–70.
94. Arendt, 'Action and the Pursuit of Happiness,' TWB, 218–19; for statists' 'frame of reference,' see Arendt, 'Authority in the Twentieth Century,' 89.
95. PP, 201.
96. *Between Friends*, 88; McCarthy's *Oasis* (New York: Melville House, 2013) was published in 1949.
97. Compare PP, 202–3 with *Liebesbegriff*, 86.
98. Jerome Kohn, 'Hannah Arendt: The Appearances of Estrangement,' *Social Ressearch* 85, no. 2 (2018), 308–9.
99. Judith Butler, *Notes Toward a Performative Theory of Assembly*, 24–5, 72–3.
100. Ibid., 216–18.
101. Ibid., 113.
102. *Liebesbegriff*, 75.
103. Ibid., 84–6.
104. HC, 75–6.
105. Augustine, *De libero arbitrio* 3.5.13; *Corpus Scriptorum Ecclesiasticorum Latinorum*, vol. 74, ed. W. M. Green (Berlin: De Gruyter, 1956).
106. LMW, 92, translating *nullam reprehendere audens nisi in comparatione melioris*.
107. OR, 272–3.
108. Arendt, 'Culture and Politics,' TWB, 170.
109. Shklar, *Political Thought*, 369.
110. *Denktagebuch*, 391–2 (*den Freuden der Pluralität*).
111. HC, 206.
112. Zapata, 'Espacio público,' 169.
113. Arendt, 'Walter Benjamin: Vortrag in Freiburg,' Essays and Lectures, 1967–1968, 022715–6; USLC.

# 5

# Why Arendt's 'New' Makes Sense Now

## Conciliar Republics?

Although much has already been said about Arendt's perceptions of statists' salesmanship and about her frustration with their attachments to conventional politics that debases communication and foregrounds competition for rule, this chapter explicitly asks why Arendtian alternatives are particularly timely. Her answer might simply have referred to the depletion of the revolutionary spirit. Yet the only alternative structure she proposed, a layered conciliar republic, oddly, would appear to have had just that effect. It would have qualified as a new beginning, to be sure, and it is more than a modest alteration of established protocols and apparatuses. But conciliar republics hardly constitute the thoroughgoing democratisation or the *novus ordo saeculorum* that founders of the republic promised. Many of their statements about the novelty of their creation have been reread at celebrations of many democracies that claim to have arrived. But, during this third decade of the twenty first century, we have reason to doubt whether any new secular order is truly new or secular or orderly. We are positioned, that is, to ask whether statists and citizens with centuries of experience with some simulacrum of democracy and others, who envy what they know about others' democracies and who work to empower citizens, are squandering the freedoms Arendt, disappointed, identified as a legacy that, in her time, seemed spent.[1]

Arendt was certain that freedom's survival in public realms depended on persistent, persuasive, plural presentations of a new brand of politics. She reiterated its importance whenever she came to define properly political performances. Her emphasis on both persistence and plurality call to mind Robert Putnam's acclaimed manifesto for what he calls 'bridging social capital,' which acknowledges diversity yet transcends, transforming loners into joiners.[2] Arendt took another tack. As we now know, she emphasised resistance or defiance, recalling young Bertolt Brecht's 'desperate need of every bit of reality he [could] catch' while assailing 'the irritating bad faith of the prophets of the people,' which made it difficult and dangerous for 'ordinariness' to derail the nonsense such 'prophets' – statists – sanctimoniously spouted during the 1920s.[3] The tribute she composed recalled that, before Brecht misjudged the Communist Party's readiness to draw 'the ordinary' into political discussions, he exhibited what she characterised as a mischievous, yet regeneratively 'reckless[,] love for earth.' To Arendt, that seemed symptomatic of the pariah's sensibility.[4] The public's loss of connection to the earth was one of the reasons why democracy had to be reconstituted. Doing so, presumably, citizens would reimagine citizenship and become citizen-statesmen, backtracking to relocate and revive Brecht's passion. Borrowing from Henri Bergson to supplement what she had teased from Brecht, Arendt contrasted instinct, vitality, the 'wild variety of nature' and plural perspectives required for meaningful deliberations, on the one hand, with the 'outstanding,' yet unbecoming 'characteristics of the modern age' ('the onslaught of modernity'), on the other. To variety, moderns prefer utility; to action, they prefer fabrication. They confuse productivity (making things to fit patterns) with innovation. They 'instrumentalise' the world, Arendt protested, and they mistake their ingenuity for intelligence.[5]

She sometimes seemed shocked at how easily emphases on commodification and utility all but suppressed virtuosity, virtue, freedom and plurality in conventional public spaces, where statists anesthetised rather than energised and empowered their citizens. Arendt denounced the 'means-ends category' prevalent in such spaces, but, as we learned, she occasionally adapted it to serve her purposes: alternative polities, plurality and agonistic exchanges were the means and citizen-statesmen were the ends. She scrambled Jefferson's elementary republics with local councils that preceded the American revolution and with subsequent councils formed during twentieth-century European revolutions as well as with collectives associated in Europe and the United States with student protests in the 1960s. Looking to harvest lessons from that jumble for the reimagination of citizenship and of democracy, she only came close, albeit not close enough, when she served up a layered set of councils, an arrangement Arendt thought compatible with her preferences for plurality, agonistic discourse and concerted action. To Ruggero D'Alessandro, it amounted to a 'conciliar republic,' yet he strangely confuses this layered confection with direct democracy.[6] But, as we suggested, she actually proposed an intriguing version of representative democracy whereby, at each layer, deliberations would be carefully monitored so that the most competent participant became that cohort's or council's emissary one level or layer up. Arendt apparently presumed that citizens would suspend or somehow dissolve disagreements to reach resolutions and give delegates something to report and advocate or oppose. She never specified whether or how envoys would be kept on a short leash. She left readers guessing to what extent they were free to reformulate the results of the deliberations they were selected to represent.[7]

The Arendt who questioned representative government should have found a conciliar republic objectionable. And, tellingly, the objections she ought to have introduced signal why not only conciliar republics but statists' *faux* republics cannot accommodate her redefinition of politics. Her layered layout, therefore, makes it difficult to absolve her of contradiction. Plausibly, she believed that, at each layer, power had been taken from the elites and returned to 'we the people.' Perhaps she looked to rectify with councils the failure of the founders of the democratic republic in the United States and the failures of would-be democrats emulating them elsewhere, for none sustained 'the revolutionary spirit ... born' of crisis by drawing 'ordinary citizens into political action – into meetings.'[8] To be sure, discussion during those meetings would have met one of Arendt's requirements 'for civilised intercourse,' broadening interlocutors' perspectives. That expansion was *de rigueur* for Arendtian citizen-statesmen.[9] But in conciliar republics, ordinary citizens rather quickly disappear behind their representatives, and that should have troubled her. Particularly within the lowest level councils, the interlocutors' participation appeared to put back into democracy an egalitarian version of what she termed the 'actualisation' and 'materialisation' of political power.'[10] Did she presume that local councils in her 'conciliar republic' would serve, as a 'first practical step to restore order ... without rigid Party control?'[11] Yet nothing in her exposition suggests what might have followed from that 'first step' to maintain deliberations once delegates were designated and dispatched to the next layer of conferences. Furthermore, Arendt left much unsaid about the culmination of those deliberations. We now know she was no friend of majority rule, which led, she said, to 'the suffocation of dissent' and to 'the suppression of the rights of minorities.'[12] 'Representative government,' she argued, had, in effect, furloughed democracy, and had, 'in fact become oligarchic government.'[13] How, then, in conciliar republics, might that transformation be avoided? Did she imagine that consensus about some incontestables – choices of both representatives and of what they must represent – would simply emerge? But that, too, jeopardises politics as Arendt defined it. The consensus at any layer that expresses the will of participants, much as 'the will of the people,' Lyndsey Stonebridge rightly concludes, becomes, for Arendt, 'a collective noun with the potential to eradicate plurality.'[14]

Perhaps the most critical problem with Arendt's scheme is its failure to factor in how shrewdly statists equivocate and how easily citizens are misled. Certainly, in the twenty-first century, the incrimination of unwanted others and, generally, polarisation profit the privileged, who control media presentations of conventional political competition for domination. Arendt knew of the misdirection from above not only from her experience with, and her studies of, statists selling fascist regimes but also from attending to the pageantry of empire that had captivated, among others, Lawrence of Arabia. The seductive fictions that imperialists marketed inspired many to go abroad, including T. E. Lawrence who, renowned for his erudition and courage would have been just the type of person selected to represent one of Arendt's lowest councils and to climb through others. Yet he was impressionable and susceptible to statists' deceit. Notwithstanding Lawrence's contributions to Arabs' independence from the Ottoman empire, he seemed to her one among other savage imperialists indifferent to the incineration of indigenous civilizations.[15]

Imperialism and nationalism were powerful drugs. Nearly everything Arendt wrote suggests that specific changes in citizens' characters must precede any significant change in political protocols or structures to detoxify the addicted. Citizens must become citizen-statesmen before becoming influential. Her conciliar republics, however, offer no guarantee that conferees would be chosen for their competence rather than for their celebrity or cunning. The ordinary citizens' characters would have to be changed if such choices were to be left to them. Statecraft and sensitivity were prerequisites for alternative collectives to work as antidotes and to counter statists' wiles. Arendt, to that end, emphasised incubating statesmanship and, to repeat, redefined politics to ensure that the virtues and virtuosity preeminent in the performances she identified as political developed a pariah's perspective and sensitivities. Otherwise, imperception ruled. The fascists in Germany presided over the Weimar Republic's 'moral disintegration,' Arendt alleged, because citizens 'with so little mental or conceptual preparation,' plumped for their patrons' principles that had been poorly, if at all, 'framed … to conditions as they actually arose.'[16] Citizens still seem easy prey for predatory statists, susceptible to misleading promises, to nationalists' banter and to the inflated expectations that, when unmet, as we discussed, lead to rage and to 'piñata politics.'

Crises *du jour* in international relations, troughs in the economy and frequent threats to the civic order lately bestirred what Anne Applebaum calls 'angry politics.'[17] Gross inequalities have been tolerated in multiple democracies even as statists, sovereign powers and influential elites promise to redistribute resources and to restore greatness or stature of some sort to lost empires; local and global economic and political conditions constitute strong headwinds, but promises are easiest to make when statists and their clients care little about keeping them. Yet their promises come with demands for deference. Arendtian alternatives promise challenges rather than consolations. With those challenges, however, come possibilities for freedom and the aforesaid 'enlargement' of the perspectives of participants. Arendt's responses to authoritarianism and 'angry' or piñata politics amounted to her faith that agonistic discourses liberated and equalised interlocutors, regardless of the socio-economic conditions of any. For each participant was prepared to see all others as peers. Arendt trusted that, to citizens prepared or transformed – as citizen-statesmen – everything of interest or importance is revealed 'under many aspects ... in the presence of peers who regard it from their various perspectives.' And, she went on, what 'materialises' from that 'regard' and from reciprocity would be 'discerning insight' as well as a new form of politics, which ensured 'nothing other than the greatest possible overview of all possible standpoints and viewpoints' emerged from collectives' deliberations. Citizen-statesmanship was defined by judgement as well as by the freedom to deploy it. No one could claim to be free while statists or ideologues insisted on one standpoint and, excluding all others, played the tyrant. No one, Arendt said, is 'free and no one is capable of insight, not even the tyrant.'[18]

Tyranny easily qualifies as one of Arendt's principal interests. Her *Origins of Totalitarianism* probed its origins, aims and techniques. She told her journal about tyrants' remarkable facility dousing dissent. They fooled their citizens into thinking of necessity as 'a basic character of being in the world.'[19] They relied on their retainers – statists and ideologues – to do the fooling, but their own charisma went a long way toward convincing crowds. To be free of tyrants' tactics required stepping beyond the statists' sphere of influence. Arendt warned that individual citizens cannot take such strides alone. Wickedness was comparable to a storm sweeping 'horizontally' (due largely to statists' salesmanship), after having descended 'from above.'[20] Its force swept through Germany and Italy during the 1920s and 1930s, as ordinary citizens, to their indelible shame, took to tyranny. What was nearly as bad as the rage, envy and resentment of some was the indifference of others. The times and tyrants then called for collective resistance. The lesson learned from the citizens' abysmal failure to resist collectively, Arendt claimed, was self-evident: individuals in isolation are 'never free.' They are unprepared for the reciprocities, which reward persons with a politics befitting their dignity when they 'become free only [as they] step ... out into the polis' to speak and act there. Furthermore, when freedom 'has a space' and 'is rooted in place,' she added, equality also has a place. Interlocutors, as just noted, forsake socio-economic conditions that breed bias.[21] Equality was a political experience. As such, it had to be performed. Virtue was based on the 'love of equality.' And, inasmuch as Arendt was sure that political life was only possible among 'equally powerful' citizens, Arendtian citizens should be prepared to measure themselves against others and, affirming the equality of all interlocutors, to 'win recognition from them.'[22] They must not be satisfied to have assembled, to have picked a candidate to represent them and then to adjourn. Why? Arendt supplied the principal reason, which remains relevant. Because statists' salesmanship – their 'Madison Avenue methods' – dominate what passes as politics, some new beginning was required. Especially now, venues where collectives encourage pariahs' sensitivities, plurality, reciprocity, freedom and citizen-statesmanship must be found or created.[23]

## 'Intermediary' Associations: Arendt's or Nisbet's?

And politics, citizenship and democracy must be reimagined. Prospects for alternative public spaces where projects of this sort might have been undertaken were not altogether bleak during the 1950s and 1960s. Ironically, perhaps, surveys of citizens in the United States concluded that they were 'less connected with one another' yet more tolerant of others.[24] Yet conflicts over the integration of schools stained those very decades. Citizens of all races were estranged from and angry with their governments. Robert Nisbet, for one, influentially proposed that 'intermediary' associations be promoted not only to reconnect individuals with each other but, more important, to mediate between citizens and their governments. Yet, whereas Arendt – somewhat similarly inclined – favoured levelling within those collectives, Nisbet required rank or disproportion and regretted what he presented as 'the erosion of place in national esteem.' Arguing for hierarchy, he maintained that equality had impaired leadership's abilities to organise democracies.[25]

Nuclear and extended families, Nisbet pointed out, traditionally distributed power unequally. And he approved. During the twentieth century, however, family life seemed to be changing. Nisbet noted and disapproved. He cited literature that predicted a questionable future for the families that unaccountably were dispensing with patriarchy or matriarchy and, therefore, he feared, were forfeiting their chances to survive as family units – forfeiting their 'indispensable' places in society. The forfeitures were especially tragic, he believed, because they made every family member's personal 'adjustments' to economic and political changes in society far more difficult.[26] In addition to rearranging authority in what had become non-traditional families, he recommended what Arendt commended, alternative, 'intermediary' collectives, but he warned that levelling or democratising experiments within them was imprudent. Within them – much as within traditionally, hierarchically structured families – members prepared for the undemocratic conditions of their workplaces and governments. Nisbet trusted rank to 'mute' factionalism and 'gnawing conflicts' that were destroying families and that characterised political organisations. He argued that military protocol and military efficiency, for which the United States was much admired after its victories in 1945, cinched his argument for distinction and against equality.[27]

Arendt's experiences with militarism and paramilitaries surely made Nisbet's fondness for military efficiency unappealing. But she could readily have warmed to his criticisms of the recurring emphasis on national community in American political discourse. Reviewing his censorious remarks will help us appreciate why she, as he, suggested alternative venues to change that discourse and to reimagine citizenship. But reconsidering Nisbet's intermediary associations will also help us appreciate how radically Arendt departed from what could be characterised as the standard response to statists' citizen capture. For his alternatives enabled 'smaller allegiances of men' to 'assume both functional and psychological significance.'[28] In Nisbet's view, 'new forms' of the heroic, democratic spirit ought to be summoned or revived. Nonetheless, he insisted that he was not scouting out a way back to the frontier and to pioneers' syndicates, which the aforementioned Turner thesis lionised. For frontiers were generally hostile to hierarchies, which he thought essential to the maintenance of his collectives. Nisbet, then, was not nostalgic, but he blamed statists for having stalled what he called (and would have welcomed as) a 'full-fledged renascence of conservatism.' Much as Arendt, he disliked the intrusion of any 'administrative bureaucracy' bent on the 'glorification of the unitary state at the expense of pluralistic society.' Statists' excitement about solidarity camouflaged their desire for citizens' conformity and complacency, even to the point of replicating what he called 'totalitarianism's fundamental structure.'[29] And, he added, to the extent that statists' misleading enthusiasm was contagious, their regimes had a 'pulverising influence' on intermediary associations.[30] He and Arendt, then, shared a sense of urgency yet doubted that incremental reforms could be effective. The two looked to more radical commitments to reverse what subsequent researchers measured as a 'striking shift in the way [persons] allocate time – towards [them]selves and ... away from' their communities.[31]

Others presumed that a dram of common sense and a bit of tinkering sufficed to set the system right. From the start, Nisbet entertained, as Arendt did, the reasons why it was important for the future of democracy to introduce alternatives to the arrangements that statists preferred. For him, those arrangements were supplemental and hierarchical; for her, they were more egalitarian and meant to be personally transformative.

Supplemental or transformative, the associations, as Nisbet and Arendt conceived or retrieved them were strenuously nonpartisan. They were free from what Rosine Kelz, in her remarks on 'non-sovereignty,' calls 'ideologically saturated party politics.'[32] Nisbet, though, attributed to Hobbesian statists' fear of factions their regime's citizens' disaffection with, and disaffiliation from, intermediary associations. Statists, he averred, were stalwart defenders of centralisation. They went about 'relentlessly eradicat[ing]' local customs and coalitions. They preferred their omnicompetent political Leviathans to the unravelling and anarchy, which, they all but promised, would follow, should the local or the parochial prevail.[33] But Nisbet was unhappy with Arendt's reading of the American republic's aversion to, yet capitulation to, federalism. By concentrating on the founders' effort to redistribute and limit political power, she missed the social causes and implications of the insurgency that, for Nisbet, textured the outcome. Channeling him, Spartaco Pupo characterises Arendt's certainty as 'extravagant.'[34] Nevertheless, Nisbet did endorse her complaints about the Hobbesian consequences of deploying Jean Jacques Rousseau's political references to a General Will that discouraged self-discoveries and self-disclosures (Arendt) and subsumed local, intermediary associations (Nisbet). For both, the preeminence of a General Will allowed statists to construe the parochial as 'interference,' to present alternative collectives as 'a flaw in the spiritual unity Rousseau prized so highly.' Statists, apparently citing Rousseau, made the case that intermediary associations had to be sacrificed to preserve the 'values of national life.' For Nisbet, such centralisation was catastrophic.[35] Anticipating statists' counter that any independent collective or coalition would create politically irresponsible citizens, he claimed quite the reverse, that the disintegration of intermediary voluntary associations encouraged political isolation and disaffection.[36]

Nisbet resented Hobbesian statists. He argued that they were keen on what he called 'the old laissez faire,' because it stressed freedoms from oppressive measures but that they were keener to abridge freedoms to assemble or associate. 'The force of the State, throwing the weight of its fast-developing administrative system' behind select 'economic elements,' he protested unfairly favoured centralisation and undermined old forms of sociability. And this was no accident. He held that the destruction of old associations and customs was 'planned.'[37] To substantiate that, Nisbet turned to Arendt, citing her accounts of totalitarianism's mendacity and efficiencies, its 'demolition of as much of civil society as possible.' He claimed that intermediary consortiums preserved civility.[38] Arendt would have had few, if any, reservations about Nisbet's perception. But his prescriptions, we now know, were different from hers.

He bristled most at statists' conceit that one only finds 'freedom, equality, fraternity and virtue' by submitting to a centralised Hobbesian regime's 'unifying' regimen. Yet one may ask whether the freedoms at stake survive – and would a civil society with Nisbet's intermediary associations become utterly unmanageable – if no central administrative apparatus intervened to lower the volume when competitions among them became noisy and noxious?[39] Arendt's answer would presumably have come as a concession of sorts. She conceded, as Nisbet would not, that 'the gigantic and still increasing sphere of social and economic life' was 'the proper sphere to take care of life's necessities.' She was as apprehensive as he was, however, about the extent of that sphere's political influence. She fretted that bulky bureaucracies, worried about dismemberment, would mistake unconventional collectives as threats. She likely figured that dismemberment was a high-risk strategy. Statists had no cause for concern. Moreover, as just noted, an administrative state could be useful, ensuring the orderly distribution of goods and services. Problems surfaced, however, when any administrative colossus attempted to play at politics.[40] And she was troubled by the probability that political patronage would determine not only bureaucratic appointments (who would be likelier to get a leg-up in bureaucratic Leviathans than a candidate with statists' imprimaturs?) but administrative priorities as well. Arendt's mistrust will seem comprehensible, if we read into her disappointments a denial that totalitarianism was either dead or irrelevant in the 1950s and 1960s. Witnessing the feeble efforts to oppose Joseph McCarthy, remembering Europe's demagogues or listening to Adolf Eichmann fluently justify bureaucrats' loyalty to their regimes may have stiffened Arendt's resolve to redefine political practice to ensure its independence from the social and administrative.[41]

Nisbet had no such intent, although he came close to accusing statists who were presiding over democratic regimes of flirting with former totalitarians' methods and of 'fully eras[ing] attributes of human plurality and spontaneity.'[42] Their nearly successful purge, he wrote, was 'the towering moral problem of the age.'[43] Arendt might have classified that erasure as a political problem with moral implications, yet she believed that solutions were 'given every day' as 'matters of practical politics.'[44] But such solutions to chronic political problems were impossible to popularise as long as statists controlled the narratives, retaining the power to inflict 'injury upon factual truth.' They were conspicuous during the twentieth century and occasioned Arendt's many disappointments. They are equally, if not more, influential in the twenty-first. They make a restoration of every citizen's awareness of the importance of – and the loss of – community more difficult when 'chances of factual truth surviving the onslaught of power' become, as Arendt reluctantly conceded, 'very slim indeed.'[45] Statists cunningly ensure that conventional politics remains focused on rule and freighted with misrepresentation rather than providing incentives for broad citizen participation. They reroute revelations that have chances of stirring dissent. Their ability to manipulate and to market their brand of democracy as politically prudent is symptomatic of democracy's decline. Arendt referred to their 'tyrannical traits' as reversions to Plato's cynical 'conviction that truth can be neither gained [from] nor communicated among the many.'[46] She might have sought 'to understand whether something like a desire for truth' could conceivably 'be at odds with the spirit of debate and discussion that animates political life. David Antonini thinks so, yet, as we argued while chronicling her disappointments, she decided early on that statists and sovereign powers, shielding their truths from ordinary citizens' discussions and debate, contrived to present just such a conflict.[47]

Rather than prompt debate and discussion, statists' truths tended to stir the embers of citizens' discontent and organise parades or – worse – pogroms to marginalise dissidents and unwanted others. Progressives in democratic republics are powerless when statists win over substantial numbers of citizens by selling their version of 'absolute goodness,' which Arendt considered 'hardly less dangerous than absolute evil.'[48] Statists' truths clamp onto citizens' imaginations and become their truths and absolutes. And that observation is one reason why unconventional, intermediary associations or collectives are vital for the survival of democratic republics. As citizen-statesmen emerge from alternative venues, where freedom is showcased in interpersonal performances that draw interlocutors into politics, those interlocutors grow interested in drawing others.[49] They defend freedom and plurality 'in matters of practical politics,' Arendt repeatedly asserted, because their challenge is not to replace one set of absolutes with another. They know absolutism poorly serves the 'down-to-earth interest[s]' of communities, which, she graded as infinitely more complex than – and worlds apart from – any principles hewn from philosophy. Such principles 'concern[ed] man in his singularity,' she explained, specifying that they were 'unpolitical by nature.'[50] Every absolute principle, Arendt went on, 'spells doom to everyone when it is introduced into the political realm.' So, she refused to be categorical, save to protest that political commitments to freedom, plurality, equality, friendship, forgiveness and natality were categorically antithetical to the categorical.[51]

During one of her final interviews, Arendt was asked if barring absolutes and abstractions from her version of politics had wrecked her reputation among philosophers. Had colleagues pressed her to be more precise about – or to renounce – her preference for 'extreme freedom' over the convictions carrying weight in one or another academic circle? 'Without a doubt,' she replied, defending what she thought was necessary for the reimagination of citizenship and democracy, specifically, the freedom 'to think critically,' if not consistently and unambiguously. Arendt's brief for critical thinking and deviating discourses, though, signalled hostility to her colleagues who placed aprioricity and their fundamental principles beyond criticism. Still, she maintained that it was incumbent on all 'thinking being[s]' to be critics and to undermine 'rigid rules [and] general convictions.' Generalisations about experience often bewildered, but the most baffling invited controversy and conversation.[52]

In effect, she proposed a distinction that should now be familiar to us between the antagonistic and the agonistic exchanges. Criticism must not be mistaken for antagonism, she said, coupling antagonism with competition for domination in what passed as conventional political discourses about rule and sovereignty. But agonistic exchanges, refined political judgement. But judgement was not what statists wanted from their citizens. 'Marching together' as obedient soldiers, those citizens lost their identities, Arendt pointed out, alluding to statists' preference for conformity and for the 'unitedness of many into one' producing what she perceived as 'the sameness prevailing in society.'[53] Wanting submissive citizens, statists glamorised acquiescence and rewarded the acquiescent. Their ideal citizens simply endorsed their governments' 'various devices of representation,' as if current protocols descended from Sinai. But the rationales for their existence were actually handed down by statists tutored by philosophers and ideologues. Arendt tried to outmanoeuvre that cabal. She plumped for what her interviewer characterised as 'extreme freedom.' Hence, her intermediary associations were quite unlike Nisbet's. Whereas civil disobedients' revolutionary spirit attracted her. To him, the disobedients appeared 'vain' and self-indulgent – caught up in the romance of revolution.[54] True, their euphoria as well as their eccentricities appealed to the romanticism threaded through some of Arendt's efforts to have philosophers take political realities seriously. Critics who refer to her as utopian noticed. Minus much of the criticism, Andreas Kalyvas designated her politics as 'extraordinary,' as a 'radical popular politics' conducted in 'politicised,' though 'extra-institutional, spontaneous popular assembles.' Nonetheless, Kalyvas looked forward to the convergence of Arendtian 'counterinstitutions' with the interests of statists and sovereign powers. But Arendt saw no chance for extraordinary politics to merge with the ordinary or conventional politics of mid-twentieth-century democracies.[55]

On that count, she agreed with Nisbet. For him, convergence would have been a betrayal of the democratic spirit his associations defended against Hobbesian statists. But, for Arendt, the reason why her unconventional collectives were necessary to reevaluate and reimagine citizenship and to reinvent democracy put such convergences well out of bounds. Permit an elaboration that reintroduces Judith Butler's discussion of gendered identity to explain why. Butler begins by adapting Arendt's placement of self-discovery and self-disclosure at the centre of her endeavour to bring 'space[s] of appearance into being.' We might represent that as Arendtian housekeeping and simply note Butler's agreement, inasmuch as Butler maintains her spaces must be set apart from conventional initiatives to 'pathologise' or 'criminalise' the 'non-normative' ways some persons 'live their gender or their sexuality.' Arendt deserves 'an assist' for helping Butler get past the prejudicial terms with which supposed 'deviance' is ordinarily discussed. Arendt, of course, located her collectives for different purposes, but nothing prohibits her unconventional spaces of appearance from enabling otherwise 'susceptible' or 'vulnerable' persons to break the 'citational chains of gender normativity' and from 'resignify[ing]' behaviour.[56] We may conclude, therefore, by replacing the liberation Butler advocates with relief from statists' 'citational chains' that define citizenship. The result: a defensible – and arguably the principal – reason why Arendt rummaged through history looking to illustrate a revolutionary spirit that survived long enough in some spaces to give 'nonnormativity' political legitimacy and resonance. By reimagining citizenship as citizen-statesmanship, she underscored the importance of political judgement, specifying the conditions necessary for its development. By redefining politics, she (and we) may reimagine democratic practices within those intermediary colloquies she envisioned. Still, by shifting her interest from political structures or systems to political agents' values, virtuosity and judgement, she tempts visionaries to extend citizen-statesmen's influence.

## Political Judgement

Arendt's collectives, as Nisbet's, were independent. But, for her, independence was also defiance. Her redefinitions were also rejections. She opposed what statists prescribed for citizens, and her prescriptions, in effect, were revisions of conventional political expectations. Borrowing a distinction she had borrowed from salonnière Rahel Varnhagen, one might classify her citizen-statesmen as warriors (*Krieger*), not gardeners. Citizen-statesmen, thinking critically at their oases and then released among statists, would abjure pruning what regimes planted. Her warriors were trained in alternative spaces, yet – and this is critical – Arendt never discouraged them from trying to change political judgement and political behaviour in the desert.[57] Of course, it would be safer to remain secluded. Change agents should count on vigorous statist opposition. Statists were certain to try to scupper whatever new beginnings citizen-statesmen made. Statists' capture and control of citizens' reactions were, as noted, considerable and formidable. So, advise change-agents to figure on unforeseen consequences. Sometime after 1969, Arendt, on reading Hans Morgenthau's short volume on the formation of foreign policy, was apparently struck, as he had been, by the inadequacy of doctrines predicated on predictions of political loyalty. She, after all, had witnessed what he reported: when German middle classes were 'proletarianised,' they did not gravitate to Marxism, as forecast, but to fascism. The last stage of capitalism, for those who had been impoverished by the economic downturns in the 1920s, was not classless; capitalism collapsed yet did not give way. Instead, it accommodated authoritarian regimes.[58]

As economic hardship spreads in the twenty-first century and as fascist political parties become popular in republican regimes, the unpredictable seems predictable – and menacing. Aggrieved citizens' clenched fists and the rhetoric of populist politicians harping on their grievances keep citizens and statists alike from getting a firm grip on what we have heard Arendt call verifiable experience. Political judgement is in short supply. She expected civil disobedients to possess it. But they were warriors, in her book, and, in battles, impulses often overtake judgement. Those she distinguished as conscientious objectors, however, more closely resembled Varnhagen's – and Arendt's – gardeners tending their dissent *in foro conscientiae*. They have more leisure to ponder. But what made them less attractive to Arendt was their relative isolation. They needed no public. But disobedients' dissent was formed along with, and reputedly informed by, others' discourses and alongside their colleagues who worked to put to the test all reasons for opposing statists' justifications for imperialist interventions in southeast Asia. Plus, all testing of that sort, notably, interpersonal performances during which it was conducted before sparse yet committed crowds, was necessary for the informed formation of political judgement.[59]

Conclusions were to be constantly tested, as were the opinions articulated enroute to their formulation, for Arendt had an abiding faith that the exposure to others' views made one's own opinions more comprehensive, more comprehensible and more defensible – without making one defensive. Such exposures, ideally, led interlocutors to respect their 'common world' yet did not routinely bring them to common ground. Strangely, for all her talk of the former, of the citizens' common world, Arendt never appears to have addressed the likelihood that interlocutors would land on the latter, would reach consensus, although she assumed that participants in conciliar republics would ultimately agree on the identity of their most competent member, the person to be sent to a higher council. The route to common ground, however, was left unmarked, probably because what mattered most to her was exposure to others' opinions, which made disobedients citizen-statesmen, made them political (on Arendt's terms) and, Hubert Faes adds, made them 'truly human.'[60]

Arendt's avid, though not uncritical, admiration of the civil disobedients was due, in large part, to her baseless reconstruction of colloquies that presumably preceded their demonstrations; she imagined each reevaluated her or his opinion while evaluating others' views. In her imagination, then, as Bethânia Assy explains, civil disobedients 'reinforce[d] the primacy of communicability, plurality and diverse viewpoints in building up [their] *doxa*.'[61] Yet, as suggested, the building up involved some tearing down. Arendt did not flinch from the violence that sometimes precipitated new beginnings or the disorientations that accompanied them.[62] For, as Dana Villa extrapolates from her statements of purpose, the objective was to break the 'habit of mechanical, unthinking judgement.' Either one frees political judgement from having to apply conventional standards and rules or one stands by as 'powers of judgement atrophy.'[63]

Reenter into evidence, Adolf Eichmann. Arendt was reminded by his remarks of the difference between applying rules and thinking. She accused the prosecution at his trial in Israel of having given him too much credit for judgement.[64] Fascism had barrelled down on him. Eichmann was politically amateurish. He received orders and proved to be clever organizing the collection of victims. That 'habit of mechanical unthinking judgement' kicked in; he devised the 'assembly line' that provided Jews' transportation to internment camps. So, in effect, he presided over the Nazis' disassembly line. He supervised the dispossession and disposal of its casualties.[65] At the trial Eichmann confided that he had been relieved to be relieved of the responsibility for passing judgement on the probity of his orders. He was, Arendt wrote, the 'perfect bureaucrat.'[66] At the trial, she learned what an 'unthinking instrument' looked like. We may presume that, during her travels in post-war Germany, she met many who lost their bearings and who found in fascism an attractive remedy to their republic's many maladies. Unfortunately, we have no evidence for her reply when asked whether trials of former Nazis should continue after the Bundestag, the lower house of the German parliament, extended the statute of limitations in 1965 to allow additional prosecutions. Yet we may guess that the spectacle of unpunished fascist statists from the 1930s and 1940s exerting influence in German politics and commerce during the 1950s and 1960s nauseated her, even if it did not whet her appetite for retribution.[67]

Arendt preferred analysis to revenge. Uninterested in branding and scourging a scapegoat, she wanted to comprehend a cog in fascism's murderous machine.[68] Recycling a phrase she earlier applied to Bertolt Brecht's detachment from all that seemed inappropriate in the Stalinist regime, Arendt referred to Eichmann's abdication of responsibility as an 'internal emigration.' Less so in Brecht's case but decisively in Eichmann's, that inner emigration, she argued, 'extinguished' the émigré's personality, although not his culpability.[69] Conformity was complicity. In conventional politics, she contended, 'obedience and support [were] the same.'[70] She acknowledged Eichmann had been 'surrounded by corruption' and had developed tunnel vision, seeing only the 'enormous tasks of organization and administration.' He 'was not used to thinking big' or to thinking at all. He could not, then would not, look beyond the immediate challenge of trafficking the regime's victims.[71] Arendt controversially thought of him as normal in appallingly abnormal times (and, therefore, as abnormal). She suspected that, had there been referenda on the fate of European Jewry during the 1930s, central and eastern Europeans would have voted to endorse fascists' plans. Antisemitic literature had been horrifyingly influential. Ethnonationalists were stoking embers of animosity before Auschwitz's ovens were in operation, but Nazis made hatred and horror public policy. In an undated lecture Arendt posted what can pass as an epitaph for the deceased but also for the diseased liberal democracies she watched dying. People killing for greed were inexcusable yet comprehensible, she said; 'murder as factory' that uncoiled with fascism from the womb of the Weimar Republic, was historical yet unimaginable.[72]

Could such unimaginable, reprehensible history be repeated? Decades into the twenty-first century, one cannot say 'no' with confidence. The prevalence of vulgar populisms bodes ill for the equilibrium in ostensibly democratic republics, old and new. One would be foolish to invest much hope that success in reimagining citizenship would make an immediate difference in most citizens' conduct. The lesson Arendt learned from Eichmann's trial, though, bears repeating, for she was not only struck by the defendant's 'non-thinking' but also by ordinary German citizens, who suspended judgement and by citizens elsewhere in Europe who colluded with the Nazis. Arendt censured members of the *Judenräte*, the councils, who bargained with Eichmann and others to save some Jews at the expense of others and whose assurances to deportees kept the deportations orderly. Colleagues scolded her for having blamed the victims. When her reports from, and reflections on, the trial were published as a volume the Anti-Defamation League of B'nai B'rith in the United States ironically circulated patently defamatory bulletins distorting Arendt's remarks, attempting to prejudice reviewers.[73] But she did not yield. Eichmann and his accomplices along with most Germans by the 1930s, including members of the *Judenräte*, were 'generally rather well informed,' she concluded. They just lacked judgement; if Eichmann was a monster, 'a large majority of the German people were monsters.' That said, Arendt also admitted that it was extraordinarily difficult in conventional public forums and realms (as it has continued to be) to form political judgement.[74]

Populists in the twenty-first century and statists serving their interests and often creating – then capitalising on – their resentments would disagree. Their politics is governed by truths and *isms* made digestible as doctrines. Capitalism comes across as a devotion to upward mobility bracing the regimes' protection of some citizens' opportunities from immigrants or dissidents. Politics, for Arendt, is 'a domain of opinions and appearances,' calling for judgement and ongoing self-discoveries rather than for adherence or acquiescence.[75] Judgement is difficult to acquire; adherence is easy. Ordinary citizens feeling left behind simply defer to statists with ready explanations for their disadvantages and with a set of culprits – progressives, immigrants, minorities, *inter alia* – who can be held responsible. Ned O'Gorman, as we saw, has been attentive to populist statists selling the dichotomy between the virtuous yet deprived and the undeserving yet privileged. Statists' salesmanship ensures that the clamour of the former, their 'partisan hyperventilation,' polarises and 'paralyses.'[76] O'Gorman's assessment is astute, to a point: Arendt's version of democratic politics cannot take hold as long as commercial interests flood conventional public realms and, as he admitted, become 'downright imperialist.' Yet, as we found, O'Gorman writes as if such developments have stalled and thinks that conventional regimes may now reserve places for Arendt's values in public life.[77]

But she was far less optimistic. Her portions of the twentieth century were forbidding. And the twenty-first fares no better. Acquiescence and deference have replaced judgement. Those well informed are in a quandary, because their colleagues are ill equipped to hold accountable the cabal of statists and power-brokers driven by their lust to dominate. Arendt lived through and then studied stretches of time when political judgement was wanting – when too few citizens were discerning and dissident. Politicised parties morphed into 'movements.' And movements' acceleration toward 'totalitarian form[s] of domination depend[ed]' on citizens' indifference to the exclusions that ended in internments and worse. Too few objected to nationalism's excesses. Later, in the aftermath of the second war to end all wars, agreements to protect minorities were either unenforced or simply binned. Arendt learned how (and why) precarious balances between nation and state could be upset 'with terrifying swiftness.'[78] But, notwithstanding the persistence of nationalisms with their incendiary rhetoric and abominable purges, her vision for, and revisions of, inclusive democratic practices, Daniela Bassi confirms, are *sempre riproponibile*, perennial. We agree, but imperatives follow. Incubate citizen-statesmen's political judgement; develop their virtuosity. Have them embody and promulgate virtues associated with Arendt's alternative politics. See that they do not shrink from competing against statist marketing and management. Why? To find new beginnings that exhibit what Arendt characterised as the revolutionary spirit and what Bassi calls political 'epiphanies.'[79]

Bassi's theologically freighted reference calls to mind a question that seems to have intrigued Arendt when she read one of Werner Jaeger's lectures. The German philosopher, who studied religion and philosophy in antiquity, asked whether 'the faith of the fishermen of Galilee' could have 'penetrated' classical civilization, had it not been conveyed as dogma. The presence of their master was sufficient for his disciples. But, if Jesus' message were to survive and win over those who had not known him, doctrine and indoctrination were necessary. Arendt took note, but, from what we have learned, we may suspect she disagreed and placed her faith in citizen-statesmen as change agents. She did not assume, as Jaeger did, that faith or in this application, a revolutionary spirit, must take shape or congeal as dogma to inspire.[80]

Still, to anyone who suspects that Arendt's revelations about politics should achieve purchase in 'mass culture' when conveyed conventionally as parts of the 'rich tradition of civic education' in western Europe and the United States, this study's discussions of Eichmann, Zionism, Socrates, Nisbet, Brecht – even of Arendt – may seem to be an unnecessary detour. Agency and virtuosity hardly matter, if, as Brook Manville and Josiah Ober maintain, there are 'growing indications of an educational shift away from a single-minded focus on efficiency' – if conventional protocols and apparatuses are, as they postulate, 'promoting the knowledge and leadership of participative democratic citizens.' But Wendy Brown discerns movement in the opposite direction and argues that concerns with increasing production and consumption have not given ground to discussions of civic responsibility. She sees that higher education follows the lead of mass culture sprinting to 'glorify uneducated and often vacuous celebrity.' The chances to reimagine citizenship and reconceive democratic practices diminish as a result. To be sure, there are breaks in the heavy weather. Promising, honourable candidates for office surface; discerning citizens rally around them. But Brown's proofs are persuasive. Her evidence is demonstrably stronger than what Manville and Ober have mustered. And her conclusion, moreover, corresponds with the requiems for the humanities typically performed in colleges and universities. Quick-witted statists captured what was once described in the United States as civics education enroute to what we called citizen capture. For Brown and Arendt, democracy 'requires a people who are educated, thoughtful, and democratic in sensibility.' Their political judgement and agency are what may prevent the 'neoliberal economisation' of political culture.[81]

If not, statists' synthesis of prejudice, profit and patriotism will increasingly make it impossible to find spaces to reimagine citizenship or to incubate the virtues and virtuosity citizen-statesmen might export to make new beginnings in that desert. Admittedly, to those ends, Arendt's legacy is more telling than her own agency. She confided to Mary McCarthy that, although she signed the occasional petition, she did not intend to 'make a profession of it.'[82] Disappointments seem to have led to her resignation that intermediary voluntary associations committed both to human dignity and to the 'performativity' of citizen-statesmanship can only flourish on the fringes; she was ill-suited for life there.[83] Arendt served us, instead, by lecturing and writing about statists' deceit, philosophers' misjudgements, and the dystopian character of 'mass culture,' which did 'not know how to take care of the world.' She served us also and well, redefining politics and setting the conditions required for making sturdy new beginnings.[84]

## Notes

1. See Tracy B. Strong, 'America as Exemplar: The *Denktagebuch* of 1951,' in *Artifacts of Thinking: Reading Hannah Arendt's 'Denktagebuch,'* eds. Roger Berkowitz and Ian Storey (New York: Fordham University Press, 2017), 127.
2. Robert D. Putnam, *Bowling Alone: The Collapse and Revival of American Community* (New York: Simon and Schuster, 2000), 22–4 and 362–3.
3. MDT, 222.
4. Ibid., 230–1.
5. HC, 305–6.
6. D'Alessandro, *La communità possibile*, 90–1.
7. CR, 232–3.
8. Arndt, *Arendt on the Political*, 258.
9. Arendt, Some Questions of Moral Philosophy,' RJ, 140.
10. HC, 200; CR, 140.
11. Arendt, 'The Hungarian Revolution and Totalitarian Imperialism,' TWB, 134–5.
12. CR, 141.
13. OR, 261.
14. Stonebridge, *We Are Free*, 243.
15. Arendt, 'The Imperialist Character,' *The Review of Politics* 12, no. 3 (1950), 316–20.
16. Arendt, 'Personal Responsibility under Dictatorship,' RJ, 24–5.
17. Applebaum, *Twilight of Democracy*, 115–17.

18. PP, 168–9.
19. *Denktagebuch*, 733.
20. Ibid., 644.
21. PP, 170.
22. Arendt, 'The Great Tradition,' TWB, 54–5.
23. OR, 267–8.
24. Putnam, *Bowling Alone*, 352.
25. Compare *Denktagebuch*, 467 with Robert Nisbet, *Twilight of Authority* (Indianapolis: Liberty Fund, 1975), 98–9. Nisbet spent most of his career on the west coast of the United States, moving to New York City in 1974, the year before Arendt died there.
26. Robert Nisbet, *Quest for Community: A Study in the Ethics of Order and Freedom* (Wilmington: Intercollegiate Studies Institute, 1990), 52–4.
27. Nisbet, *Twilight*, 145.
28. Nisbet, *Quest for Community*, 63–4.
29. Robert Nisbet, 'Arendt on Totalitarianism,' *The National Interest* 27 (Spring, 1992), 87.
30. Robert Nisbet, 'Still Questing,' *The Intercollegiate Review* 29, no. 1 (1993), 41–4.
31. For which, see Putnam, *Bowling Alone*, 107.
32. Rosine Kelz, *The Non-Sovereign Self, Responsibility, and Otherness: Hannah Arendt, Judith Butler, and Stanley Cavell on Moral Philosophy and Political Agency* (New York: Palgrave Macmillan, 2016), 139–41.
33. Nisbet, *Quest for Community*, 121.
34. Spartaco Pupo, *Libertà é conservazione: Robert Nisbet e la critica al progressismo* (Rome: Idrovolante Edizioni, 2016), 34–6 (*l'ostentata sicurrezza della Arendt*).
35. Nisbet, *Quest for Community*, 135–7. For Arendt's remarks on Rousseau's General Will and on its contributions to 'a general human solidarisation' leading to a loss of one's self, see OR, 69–71.
36. Robert Nisbet, 'What to do when you don't live in a Golden Age,' *The American Scholar* 51, no. 2 (1982), 233.
37. Nisbet, *Quest for Community*, 257.
38. Ibid., 181–2; Nisbet, 'Arendt on Totalitarianism,' 89–90.
39. See Nisbet, *Quest for Community*, 144, for the conceit that freedom in a supposedly 'all-benign state' requires freedom from other and intermediate collectives.
40. For example, BPF, 154.
41. For her perception of the persistence of totalitarianism, see Auer and Burdach, 'Der verlorene Schatz,' 88; Truc, *Assumer l'humanité*, 119 and

Richard Bernstein, 'The Illuminations of Hannah Arendt,' *New York Times*, June 20, 2018, accessed October 11, 2020, at https://www.nytimes.com/2018/06/20/opinion/why-read-hannah-arendt-now.html

42. For which, consult Peter Baehr, 'Totalitarianism in America? Robert Nisbet on the "Wilson War State" and Beyond,' *American Sociology* 45, no. 1 (2014), 99.
43. Nisbet, *Quest for Community*, 23.
44. HC, 5.
45. BPF, 226–7.
46. BPF, 231.
47. Compare Antonini, *Public Space*, 126–7.
48. OR, 72.
49. For which, see Nils Baratella, 'Der immerwährende Anfang: Űber Hannah Arendts Augustinus-Rezeption,' in *Existenz und Freiheit: Karl Jaspers, Hannah Arendt und Heinrich Barth zur Freiheitslehre Augustins*, ed. Baratella, Johanna Hueck and Kristin Zeyer (Basel: Schwabe, 2022), 44.
50. BPF, 241.
51. OR, 74–5.
52. LIOC, 122–3.
53. HC, 214.
54. Pupo, *Libertà é conservazione*, 176.
55. Compare Kalyvas, *Democracy and the Politics of the Extraordinary*, 298–300.
56. Butler, *Notes Toward a Performative Theory*, 59–64.
57. RV, 83.
58. See the marks in the margins in Arendt's copy of Hans J. Morgenthau, *A New Foreign Policy for the United States* (New York: Praeger, 1969), 44; BCSL.
59. CR, 65–8.
60. Hubert Faes, *La paradoxe de la condition humaine selon Hannah Arendt* (Leuven: Peeters, 2016), 36.
61. Bethânia Assy, 'Hannah Arendt's *Doxa* Glorifying Judgment and Exemplarity: A Potentially Public Space,' *Veritas* 50, no. 1 (2006), 12–13.
62. For which, see Albanel, *Amour du monde*, 308.
63. Dana Villa, 'The Philosopher versus the citizen,' 154.
64. EJ, 81.
65. Ibid., 45–6.
66. Ibid., 135–7.
67. The question was posed in a letter from Heinz Wewer, a Berlin professor, USLC, 021464.
68. EJ, 286.

69. LIOC, 59.
70. EJ, 279.
71. EJ, 142–4.
72. 'Remarks to European Jewry,' 1 (undated), Speeches and Writings File, 1923–1975; USLC.
73. For which, see Young-Bruehl, *Hannah Arendt*, 337–78 (for the ADL's 'bulletins,' 348).
74. Arendt's 'Answer to Questions submitted by Samuel Grafton,' JW, 482.
75. Genel, *L'expérience de la liberté*, 245.
76. O'Gorman, *Politics*, 8.
77. Ibid., 21.
78. Consult OT, 275–7; Arendt, 'Authority in the Twentieth Century,' TWB, 73–4; and Vicky Iakovou, 'La critique entre Hannah Arendt et l'École de Frankfort,' *Tumultes* 17/18 (2002), 259–60.
79. Bassi, *Verso una politica del limite*, 91.
80. See the margins of Arendt's copy of Werner Jaeger, *Humanism and Theology* (Milwaukee: Marquette University Press, 1943), 59–60; BCSL.
81. Compare Brown, *Undoing the Demos*, 190–2, 196, 199–200 with Brook Manville and Josiah Ober, *The Civic Bargain: How Democracy Survives* (Princeton: Princeton University Press, 2023), 237–9.
82. *Between Friends*, 217.
83. *Briefwechsel*, 65 (*Bin mehr denn je der Meinung, dass man eine menschenwürdige Existenz nur am Rande der Gesellschaft sich heute ermöglichen kann*).
84. Arendt, 'Society and Culture,' 286.

# Conclusion: Arendt on Controlling the New

Arendt was primarily interested in agency. Desirable policies were afterthoughts. She was intensely disappointed in conventional political structures, but the conciliar structure she found congenial was not, for her, as scholars often claim, 'a new form of government.'[1] Interpersonal performances constituted (or enacted) her alternative politics, not the systems or structures that contained them. She was not looking to improvise and commend a new normal for her oases or for the desert, yet she advocated the pariah's perspective to counter temptations to conformity. She counselled resistance that amounted to more than a rejection of statists' salesmanship and, ideally, would issue in places, and inspire occasions for, citizen-statesmen to be free, to sift various opinions, to reimagine democracy and to contemplate new beginnings. But Arendt refrained from giving us more, because they were to be our new beginnings.

Her restraint is hardly uncontroversial. To some, she seemed 'unduly neglectful.'[2] During a colloquy on her work, one conferee tried to pry from Arendt instructions or rules for citizen-statesmen in alternative political collectives. But she pointedly refused. For the 'real political action,' she said, 'arises as a group act.'[3] Persistently offering argument as the option to both authoritarianism and anarchy, however, she can hardly be accused of holding back. Rather, she identified political action's most conspicuous characteristic as 'the freedom of spontaneity' and declined to script debates about citizenship. She just stipulated the virtues enabling it to flourish.[4] She made no secret of her impatience with progressives who claimed that specific structures and institutions were necessary conditions for the survival or the revival of democracy. 'We destroy everything,' Arendt warned, 'if we try to control the new.'[5]

To avoid such destruction, she distinguished politics as experience and performance. Nearly all the best contemporary studies of her enterprise acknowledge as much yet seem unable to resist theorising her legacy and, against her advice, controlling 'the new.' David Arndt sifts Arendt's objections to philosophies that 'obscure the essential link between politics and freedom.' Still, Arndt appears not to see how frail or fragile that 'link' becomes if social theories and social problems are not excluded from politics. For Arendt, politics prepares change agents whose subsequent steps could then address inequities. But, when unprepared, citizens blunder. Her principal example, eighteenth-century French insurgents, who rushed nonstop from revolution into the Reign of Terror.[6] But, when prepared, citizen-statesmen brought generous or capacious political judgement – for Arendt [following Kant], an enlarged mentality – from their oases into the desert to wrestle with their republics' civic problems. As Jonathan Peter Schwartz says, they had learned to judge in the absence of a 'sovereign theorist,' yet when Schwartz designates the contributions Arendt's citizen-statesmen make, laying 'new foundation[s] for modern politics,' he refers to some elusive 'impartiality' rather than to their acquired perspicacity.[7]

The reservations expressed in this study about others' interpretations and clarifications should not be interpreted as signs of my diminished respect for what their authors have contributed to what has been called an Arendt renaissance. But by dating Arendt's disappointments to the late 1920s and emphasising their influence on her perceptions of statists' captivation and capture of citizens during 'the onslaught of modernity,' our study underscores her resistance to politics as practised from then to now. Ordinary citizens were fed a steady diet of clichés, in effect, depriving them of political judgement. Arendt occasionally intimated that the statists' strategy had been calculated to promote constituents' 'inability to think.' Any dissidents among them would be written off as petulant and petty, while those disinclined to dissent, grew accustomed to 'the monstrous process of expropriation' that impounded their freedoms.[8] Citizen-statesmen, as Arendt conceived of them, were obliged to make other citizens aware of such circumstances. Nonetheless, she did not expect them to proceed from their oases and make the desert bloom. The cumulative effect of her disappointments led her to conclude that radical new beginnings rather than structural modifications, however, promised some relief. Clearly, though, she was excited to see some spurts of citizen concern about political improprieties. She wrote to Karl Jaspers in the late 1960s, tentatively suggesting that 'the republic still has a chance.' Yet one statement in her letter, referring to student protests, nearly recants, inasmuch as she predicted that 1968 would be commemorated in the twenty-first century as 1848 was in the twentieth.[9]

True, rival readings of the revolutions of 1848 still compete with each other, but, during her career, much as now, few scholars quarrelled with the conclusion that the nineteenth-century European insurgents' grievances were inadequately addressed in the aftermath of 1848, and, Christopher Clark claims, the post-revolutionary synthesis appeased the statists interested in continuing to disempower 'the popular classes.'[10]

The conceit of this study has been that, because we looked first to learn about Arendt before learning from her, we can understand how disappointments conditioned her mistrust of statist rhetoric and why she came to believe, for example, that the dismantling of dissent in the 1960s revealed more about democracy's deterioration than about the dissidents. We argued that those disappointments predated her experiences in, and studies of, the United States. Alfons Söllner, among others, however, inaccurately proposes that her interest in the relationship between new beginnings and statist machinations as well as her determination to redefine politics originated with her fascination with the founding of the American republic.[11] But, studying the effects of alienation on early Christianity and, specifically, on Augustine, Arendt grew interested in what occurs when alternatives to conventional understandings of power and sovereignty break ground in an inhospitable world. From the late 1920s, she was weighing the cost incurred by defiance or simply by being different against the virtues of pariah collectives.[12] When it seemed impossible to mobilise conventionally against cruelties and to challenge statists' definitions of citizenship, she conceded that some degree of distance and defiance was proper for citizens who esteemed judgement, plurality and freedom. She witnessed much to contest and protest: the pressures to assimilate, prejudice against pariahs, expressions of xenophobia and racism in Europe and the United States. She saw the Weimar Republic collapse, looked on while the Zionists colonised Palestine and watched as statists in purported democratic republics managed or manipulated – rather than empowered – their *demos*. Or, to borrow Wendy Brown's characterisation of that process, Arendt discerned and deplored statists' determination to ensure 'both individual and state become projects of management.'[13]

To learn from Arendt's perceptions is not to cast all statists as sinister. But the resistance to resistance of most and what we identified as the opposition of salesmanship to statesmanship signals that efforts to minimise statists' damaging influence are ill-considered, especially now that their marketing has been made easier, as Eric Foner reports, insofar as news has 'migrated' from print to social media and to partisan blogs. On the internet, algorithms push people to sites reinforcing their prejudices, precluding 'the public-spirited dialogue necessary in a democracy.'[14] Foner's is a familiar refrain. It betrays a nostalgia for what passed as objective journalism during the late twentieth century and assumes that, absent 'systematic [statist] domination,' 'egalitarian civic dialogue in public spaces should – almost naturally – flourish.'[15] But this assumption holds only if statists' nearly ubiquitous and generally invidious influence somehow diminishes. Fausto Proietti, though, claims the need for attenuation has been exaggerated, that, contrary to Arendt's analysis, statists are sensible curators or managers, more often prudent and benevolent managers than treacherous Machiavellians.[16] Arendt, we have argued, thought otherwise, and the marginal lines she added to Peter Laslett's edition of John Locke's treatises on government may serve as her reply to Proietti (as well as to Locke), reminding us of the remarks this study harvests from her essays, books, journal, correspondence and marginalia. Laslett says that Locke understated the early modern statists' exertions to maintain control over constituents, and Arendt's marker appears to signal her agreement. For, during the twentieth century, she was stunned by statists' superficially camouflaged attempts to undermine what remained of their democratic republics. Even if journalism stepped back across the threshold and reversed Foner's 'migration' of the news, in Arendt's view, there could be no return to 'egalitarian civic dialogue' in politics as conventionally conceived.[17]

Her realisation likely was what moved her to confide to her journal that it was 'so hard to love the world.'[18] Most conventional political deliberations then were – and remain – acrimonious contests for dominance. Citizens are unprepared for the agonistic exchanges that define politics for Arendt. Jason Brennan collates relatively recent empirical research on political deliberations, making precisely that point to clinch his case 'against democracy.' Conversations about politics, he concludes, neither enlighten nor 'ennoble' interlocutors but corrupt them.[19] Arbiters may set rules but cannot rule out biases: 'confirmation bias[es],' which drive citizens to accept only the evidence corroborating their preexisting views, and 'disconfirmation bias[es],' which lead them to reject evidence inconsistent with those views. Interlocutors become irrational and demonise each other. Brennan admits that deliberations afford citizens a unique opportunity 'to confront new ideas … in a rational way' but stresses how infrequently citizens do.[20]

Brennan is frustrated by the failure of citizens to engage in discourse without uncrating and brandishing their biases. At the top of the ticket, though, leaders of democratic republics also seem to have no stomach for Arendt's 'give-take-and up against.' At a recent symposium on democracy, which claimed democracy was 'on the rebound,' they enumerated the deliverables they associated with their protocols. Featured speakers, a few of whom were notorious for having turned elections in their territories into coronations, were exceptionally gifted statists, reinforcing citizens' conformity and concentrating power in ruling elites. Narendra Modi had marginalised a significant portion of India's population. Benjamin Netanyahu just then was confronting protests against his efforts to weaken the Supreme Court of Israel, which traditionally monitored abuses of power. One journalist covering the virtual colloquy wryly concluded that, notwithstanding their promises to deliver justice and prosperity, the ostensible advocates of democracy, as a 'political system,' could only deliver 'regular ... opportunities for changing the governing officials.' And, given the influence of statists and the marketplace over citizens and change, elections may sift and replace candidates but seldom supply the changes that meaningfully challenge the shape or conduct of that 'system' and that would qualify as Arendtian new beginnings.[21]

They begin by making citizens statesmen and stateswomen. To do so, Sophie Loidolt explains, plurality and freedom are 'actualised,' encouraging citizens to create in betweens (or *inter-ests*), as we have repeatedly explained, and in those in betweens, self-discoveries and self-disclosures become possible. Loidolt, though, is at pains to maintain Arendt's disinterest in the results that reach beyond those 'spaces of appearance.' Arendt, she says, advocates 'a non-purpose-bound activity that finds an end in itself.'[22] Yet, despite Arendt's aversion to instrumentalism and her increasingly explicit efforts to distinguish politics from the formulation and implementation of policy, her controversial redefinition of politics as performance and her stipulation of what she expected of new beginnings focused on the virtuosity and virtues summoning citizen-statesmen to make a difference. Becoming somebody or, as she said, a 'who' was not 'an end in itself.' It was a new beginning that did not bring governments down but, ideally, started to make course corrections.[23] New beginnings that raised voices to that end and assisted citizens to become somebodies were miraculous. Arendt specified that each new beginning was 'like a second birth.' The odds were that the colloquies and collectives serving as makeshift cradles would periodically dissolve, then regroup and, in different forms and settings, 'actualise ... the human condition[s] of natality [and] ... plurality.' But, in every iteration, reborn citizens 'appear ... in the guise of miracle[s].'[24] And, with each 'rebirth' in Arendt's alternative, 'intermediary' venues, as André Enegrén remarks, political judgement was 'resuscitated.'[25] 'The miracle that saves the world, the realm of human affairs, from its normal, "natural" ruin,' she proposed, 'is ultimately the fact of natality.'[26]

Ruin? It seemed possible. During the late 1960s, perhaps soon after protests failed to impress government and university officials, Arendt recalled one of Heidegger's 'inner circle' asking whether the term 'humanism' could have any meaning in such an inhumane world.[27] Without new beginnings, how could she have answered other than 'yes.' And, as we have learned, she often doubted whether the need for natality or new beginnings would be widely acknowledged while statists' retained control over their public forums. In her view, then, the new beginnings would only begin in intermediary associations or collectives where interlocutors adapted the pariahs' perspective and their challenges to inhumanity, which we found her recoding in her remarks on Augustine, Varnhagen, Lessing, Brecht, Jaspers and others. Asked in 1970 what concept of the state she favoured, she refused to play statist. She responded that 'we need a number of political spaces.'[28] Dissatisfaction with that sort of answer often surfaces. Francis Moreault is displeased that Arendt had not urged readers to patch up the existing regimes and explicitly set out plans for renovations that would reduce distances between the governed and their governments.[29] One could argue that this study was conceived to register dissatisfaction similar to Moreault's but also to ascertain why she left so much unstipulated. She lucidly and comprehensively discussed the need for new beginnings, which we related to disappointments and indignation that she experienced and expressed, respectively, during her entire career. Yet she left readers to make them their new beginnings – to make them our new beginnings. She did not unequivocally rule out the possibility that incremental political changes might make regimes more humane. Arendt accepted that the future was too poorly lit to see whether statists would be as successful in what remained of her century (and in ours) as they had been through the history of political practice in Europe and the United States. Too poorly lit to see what affects, if any, multiple 'political spaces' and citizen-statesmen might have. But she suggested that, in those political spaces, 'deliberation, discussion and persuasion,' if ever tried, could inspire citizen-statesmen to share their 'passion for public freedom' with others elsewhere.[30]

## Notes

1. Compare Shmuel Lederman, 'Philosophy, Politics, and Participatory Democracy in Hannah Arendt's Political Thought,' *History of Political Thought* 37, no. 3 (2016), 504.
2. Benhabib, *Reluctant Modernism*, 208.
3. Arendt, 'Hannah Arendt on Hannah Arendt, TWB, 450.
4. PP, 127.
5. BPF, 189.
6. Compare Arndt, *Arendt on Politics*, 77–81, and consult OR, 97–103, 238–40.
7. See Schwartz, Arendt's *Judgment*, 184–6, but also note our previous appreciation for his foregrounding political judgement. Nonetheless, as

mentioned there, Schwartz's efforts to extend Arendt's ambitions from local to global political transformations seem unwarranted.

8. CR, 210–11.
9. *Briefwechsel*, 716.
10. For which, see Clark, *Revolutionary Spring*, 746–7. Hiruta, *Hannah Arendt*, 181–5 and Truc, *Assumer l'humanité*, 73–4 insightfully comment on Arendt's reactions to the protest against what Hiruta calls citizens' 'retreat … to the sphere of production and consumption.'
11. Compare Alfons Söllner, 'Zwischen Europa und Amerika: Hannah Arendts Wanderungen durch die politische Ideengeschichte,' *Leviathan* 36, no. 2 (2008), 303.
12. For which, see Beatrice Magni, *Hannah Arendt et la condition politique: Le réel dans la pensée philosophique du XXe siècle* (Turin: Harmattan Italia, 2018), 63–5.
13. Brown, *Undoing the Demos*, 22.
14. Eric Foner, 'Seeing Was Not Believing,' *The New York Review of Books* 70 (September 21, 2023), 43.
15. Adut, *Reign of Appearances*, 9.
16. Fausto Proietti, 'Su un'accezione repubblicana dei termini 'libertà' e 'politica' in Hannah Arendt,' *Il pensiero politico* 30, no. 3 (1997), 526–7, 531.
17. See Arendt's copy of Peter Laslett's *Locke's Two Treatises of Government* (Cambridge: Cambridge University Press, 1963), 69; BCSL.
18. *Denktagebuch*, 522.
19. Jason Brennan, *Against Democracy* (Princeton: Princeton University Press, 2016), 54–5.
20. Ibid., 72; Kimberley Curtis, *Our Sense of the Real: Aesthetic Experience and Arendtian Politics* (Ithaca, NY: Cornell University Press, 1999), 137–52 reports on an instance of 'direct political engagement,' which began as partisans articulated opposing views packed with prejudices during a 'charrette' or conference called to solve a problem caused by a school fire in Durham, North Carolina. The debate concerned the desegregation of the one remaining high school to accommodate the displaced youngsters. Curtis does well to show how the leading civil rights activist and spokesman for the local Ku Klux Klan, becoming 'the best of enemies,' document what Arendt intended, although the personal reconciliation does not substantiate Curtis's faith, which was clearly not Arendt's, that 'the courage and generosity' of the protagonists were contagious and that changes in the world around proved democracy had been 'renewed' and was 'renewable.'
21. For the summit, hosted by President Joseph Biden, see Benjamin Wallace-Wells, 'Democracy Calling,' *The New Yorker* (April 10, 2023), 11–12.

Two other featured speakers, Presidents Mohamed Bazoum of Niger and Zuzana Čaputová of Slovakia were dislodged by authoritarians within months of adjournment.

22. Loidolt, *Phenomenology of Plurality*, 187.
23. Arendt, 'Legitimacy of violence,' 014380–81, Speeches and Writings File, 1923–1975; USLC.
24. HC, 176–8.
25. André Enegrén, *La pensée politique de Hannah Arendt* (Paris: Universitaires de France, 1984), 249.
26. HC, 247.
27. *Denktagebuch*, 1132.
28. CR, 229, for the question; 232, for her answer.
29. Francis Moreault, 'Citoyenneté et représentation dans la pensée politique de Hannah Arendt,' *Sociologie et sociétés* 31, no. 2 (1999), 177, 187–8.
30. Arendt, 'The Freedom to be Free,' TWB, 378.

# Bibliography


Adams, Henry. *The Education of Henry Adams.* New York: Random House, 1996.

Adelman, Jeremy. 'Pariah: Can Hannah Arendt Help us Rethink our Global Refugee Crisis,' *Wilson Quarterly* 40, no. 2 (2016).

Adut, Ari. *Reign of Appearances: The Misery and Splendor of the Public Sphere.* Cambridge: Cambridge University Press, 2018.

Albrecht, Tobias. 'Arendt und Adorno: Ein Forschungsprogramm,' *Zeitschrift für Politikwissenschaft* 31, no. 3 (2021), 487–505.

Antonini, David. *Public Space and Political Experience: An Arendtian Interpretation.* Lanham, MD: Lexington, 2021.

Applebaum, Anne. *Twilight of Democracy: The Seductive Lure of Authoritarianism.* New York: Doubleday, 2020.

Arendt, Hannah. 'Adolf Eichmann File: 1938–1968.' USLC, correspondence.

Arendt, Hannah. 'Is America by Nature a Violent Society?' USLC, speeches and writings files.

Arendt, Hannah. *Between Friends: The Correspondence of Hannah Arendt and Mary McCarthy, 1949–1975*, ed. Carol Brightman. New York: Harcourt Brace, 1995.

Arendt, Hannah. *Between Past and Future: Eight Exercises in Political Thought.* New York: Penguin, 2006.

Arendt, Hannah. 'Beyond Personal Frustration: The Poetry of Bertolt Brecht,' *Kenyon Review* 10, no. 2 (1948), 304–12.

Arendt, Hannah. 'Breakdown of Authority.' USLC, speeches and writings files.

Arendt, Hannah. 'Concern for Politics in Recent European Thought.' USLC, speeches and writings files.

Arendt, Hannah. 'Contracts and Royalties.' USLC.

Arendt, Hannah. Correspondence: David Riesman, 1947–1956. USLC.

Arendt, Hannah. *Crises of the Republic*. New York: Harcourt Brace, 1972.

Arendt, Hannah. *Denktagebuch*, 2 vols, eds. Ursala Lutz and Ingeborg Nordmann. Munich: Piper, 2016.

Arendt, Hannah. Difficulties of Understanding.' USLC, speeches and writings files.

Arendt, Hannah. *Eichmann in Jerusalem: A Report on the Banality of Evil*. New York: Penguin, 2006.

Arendt, Hannah. 'Emerson – Thoreau Medal Lecture.' USLC, speeches and writings files.

Arendt, Hannah. *Essays in Understanding, 1930–1954: Formation, Exile, and Totalitarianism*, ed. Jerome Kohn. New York: Schocken Books, 2005.

Arendt, Hannah. 'Europe's Image of America.' USLC, speeches and writings files.

Arendt, Hannah. *Hannah Arendt/Karl Jaspers, Briefwechsel, 1926–1969*, eds. Lotte Köhler and Hans Saner. Munich: Piper, 1993.

Arendt, Hannah. *The Human Condition*. Chicago: University of Chicago Press, 1998.

Arendt, Hannah. 'Ideology and Propaganda.' USLC, speeches and writings files.

Arendt, Hannah. 'Imperialism, Nationalism, Chauvinism,' *The Review of Politics* 7, no. 4 (1945), 441–63.

Arendt, Hannah. 'The Imperialist Character,' *The Review of Politics* 12, no. 3 (1950), 303–20.

Arendt, Hannah. *The Jewish Writings*, eds. Jerome Kohn and Ron H. Feldman. New York: Schocken Books, 2008.

Arendt, Hannah. 'Der jüdische Armee.' USLC, speeches and writings files.

Arendt, Hannah. 'Karl Marx and the Tradition of Western Thought,' *Social Research* 69, no. 2 (2002), 273–319.

Arendt, Hannah. 'Krieg und Revolution.' USLC, speeches and writings files.

Arendt, Hannah. *The Last Interview and Other Conversations*. New York: Melville House, 2013.

Arendt, Hannah. *Lectures on Kant's Political Philosophy*, ed. Ronald Beiner. Chicago: University of Chicago Press, 1982.

Arendt, Hannah. *Der Liebesbegriff bei Augustin: Versuch einer philosophischen Interpretation*. Berlin: Springer, 1929.

Arendt, Hannah. *The Life of the Mind*. New York: Harcourt, 1981.

Arendt, Hannah. *Men in Dark Times*. New York: Harcourt, 1970.

Arendt, Hannah. *On Revolution*. New York: Penguin, 1977.

Arendt, Hannah. 'Organized Guilt and Universal Responsibility,' in *The Jew as Pariah: Jewish Identity and Politics in the Modern Age*, ed. Ron H. Feldman. New York: Grove, 1978, 225–36.

Arendt, Hannah. *The Origins of Totalitarianism*. New York: Harcourt, 1985.

Arendt, Hannah. 'Outlines and Research Memoranda.' USLC.

Arendt, Hannah. 'Peace or Armistice in the Near East,' *The Review of Politics* 12, no. 1 (1950), 56–82.

Arendt, Hannah. 'Philosophy and Politics,' *Social Research* 71, no. 3 (2004), 427–54.

Arendt, Hannah. *The Promise of Politics*, ed. Jerome Kohn. New York: Schocken Books, 2005.

Arendt, Hannah. *Rahel Varnhagen: Lebensgeshcichte einer deutschen Jüdin aus der Romantik*. Munich: Piper, 2018.

Arendt, Hannah. 'Reflektionen über den Dichter Bertolt Brecht und sein Verhältnis zur Politik.' USLC, speeches and writings files.

Arendt, Hannah. 'Remarks' (to the American Society of Christian Ethics [1973]). USLC, speeches and writings files.

Arendt, Hannah. 'Remarks to European Jewry,' USLC, essays and lectures.

Arendt, Hannah. *Responsibility and Judgment*, ed. Jerome Kohn. New York: Schocken Books, 2003.

Arendt, Hannah. 'Revolution: Spurious and Genuine.' USLC, speeches and writings files.

Arendt, Hannah. 'Society and Culture,' *Daedalus* 89, no. 2 (1960), 278–87.

Arendt, Hannah. *Thinking Without a Bannister: Essays in Understanding, 1933–1975*, ed. Jerome Kohn. New York: Schocken Books, 2015.

Arendt, Hannah. 'Threat of Conformism.' *The Commonweal* 60 (September, 1954), 607–10.

Arendt, Hannah. 'Understanding Politics,' *Partisan Review*, 20, no. 4 (1953), 377–92.

Arendt, Hannah. 'Walter Benjamin: Vortrag in Freiburg,' USLC, speeches and writings files.

Arendt, Hannah. 'Der Zionismus aus heutiger Sicht,' USLC, speeches and writings files.

Arens, Katherine. 'Hannah Arendt Translates Culture: *Men in Dark Times*,' *Monatshefte* 108, no. 4 (2016), 535–59.

Arndt, David. *Arendt on the Political*. Cambridge: Cambridge University Press, 2019.

Arnold, Jeremy. 'Arendt's Jeremiad: Reading *On Revolution* in a Time of Decline,' *The Review of Politics* 76, no. 3 (2014), 361–87.

Assy, Bethânia. 'Hannah Arendt's *Doxa* Glorifying Judgment and Exemplarity: A Potentially Public Space.' *Veritas* 50, no. 1 (2006), 5–21.

Auer, Stefan and Burdach, Kurt. 'Der verlorene Schatz der Revolution: Hannah Arendt und die Revolutionen 1956, 1968, und 1989,' *Osteuropa* 56, no. 9 (2006), 85–97.

Augustine, Aurelius. *De libero arbitrio libri tres. Corpus Scriptorum Ecclesiasticorum Latinorum*. vol. 74, ed. W. M. Green. Berlin: De Gruyter, 1956.

Baehr, Peter. 'Totalitarianism in America? Robert Nisbet on the "Wilson War State" and Beyond,' *American Sociology* 45, no. 1 (2014), 84–102.

Ballaci, Giuseppe. 'Deliberative Agonism and Agonistic Deliberation in Hannah Arendt,' *Theoria* 66, no. 161 (2019), 1–24.

Baratella, Nils. 'Der immerwährende Anfang: Über Hannah Arendts Augustinus-Rezeption,' in *Existenz und Freiheit: Karl Jaspers, Hannah Arendt und Heinrich Barth zur Freiheitslehre Augustins*, ed. Baratella, Johanna Hueck and Kristin Zeyer. Basel: Schwabe, 2022, 37–49.

Bassi, Daniela. 'Verso una politica del limite? Note sur potere e l'azione nel lessico politico di Hannah Arendt,' *Jura Gentium* 15, no. 1 (2018), 76–91.

Beiner, Ronald. 'Hannah Arendt on Judgment,' LKPP, 89–156.

Beiner, Ronald. 'Rereading "Truth and Politics"' *Philosophy and Social Criticism* 34, no. 1–2 (2008), 123–36.

Beiner, Ronald. Review of Linda M. G. Zerilli's *A Democratic Theory of Government*, in *Perspectives on Politics* 16, no. 3 (2018), 819–21.

Benhabib, Seyla. *Exile, Statelessness, and Migration: Playing Chess with History from Hannah Arendt to Isaiah Berlin*. Princeton: Princeton University Press, 2018.

Benhabib, Seyla. *The Reluctant Modernism of Hannah Arendt*. Lanham, MD: Rowman and Littlefield, 2000.

Ben-Israel, Hedva. 'Bi-Nationalism versus Nationalism: The Case of Judah Magnes,' *Israel Studies* 23, no. 1 (2018), 86–103.

Berkowitz, Roger. 'Protest and Democracy: Hannah Arendt and the Foundation of Freedom,' *Stasis* 6, no. 1 (2018), 36–55.

Berlato, Roberto. *Il buio del tunnel e la strada della libertà: Hannah Arendt e il XII secolo ronnovata eopca di fascino dei totalitarismi*. Bologna: Diogene Multimedia, 2022.

Bernstein, Richard J. 'The Illuminations of Hannah Arendt,' *New York Times* (June 20, 2018), https://www.nytimes.com/2018/06/20/opinion/why-read-hannah-arendt-now.html

Bernstein, Richard J. 'Provocation and Appropriation: Hannah Arendt's Response to Martin Heidegger,' *Constellations* 4, no. 2 (1997), 153–76.

Bernstein, Richard J. *Why Read Hannah Arendt Now*. Cambridge: Polity, 2018.

Birulés, Fina. *Hannah Arendt: Liberdad politica y totalitarismo*. Barcelona: Gedisa, 2019.

Brecht, Bertolt. *Poetry and Prose*, ed. Reinhold Grimm. New York: Continuum, 2003.

Brennan, Jason. *Against Democracy*. Princeton: Princeton University Press, 2016.

Brown, Wendy. *Nihilistic Times: Thinking with Max Weber*. Cambridge, MA: Harvard University Press, 2023.

Brown, Wendy. *Undoing the Demos: Neoliberalism's Stealth Revolution*. New York: Zone Books, 2015.

Buckler, Steve. *Hannah Arendt and Political Theory: Challenging the Tradition*. Edinburgh: Edinburgh University Press, 2011.

Butler, Judith. *Notes Toward a Performative Theory of Assembly*. Cambridge, MA: Harvard University Press, 2015.

Canovan, Margaret. 'Hannah Arendt as a Conservative Thinker,' in *Hannah Arendt Twenty Years Later*, eds. Larry May and Jerome Kohn. Cambridge MA: MIT Press, 1996, 11–32.

Canovan, Margaret. *Hannah Arendt: A Reinterpretation of her Political Thought*. Cambridge: Cambridge University Press, 1992.

Chernow, Ron. *Alexander Hamilton*. New York: Penguin, 2004.

Chiba, Shin. 'Hannah Arendt on Love and the Political: Love, Friendship, and Citizenship,' *Review of Politics* 57, no. 3 (1995), 505–35.

Chrostowska, S. D. *Utopia in the Age of Survival: Between Myth and Politics*. Stanford, CA: Stanford University Press, 2021.

Clark, Christopher. *Revolutionary Spring: Europe Aflame and the Fight for a New World, 1848–1849*. New York: Crown, 2023.

Connolly, Joy. 'The Promise of the Classical Canon: Hannah Arendt and the Romans.' *Classical Philology* 113, no. 1 (2018), 6–19.

Curtis, Kimberley. *Our Sense of the Real: Aesthetic Experience and Arendtian Politics*. Ithaca, NY: Cornell University Press, 1999.

D'Alessandro, Ruggero. *La communità possible: la democrazia consiliare in Rosa Luxemburg e Hannah Arendt*. Milan: Mimesis, 2011.

Davidson, Osha Gray. *Best of Enemies: Race and Redemption in the New South*. New York: Scribner, 1996.

Dünckmann, Florian. 'Nur für Schwindelfreie? Eine Geographie politischer Praktiken nach Hannah Arendt.' *Geographica Helvetica* 75, no. 2 (2020), 81–91.

Enegrén, André. *La pensée politique da Hannah Arendt*. Paris: Universitaires de France, 1984.

Evans, Richard J. 'Why did he not Speak Out?' *London Review of Books* 45 (October 19, 2023), 33–4.

Faes, Hubert. *Le paradoxe de la condition humaine selon Hannah Arendt*. Leuven: Peeters, 2016.

Foner, Eric. 'Seeing Was Not Believing.' *The New York Review of Books* 70 (September 21), 2023, 43–5.

Fossen, Thomas. 'Agonistic Critiques of Liberalism' in *Contemporary Political Theory* 7, no. 4 (2008), 376–94.

Fuss, Peter. 'Hannah Arendt's Concept of Political Community,' *Idealistic Studies* 3, no. 3 (1973), 252–65.

Genel, Katia. *Arendt: L'expérience de la liberté*. Paris: Belin, 2016.

Gines, Kathryn. 'Race Thinking and Racism in Hannah Arendt's *The Origins of Totalitarianism*,' in *Hannah Arendt and the Uses of History: Imperialism, Nation, Race, Genocide*, eds. Richard H. King and Dan Stone. New York: Berghahn, 2007, 38–53.

Gregory, Eric. 'Augustine and Arendt on Love: New Dimensions in the Religion and Liberalism Debates,' *The Annual Society of Christian Ethics* 21 (2001), 155–72.

Gregory, Eric. *Politics and the Order of Love: An Augustinian Ethic of Democratic Citizenship*. Chicago: University of Chicago Press, 2008.

Herrmann, Steffen. 'Demokratische Urteilskraft nach Arendt,' *Zeitschrift für praktische Philosophie* 6, no. 1 (2019), 179–210.

Hinchman, Sandra K. 'Common Sense and Political Barbarism in the Theory of Hannah Arendt,' *Polity* 17, no. 2 (1984), 317–39.

Hiruta, Kei. *Hannah Arendt and Isaiah Berlin: Freedom, Politics, and Humanity*. Princeton: Princeton University Press, 2021.

Holman, Christopher. *Politics as Radical Creation: Herbert Marcuse and Hannah Arendt on Political Performativity*. Toronto: University of Toronto Press, 2013.

Bonnie Honig, *Political Theory and the Displacement of Politics*. Ithaca, NY: Cornell University Press, 1993.

Iakovou, Vicky. 'La critique entre Hannah Arendt et l'École de Francfort,' *Tumultes* 17/18 (2002), 259–78.

Jacobitti, Susan Duvall. 'Thinking about the Self,' in *Hannah Arendt: Twenty Years Later*, eds. Larry May and Jerome Kohn. Cambridge, MA: MIT Press, 1992, 119–219.

Jay, Martin. *Permanent Exiles: Essays on the Intellectual Migration from Germany to America*. New York: Columbia University Press, 1985.

Jones, David Martin. *History's Fools: The Pursuit of Idealism and the Revenge of Politics*. Oxford: Oxford University Press, 2020.

Kalyvas, Andreas. *Democracy and the Politics of the Extraordinary: Max Weber, Carl Schmitt, and Hannah Arendt*. Cambridge: Cambridge University Press, 2008.

Kateb, George. 'Arendt and Representative Democracy,' *Salmagundi* 60 (Spring–Summer, 1983), 20–59.

Kateb, George. *Hannah Arendt: Politics, Conscience, Evil*. Totowa, NJ: Rowman and Allanheld, 1989.

Kaufman, Peter Iver. *On Agamben, Arendt, Christianity and the Dark Arts of Civilization*. London: Bloomsbury, 2020.

Keedus, Liisi. *The Crisis of German Historicism: The Early Political Thought of Hannah Arendt and Leo Strauss*. Cambridge: Cambridge University Press, 2015.

Kelz, Rosine. *The Non-Sovereign Self, Responsibility, and Otherness: Hannah Arendt, Judith Butler, and Stanley Cavell on Moral Philosophy and Political Agency*. New York: Palgrave Macmillan, 2016.

Kimball, Roger. 'Heidegger at Freiburg,' *The New Criterion* 3 (June, 1985), 9–13.

King, Richard. *Arendt and America*. Chicago: University of Chicago Press, 2015.

Klarman, Michael J. 'How Brown Changed Race Relations: The Backlash Thesis,' *The Journal of American History* 81, no. 1 (1994), 81–118.

Klausen, Jimmy Casas. 'Hannah Arendt's Antiprimitivism,' *Political Theory* 38, no. 3 (2010), 394–423.

Klein, Steve. 'Fit to Enter the World:' Hannah Arendt on Politics, Economics, and the Welfare State,' *American Political Science Review* 108, no. 4 (2014), 856–69.

Klusmeyer, Douglas. 'Beyond Tragedy: Hannah Arendt and Hans Morgenthau on Responsibility, Evil, and Political Ethics,' *International Studies Review* 11, no. 2 (2009) 332–51.

Klusmeyer, Douglas. 'Hannah Arendt's Case for Federalism,' *Publius: The Journal of Federalism* 40, no. 1 (2010), 31–58.

Kohn, Jerome. 'Freedom: The Priority of the Political,' in *The Cambridge Companion to Hannah Arendt*, ed. Dana Villa. Cambridge: Cambridge University Press, 2000, 113–29.

Kohn, Jerome. 'Hannah Arendt: The Appearances of Estrangement,' *Social Ressearch* 85, no. 2 (2018), 301–21.

Kohn, Jerome. 'Loyalty as Betrayal: Hannah Arendt's Judgment of the Poet Bertolt Brecht,' *Social Research* 86, no. 3 (2019), 651–69.

König, Helmut. 'Die Gründung der Freiheit: Hannah Arendt und die Theorie der Revolution,' *Osteuropa* 67, no. 6–8 (2017), 185–209.

Krimstein, Ken. *The Three Escapes of Hannah Arendt*. New York: Bloomsbury, 2018.

Kuttner, Robert. *Going Big: FDR's Legacy, Biden's New Deal, and The Struggle to Save Democracy*. New York: The New Press, 2018.

La Porta, Lelio. *Hannah Arendt: Il problema storico della libertà*. Milan: Unicopli, 2017.

Lechte, John and Newman, Saul. *Agamben and the Politics of Human Rights: Statelessness, Images, Violence*. Edinburgh: Edinburgh University Press, 2013.

Lederman, Shmuel. 'Agonism and Deliberation in Arendt,' *Constellations* 21, no. 3 (2014), 327–37.

Lederman, Shmuel. 'Philosophy, Politics, and Participatory Democracy in Hannah Arendt's Political Thought.' *History of Political Thought*. 37, no. 3 (2016), 481–508.

LeSure, Ainsley. 'The White Mob (in) Equality Before the Law, and the Racial Common Sense: A Critical Race Reading of the Negro Question in [Arendt's] "Reflections on Little Rock."' *Political Theory* 49, no. 1 (2021), 3–27.

Levy, David M. and Peart, Sandra J. *Escape from Democracy: The Role of Experts and the Public in Economic Policy*. Cambridge: Cambridge University Press, 2017.

Lippmann, Walter. *Public Opinion*. New York: Macmillan, 1929.

Lipset, Seymour Martin. 'Some Social Requisites of Democracy: Economic Development and Political Legitimacy.' *American Political Science Review* 53, no. 1 (1959), 69–105.

Loidolt, Sophie. *Phenomenology of Plurality: Hannah Arendt on Political Intersubjectivity*. London: Routledge, 2018.

Losurdo, Domenico. 'Hannah Arendt e l'analisi delle rivoluzioni,' in *La pluralità irrappresentabili: Il pensiero politico di Hannah Arendt*, ed. Roberto Esposito. Uribino: Edizioni QuattroVenti, 1987, 139–53.

Lugaresi, Leonardo. *Il teatro di Dio: Il problema degli spettacoli nel cristianesimo antico (II – IV secolo)*. Brescia: Morecelliana, 2008.

Macready, John Douglas. 'Hannah Arendt and the Political Meaning of Human Dignity,' *Journal of Social Philosophy* 47, no. 4 (2016), 399–419.

Magni, Beatrice. *Hannah Arendt et la condition politique: Le réel dans la pensée philosophique du XX^e^ siècle*. Turin: Harmattan Italia, 2018.

Manville, Brook and Ober, Josiah. *The Civic Bargain: How Democracy Survives*. Princeton, NJ: Princeton University Press, 2023.

Marantz, Andrew. 'Minority Rules: The Once Fringe Legal Theory that Became a Threat to Democracy,' *The New Yorker* (June 12, 2023), 51–6.

Markell, Patchen. 'Politics and the Case of Poetry: Arendt and Brecht,' *Modern Intellectual History* 15, no. 2 (2018), 503–33.

Markell, Patchen. 'The Rule of the People: Arendt, *Archê*, and Democracy,' *American Political Science Review* 100, no. 1 (2006), 1–14.

Marshall, David L. 'The Polis and Its Analogues in the Thought of Hannah Arendt,' *Modern Intellectual History* 7, no. 1 (2010), 123–49.

McCarthy, Mary. *The Oasis*. New York: Melville House, 2013.

McCarthy, Mary. *The Seventeenth Degree*. New York: Harcourt, Brace Jovanovich, 1974.

McCarthy, Mary. *Vietnam*. New York: Harcourt, 1967.

McMaster, H. R. *Dereliction of Duty: Lyndon Johnson, Robert McNamara, the Joint Chiefs of Staff, and the Lies that Led to Vietnam*. New York: Harper, 1997.

Menand, Louis. 'Joseph McCarthy and the Force of Political Falsehoods,' *The New Yorker* (August 3 and 10, 2020), 71–5.

Mewes, Horst. 'L'action politique selon Hannah Arendt,' *Cités* 67, no. 3 (2016), 79–92.

Mills, C. Wright, *The Power Elite*. New York: Oxford University Press, 1956.

Moreault, Francis. 'Citoyenneté et représentation dans la pensée politique de Hannah Arendt,' *Sociologie et sociétés* 31, no. 2 (1999), 175–90.

Moruzzi, Norma Claire. *Speaking through the Mask: Hannah Arendt and the Politics of Social Identity*. Ithaca, NY: Cornell University Press, 2000.

Moses, Dirk. '*Das römische Gespräch* in a New Key: Hannah Arendt, Genocide and the Defense of Republican Civilization,' *The Journal of Modern History* 85, no. 4 (2013), 867–913.

Moyn, Samuel. 'Hannah Arendt on the Secular,' *New German Critique* 105 (Fall, 2008), 71–96.

Muldoon, James. 'The Lost Treasure of Arendt's Council System,' *Critical Horizons* 12, no. 3 (2011), 396–417.

Musso, Luisa G. 'Formazione della persona ed educazione alla cittadinanza spunti a partire da H. Arendt,' *Rivista di filosofia Neo-Scolastica* 108, no. 3 (2016), 521–42.

Nisbet, Robert. 'Arendt on Totalitarianism,' *The National Interest* 27 (1992), 85–91.

Nisbet, Robert. 'Hannah Arendt and the American Revolution.' *Social Research* 44, no. 1 (1977), 63–79.

Nisbet, Robert. *Quest for Community: A Study in the Ethics of Order and Freedom*. Wilmington, NC: Intercollegiate Studies Institute, 1990.

Nisbet, Robert. 'Still Questing,' *The Intercollegiate Review* 29, no. 1 (1993), 41–5.

Nisbet, Robert. *Twilight of Authority*. Indianapolis: Liberty Fund, 1975.

Nisbet, Robert. 'What to do when you don't live in a Golden Age,' *The American Scholar* 51, no. 2 (1982), 229–41.

Nordmann, Ingeborg. '"Fremdsein ist Gut": Hannah Arendt über Rahel Varnhagen,' in *Rahel Varnhagen: Die Wiederentdeckung einer Schriftstellerin*, eds. Barbara Hahn and Ursala Isselstein. Göttingen: Vandenhoeck und Ruprecht, 1987, 196–207.

O'Gorman, Ned. *Politics for Everybody: Reading Hannah Arendt in Uncertain Times.* Chicago: University of Chicago Press, 2020.

Owens, Patricia. 'Racism in the Theory Canon: Hannah Arendt and "the One Great Crime in which America Was Never Involved,"' *Millennium: Journal of International Studies* 45, no. 3 (2017), 403–24.

Passerin d'Entreve, Maurizio. *The Political Philosophy of Hannah Arendt.* London: Routledge, 1994.

Pitkin, Hanna Fenichel. *The Attack of the Blob: Hannah Arendt's Concept of the Social.* Chicago: University of Chicago Press, 1998.

Presby, Gail. 'Critic of Boers or Africans? Arendt's Treatment of South Africa in *The Origins of Totalitarianism*, in *Postcolonial African Philosophy: A Critical Reader*, ed. Emmanuel Chukwudi Eze. Oxford: Blackwell, 1997, 173–7.

Proietti, Fausto. 'Su un'accezione repubblicana dei termini 'libertà' e 'politica' in Hannah Arendt,' *Il pensiero politico* 30, no. 3 (1997), 525–37.

Pupo, Spartaco. *Libertà é conservazione: Robert Nisbet e la critica al progressismo.* Rome: Idrovolante Edizioni, 2016.

Putnam, Robert D. *Bowling Alone: The Collapse and Revival of American Community.* New York: Simon and Schuster, 2000.

Runciman, David. *How Democracy Ends.* New York: Basic Books, 2018.

Rustin, Bayard. '"Black Power" and Coalition Politics,' *Commentary* 42 (September, 1966), 35–40.

Schmitt, Carl. *Der Begriff des Politischen.* Hamburg: Hanseatische Verlagsanstalt, 1933.

Schoonheim, Liesbeth. 'Among Lovers,' *Arendt Studies* 2 (2018), 99–124.

Schwartz, Jonathan Peter. *Arendt's Judgment: Freedom, Responsibility, Citizenship.* Philadelphia: University of Pennsylvania Press, 2016.

Shklar, Judith. *Political Thought and Political Thinkers*, ed. Stanley Hoffman. Chicago: University of Chicago Press, 1998.

Siegelberg, Mira. 'Things Fall Apart: J. G. A. Pocock, Hannah Arendt, and the Politics of Time,' *Modern Intellectual History* 10, no. 1 (2013), 109–34.

Sigwart, Hans-Jörg. *The Wandering Thought of Hannah Arendt.* New York: Palgrave Macmillan, 2015.

Sjöholm, Cecilia. 'Voicing Thought: Arendt, Poetry, and Philosophy,' in *Philosophy and Poetry: Continental Perspectives*, ed., Ranjan Gosh. New York: Columbia University Press, 2019, 69–83.

Söllner, Alfons. 'Zwischen Europa und Amerika: Hannah Arendts Wanderungen durch die politische Ideengeschichte,' *Leviathan* 36, no. 2 (2008), 292–310.

Stears, Marc. *Out of the Ordinary: How Everyday Life Inspired a Nation and How It Can Again.* Cambridge, MA: Harvard University Press, 2021.

Storey, Ian. 'The Restless Unsaid: Arendt on Political Poetics,' *Critical Inquiry* 41, no. 4 (2015), 869–92.

Strong, Tracy B. 'America as Exemplar: The *Denktagebuch* of 1951,' in *Artifacts of Thinking: Reading Hannah Arendt's 'Denktagebuch,'* eds. Roger Berkowitz and Ian Storey. New York: Fordham University Press, 2017, 124–42.

Tamir, Yael. *Why Nationalism*. Princeton: Princeton University Press, 2019.

Taylor, Dianna. 'Butler and Arendt on Appearance, Performativity, and Collective Political Action,' *Arendt Studies* 1 (2017), 171–6.

Ternisien d'Ouville, Thierry. *Réinventer la politique avec Hannah Arendt*. Paris: Utopia, 2010.

Thaa, Winfried. *Politisches Handeln: Demokratietheoretische Űberlegungen im Anschluss an Hannah Arendt*. Baden-Baden: Nomos, 2011.

Tomba, Massimiliano. *Insurgent Universality: An Alternative Legacy of Modernity*. Oxford: Oxford University Press, 2019.

Topolski, Anya. *Arendt, Levinas, and a Politics of Relationality*. London: Rowman and Littlefield, 2015.

Truc, Gerome. *Assumer l'humanité: Hannah Arendt, la responsabilité face â la pluralité*. Brussels: Editions de l'universite de Bruxelles, 2008.

Turner, Bryan S. 'Robert Nisbet and the Problem of Community,' *American Sociologist* 45, no. 1 (2014), 68–83.

Turner, Frederick Jackson. *The Frontier in American History*. New York: Holt, 1921.

Vázquez-Arroyo, Antonio Y. *Political Responsibility: Responding to Predicaments of Power*. New York: Columbia University Press, 2016.

Villa, Dana. *Arendt*. London: Routledge, 2021.

Villa, Dana. *Arendt and Heidegger: The Fate of the Political*. Princeton: Princeton University, 1995.

Villa, Dana. 'Arendt, Heidegger, and the Tradition,' *Social Research* 74, no. 4 (2007), 983–1002.

Villa, Dana. 'From the Critique of Identity to Plurality in Politics: Reconsidering Adorno and Arendt,' in *Arendt and Adorno Political and Philosophical Investigations*, eds. Lars Rensmann and Samir Gandesha. Stanford, CA: Stanford University Press, 2012, 78–104.

Villa, Dana. 'The Philosopher versus the Citizen: Arendt, Strauss, and Socrates,' *Political Theory* 26, no. 2 (1998), 147–72.

Volk, Christian. 'Hannah Arendt und die Kritik der Macht,' Deutsche Zeitschrift für Philosophie 61, no. 4 (2013), 505–28.

Von Tevenar, Gudrun. 'Invisibility in Arendt's Public Sphere,' in *The Politics of Compassion*, eds. Michael Ure and Mervyn Frost. London: Routledge, 2014, 37–50.

Vowinckel, Annette. *Geshichtsbegriff und historisches Denken bei Hannah Arendt.* Cologne: Böhlau, 2001.

Wagner, Peter. 'Die westliche Demokratie und die Möglichkeit des Totalitarianismus: Űber die Motive der Gründung und der Zerstörung in *The Origins of Totalitarianism*,' in Totalitäre Herrschaft und republikanische Demokratie, ed. Antonia Grunenberg. Frankfurt am Main: Peter Lang, 2003), 131–45.

Wallace-Wells, Benjamin. 'Democracy Calling,' *The New Yorker* (April 10, 2023), 11–12.

Walter, Marco. 'Das Politische: eine Begriffsbestimmung mit Hannah Arendt und Carl Schmitt,' *Leviathan* 44, no. 3 (2016), 515–35.

Wurghaft, Benjamin Aldes. *Thinking in Public: Strauss, Levinas, Arendt.* Philadelphia: University of Pennsylvania Press, 2016.

Young-Bruehl, Elisabeth. *Hannah Arendt: For Love of the World*, 2nd edn. New Haven: Yale University Press, 2004.

Zapata, Guillermo. 'El espacio público y su fundamento en la libertad: Pensamiento político de Hannah Arendt,' *Papel Politico* 17, no. 1 (2012), 159–74.

Zerilli, Linda M. G. *A Democratic Theory of Judgment.* Chicago: University of Chicago Press, 2016.

Zerilli, Linda M. G. '"We Feel our Freedom": Imagination and Judgment in the Thought of Hannah Arendt,' in *The Aesthetic Turn in Political Thought*, ed. Nikolas Kompridis. London: Bloomsbury, 2014, 29–60.

# Index

EU Authorised Representative:
Easy Access System Europe Mustamäe tee 50, 10621 Tallinn, Estonia
gpsr.requests@easproject.com

Printed and bound by CPI Group (UK) Ltd, Croydon, CR0 4YY
29/09/2026
02224981-0008